Your Complete Guide to Enjoying Wine

Millions of people the world over drink wine as casually as we drink coffee or soda. Yet many Americans still assume that wine drinking is a complicated ritual, requiring specialized knowledge and elaborate equipment. Since all the equipment you really need is a corkscrew and a glass, serving wine at dinner should be as simple as pouring a glass of beer—and it's a lot more fun.

THE NEW SIGNET BOOK OF WINE is your complete guide to enjoying wines. It gives you the basic knowledge you need for developing your own personal preferences, and it serves as a handy reference source for any questions you may have about wine. As sensible in approach as it is comprehensive in outlook, THE NEW SIGNET BOOK OF WINE is a four-star introduction to one of life's greatest pleasures.

"Fills a long-felt need for a paperback guide that is informative and accurate. This eminent authority has condensed the lore of wine into a fascinating volume that contains the answers to a tremendous number of questions about wines."

—James Beard

"Clear, understandable and practical . . . remarkably sound."

—*San Francisco Chronicle*

"A 'BASIC' BOOK ON
WINE THAT THE NOVICE CAN
ACTUALLY UNDERSTAND"

THE NEW SIGNET BOOK OF WINE ". . . is a pleasure to recommend. It is written with clarity, charity and understanding for those who may want to know more about wine without having gone beyond a gallon of Gallo. The introduction . . . is an informal, common sense, dissertation on the approach to the tasting of wine with the goal of a respectable understanding of what it's all about. It deals with such basics as reading wine labels, fascinating statistics on drinking habits in various countries, and the various types of wine that exist."

—Craig Claiborne, *The New York Times*

"This well organized, readable book written by an expert is an excellent introduction to wines."

—*Publishers Weekly*

"Best new book in many a year . . . strongly recommended."

—*Bon Appetit*

THE
NEW
SIGNET BOOK
OF

A COMPLETE
INTRODUCTION

by Alexis Bespaloff

A SIGNET BOOK
NEW AMERICAN LIBRARY
TIMES MIRROR

Copyright © 1971, 1980 by Alexis Bespaloff

Library of Congress Catalog Card Number: 79-90084

Maps drawn by Elizabeth van Itallie

SIGNET, SIGNET CLASSICS, MENTOR, PLUME, MERIDIAN AND NAL
BOOKS are published by The New American Library, Inc.,
1633 Broadway, New York, New York 10019

First Printing, April, 1971
Fourteenth Printing, February, 1978
First Printing Revised Edition, February, 1980

5   6   7   8   9   10   11

PRINTED IN THE UNITED STATES OF AMERICA

PREFACE TO THE REVISED EDITION

The number of important changes that have occurred in the world of wine since 1971, when the first edition of this book was published, have made a completely revised edition long overdue. For the American consumer, the most dramatic events have occurred in California, where a remarkable number of exceptional wines have been produced, many of them by wineries that did not even exist when this book first appeared. In Germany, the new laws that went into effect in 1971 completely altered the vineyard map of that country and the way in which its wines are labeled. A much greater variety of Italian wines are now shipped here than ever before, including many excellent wines that were previously available only to those who visited that country. The chapters on these wines have been completely rewritten and expanded, as have many other parts of this book, and there are very few pages that have not been revised and updated.

I have tried to make this edition as complete and accurate as possible, and would like to thank those who were kind enough to read certain parts of the manuscript: Gerald Asher, William Bolter, Paul Bouchard, Arthur Brody, Darrell Corti, David Cossart, Mario Daniele, José Ignacio Domecq, Jr., Robert Drouhin, Tom Ferrell, Victor Hazan, Ben Howkins, Jean Hugel, Hans-Walter Kendermann, Pierre Lanson, Louis Latour, Robert Lescher, John Lockwood, Tim Marshall, Mary Mulligan, David Orr, Richard Peterson, Hank Rubin, C. Frederic Schroeder, Peter A. Sichel, Peter M. F. Sichel, Claude Taittinger, and Hubert Trimbach.

CONTENTS

MAPS

ILLUSTRATIONS

INTRODUCTION

Even a teetotaler must be aware of the increased interest in wine that has taken place in America in recent years. Consumption has more than doubled in a decade, and perhaps more significantly, in 1979 the sale of wines in this country exceeded that of spirits for the first time in this century. Despite the greater number of people who now enjoy wine with their meals or as an aperitif, however, wine is not yet the daily beverage of most Americans. The most popular beverage in this country is soda, followed by milk, coffee, and beer. The annual consumption of wine is more than 135 bottles per person in France and Italy, more than one hundred bottles in Portugal, Spain, and Argentina. The average American drinks six bottles of table wine a year.

We simply lack a tradition that encourages people to take for granted a bottle of wine on the dinner table, and to regard wine drinking as one of life's most accessible casual pleasures. Compared to Europe, we had a late start in the production and consumption of wine, and our momentum was then cut short by Prohibition. We made a second start less than fifty years ago, both as wine producers and as consumers, and we have gone about it with great enthusiasm. Although many Americans still think of wine as something special and out of the ordinary, there is now a greater variety of the world's fine wines to be found in almost any American city than in Paris, London, or Rome. Wines of all kinds are readily available in nearly every state, and an interested American's approach to wine is much more adventurous than that of the average European. Most Frenchmen, for example, are familiar only with wines from their own part of the country and tend to be condescending about wines from other regions, not to mention wines from other countries. When I lived in Bordeaux I chatted from time to time with the sommelier, or wine steward, at one of the city's finest restaurants. He was familiar with all the great châteaux of Bordeaux, and in fifteen years on the job had tasted hundreds of wines in any number of different vintages. In all that time, he had never tasted a Beaujolais or a Chablis: those wines come from the other side of France, and as a Bordelais, he had never had the curiosity or the opportunity to try them.

By comparison, an American who drinks wine even occasionally will probably have tasted some of the following: a Chianti or Soave from Italy; a Beaujolais, Chablis, Châteauneuf-du-Pape, or regional Bordeaux from France; a Portuguese rosé; and a Liebfraumilch or Piesporter Riesling from Germany, as well as a number of different wines from California. Many of the best wines from the world's most famous viticultural regions find their way here, so we tend to be more receptive to a variety of wines and more willing to learn than the people who produced them.

Because wine is only now beginning to be treated casually in this country, there are those who go to the other extreme and create a mystique out of drinking a glass of wine. Such people tend to discourage those who come into contact with them, and many people who would enjoy wine have been led to believe that you must know a great deal both about wine and about its proper presentation even before you begin. The fear of doing something incorrect has surely kept many people from taking their first steps in wine. In Europe there is no fuss made about drinking wines, just as no one here makes a fuss about drinking coffee. A few Europeans may look into wine more deeply as a hobby, just as there are some Americans who buy fresh coffee beans and grind them to their own specifications. That's no reason for the rest of us to hesitate before drinking a cup of coffee. The only equipment you need to drink wine is a corkscrew and a glass. Two glasses are better, as one of the most agreeable aspects of wine is that it seems to taste better when shared.

There are people who will tell you that good wines don't travel, or that the best wines can be found only where they are made. It may be true that a wine that tasted superb when drunk on a terrace in a seacoast village in the south of France will not taste as good over here, but in this case it's probably the view that doesn't travel. If a wine cannot travel, it is because it doesn't have quite enough alcohol to stabilize it for a long journey, but this applies almost invariably to the pleasant wines that are served in carafes in holiday resorts. To vinify them so as to increase their alcoholic content by the necessary degree or two would be to deprive them of their charm, and in any case these wines are usually undistinguished in the first place. Someone on holiday is not the most critical and objective of tasters, especially if he or she does not normally drink wine at home. There are, it is true, some delightful country wines that are not often seen here, but they are rarely produced in sufficient quantity to make it commercially worthwhile to export them, and they are usually consumed in their entirety within the region where they are made.

The fact is that all good, soundly made wines can travel, and they do. The best wines in the world can be found here, and they will taste every bit as good as on their home ground. As a matter of fact, the fine wines that are the most difficult to find in this country are certain premium varietal wines from California that are made in very limited quantities.

Wine can be broadly classified into three main groups: table wines, fortified wines, and sparkling wines. *Sparkling wines* obviously include Champagne and various other sparkling and bubbling Champagne-style wines made in most countries in several ways. Sparkling wines are specially taxed in this country, both by the federal government and individually by most states, which partly accounts for their comparatively high price.

Fortified wines are those to which alcohol has been added at some point in their production, and they generally contain between 17 and 21 percent alcohol by volume. Wines thus fortified include Sherry, Port, Madeira, and Marsala. Vermouth and various aperitif wines are both fortified and flavored. Fortified wines, which range in taste from dry to very sweet, are served before or after a meal and can be enjoyed any time during the day. They are not usually served with a meal.

The term *table wines* properly refers to all wines that contain 14 percent or less of alcohol, and thus includes every kind of natural (unfortified), still (not sparkling) wine that might be served with meals. It is with table wines that this book is primarily concerned, although chapters on both fortified and sparkling wines are included. A few pages are also devoted to brandy, which is usually distilled from wine.

It may be appropriate here to mention two terms that sometimes crop up in conversations about wine. People will occasionally refer to a moderately priced imported wine as a *vin ordinaire*, to distinguish it, perhaps, from the very greatest wines. Actually, *vin ordinaire* more correctly describes the cheap, agreeable, undistinguished wines of anonymous origin that are drunk every day by most Europeans. Although a certain amount of anonymous wine is shipped here, most of the wines that are exported to this country are of a higher class, and come from specifically defined districts of origin. Perhaps the closest thing we have to *vin ordinaire* in America are the least-expensive jug wines from California that provide pleasant wine at a modest price. It's also inaccurate to refer to an inexpensive wine as "just a table wine," as both a two-dollar bottle of wine and Château Mouton-Rothschild 1970 are "just table wines."

The only way to learn about wines is to taste them, and there is no substitute for pulling a cork. Go into any store that seems to have a reasonably large selection of wines, buy a few different bottles, and then try them one after the other. Even if you come across a wine you don't care for, you will have added to your knowledge without having spent much money. A bottle of wine costs less than a ticket to a new movie these days, and you don't have to stand in line to enjoy it.

Never buy the cheapest wine in any category, as its taste may discourage you from going on. The glass, corks, cartons, and labor are about the same for any wine, as are the ocean freight and taxes for imported wines (which are based on total gallonage, not on value).* Consequently, if you spend a little more, you are buying better wine, because the other costs remain fixed. Cheap wines will always be too expensive.

Learn to trust your own palate and to determine your own preferences by tasting, not by responding to a label. The other side of this rule is not to assume that what you like, at first, is either very good or, more important, very good value. Only as you taste different wines will you begin to understand what you like and why. You will also recognize what makes one wine better than another, and you will appreciate the distinctive taste and complexity of flavor that characterize the finest wines.

To learn even a minimum amount about wine you must do two simple things: take a moment to really taste the wine in front of you, and look carefully at the label to determine just what it is you are tasting. Tasting is discussed in another chapter, but here are some general guidelines to reading wine labels.

READING WINE LABELS

Labels for most of the world's wines, and certainly the best of them, indicate either the wine's place of origin or, in some cases, the name of the grape variety from which it is made. Most European wine names are place-names, so you are being told, most of the time, just where the wine comes from. Chablis, Sauternes, Saint-Emilion, Pommard, Vouvray, and Tavel are villages in France; Soave, Bardolino, Barolo, Orvieto, and Frascati are in Italy; German villages include Bernkastel, Piesport, Johannisberg, and Nierstein; other wine villages include Tokay in Hungary, Neuchâtel in Switzerland, and Valdepeñas in Spain. Wines whose names are those of their district of origin include Beaujolais, Anjou, Côtes du Rhône, Médoc, Chianti, and Rioja. Geography is the key to understanding wines so labeled. If you can focus on the wine's place of origin, rather than on the appearance of the label as a whole, and

---

* Federal taxes and U.S. customs duties on table wine are fairly low and amount to about $1.25 per case of twelve bottles. State taxes vary from as low as 2¢ per case in California, to 23¢ in New York and New Jersey, to more than $2.00 in a few states.

gradually build up a mental wine map for each country as you taste its wines, you will more easily recall the wines you enjoy.

The wine laws now in effect in many European countries not only define the geographical limits of specific appellations of origin, but also take into account the grape varieties that are permitted, the maximum quantity produced per acre, the wine's minimum alcoholic content, and other elements of winemaking that affect its quality. The laws simply reflect certain observations about quality based on long periods of trial and error. For example, in many wine regions, specific grape varieties are best suited to certain soils, and these are the ones that produce the finest wines. Some classic combinations of grape and soil include the Pinot Noir and Chardonnay in Burgundy, the Nebbiolo in northern Italy, and the Riesling along the Rhine and Moselle. Elsewhere, the finest wines are produced from a combination of several grape varieties, but the specific varieties, and sometimes the proportions of each, are strictly defined. Chianti, Rioja, and Châteauneuf-du-Pape are three familiar examples, as is Bordeaux, where Merlot and Cabernet Franc are planted along with the classic Cabernet Sauvignon grape. (In California, a number of different red and white grapes are often cultivated side by side, but many winemakers believe that even within one area, such as the Napa Valley, specific sites are more suited to one variety than to another.)

Wine laws limit the quantity of wine that can be produced from an acre of vines because quantity and quality have traditionally been mutually exclusive, and the most fertile soils, producing the most grapes, are rarely noted for the quality of their wines. A vineyard in Bordeaux, Burgundy, or the Napa Valley may produce less than two hundred cases of fine wine per acre; fertile districts in the south of France or in central California are capable of producing a thousand cases of undistinguished wine per acre.

A label that reflects the geographical origin of a wine may indicate not only a region, an inner district within that region, or an individual village, but also the ultimate geographical entity, the name of a specific vineyard. Every wine comes from a vineyard, of course, but most of the world's wines are blended together from many plots within a village or from several villages within a district. There are vineyards throughout the world, however, whose wines are vinified, aged, and bottled separately from those of adjoining plots of land. The most famous individually named vineyards are in Bordeaux, Burgundy, and along the Rhine and Moselle; some are less than five acres in size, others extend for 150 or 200 acres. Although it is standard wine humor to satirize the taster who tries to guess whether a wine comes from the right slope or the left slope, the fact is that the exact position of a plot of vines will have a recognizable effect on the quality of its wines year after year. A vineyard's exposure to the sun, its ability to absorb heavy rains without flooding, the elements in its subsoil that nourish its vines, all these factors and more account for the astonishing fact that the wines of one vineyard plot will consistently sell for two or three times as much as those of an adjoining plot.

Although labeling wines with their place of origin is the most traditional approach, and is used throughout most of Europe, there is another approach that has become increasingly familiar to wine drinkers. That is the use of varietal names, in which wines are labeled with the name of the grape variety from which they are primarily, or entirely, made. This method is used in Alsace, in parts of Italy, and most notably in California, because the grape variety is a more useful indication of the style of a wine than is the name of the village or region from which the wine comes. Cabernet Sauvignon, Pinot Noir, Chardonnay, Zinfandel, and Grenache Rosé are among the best-known varietal wines of California. Other varietal wines include Chelois, Concord, and Catawba in New York State; Riesling and Gewürztraminer in Alsace; Lambrusco, Barbera, and Verdicchio in Italy; and Fendant in Switzerland. Sometimes a label will indicate both the variety and the place of origin: Bernkastel Riesling, Cabernet of Istria, Debröi Hárslevelü, and Sonoma Zinfandel are some examples from Germany, Yugoslavia, Hungary, and California, respectively.

The names by which most of the inexpensive wines produced in this country are sold are, unfortunately, the least useful to the consumer. These are generic names—that is, specific place-names, usually European, that are so well known to the public that they have been adopted to market wines from somewhere else. California and New York State Chablis, Burgundy, Rhine Wine, and Sauterne (usually spelled without the final *s*) are the best-known examples of wines whose names have no relation to their origin, and whose characteristics may be similar only in the vaguest way to the wines whose names are being usurped. Chilean Rhine Wine, Argentine Burgundy and Australian Moselle are other examples of generic labeling. In recent years, a number of producers have turned away from generic labeling to the use of such terms as Red Table Wine or Mountain White Wine. The better wines produced in all these countries, however, bear the name of the grape variety from which they are made or the district from which they come, which gives the consumer a much more accurate idea of what the wine tastes like.

Another approach to labeling wines is the use of proprietary brand names created by individual producers for their own wines. A proprietary name is likely to be better known to consumers than that of the producer or the wine's place of origin. Emerald Dry, Chateau La Salle, Paisano, Lake Country Red, Blue Nun, Mouton-Cadet, Nectarose, Prince Noir, and Brillante are some proprietary brands.

HOW WINE IS MADE

Wine is commonly defined as the fermented juice of fresh grapes. This obviously leaves out such specialty products as cherry wine, dandelion wine, or a beverage made from dehydrated grapes to which water has been added.

Grape juice is transformed into wine by the process of fermentation, in which the natural sugar present in grapes is converted into almost equal parts of alcohol and carbon-dioxide gas. The normal sequence in the making of red wines is for the grapes to be brought to the vinification shed or winery, stripped of their stems, and lightly crushed to release their juice. The time-honored process of treading on the grapes by foot (which is pretty rare these days) was carried out, not to press the grapes, but to crush them so that the released juice could begin to ferment. Effective presses have been in existence since primitive times, and stamping on grapes would be a pretty ineffective way of getting all the juice out of them.

The crushed red grapes are transferred to fermentation tanks. These may be open wooden vats, large cement tanks, or stainless-steel cylinders. In recent years, many wine producers throughout the world have been replacing the traditional wooden vats with large plastic-lined, fiberglass, or stainless-steel tanks. They are much easier to keep clean and the stainless-steel tanks in particular permit the temperature of the fermenting juice to be more carefully controlled. Temperature-controlled tanks are now used by a majority of California wineries, and in Bordeaux, for example, even such famous vineyards as Château Latour and Château Haut-Brion now use stainless-steel tanks for fermentation.

The juice now begins to ferment as a result of various chemical transformations effected by yeast cells that were already present on the grape skins. (In some regions where modern techniques are used, the natural yeasts are inhibited, and special strains of cultured yeasts added to the juice.) As the sugar/water solution becomes an alcohol/water solution (with carbon-dioxide gas escaping into the atmosphere), coloring matter and tannin are extracted from the skins. The amount of color and tannin that is desired determines the length of time that the juice is left in contact with the skins, and this vatting, or *cuvaison*, may vary from two or three days to two or three weeks. Short vatting is traditional for wines whose principal attraction is their fruit and charm, longer vatting for wines noted for their depth of flavor and longevity. With very few exceptions, grape juice is clear and untinted. When a white wine is made from black grapes, as in Champagne, the grapes are pressed immediately, before the skins can impart excessive color to the juice. Rosés are traditionally made by keeping the juice and skins together just long enough to impart the desired amount of color to the evolving wine, although cheap rosés are sometimes made by mixing red and white wines.

Fermentation normally continues until all of the sugar is converted into alcohol. The resulting wine generally varies in alcoholic content from as low as 7 or 8 percent to as high as 15 or 16 percent, depending on the wine region and the nature of the vintage. Even if the juice is especially rich in sugar, an alcoholic content of 15 or 16 percent kills the yeast cells that produced it, thus stopping fermentation. Almost all the table wines we drink, however, contain 11 to 14 percent alcohol, and in this country a natural table wine is legally defined as one with a maximum alcoholic content of 14 percent. Some, such as the white wines of Germany, may contain only 8 or 9 percent.

The alcohol content listed on a wine label, incidentally, is not necessarily an accurate indication of what is in the bottle. Federal law permits a leeway of 1.5 percent, so that a wine labeled as 12 percent alcohol may in fact contain anywhere from 10.5 to 13.5 percent. Labels with precise indications, such as 12.8 percent or 13.9 percent, are more likely to be accurate.

With very few exceptions, red table wines are fermented until they are completely dry: the minute trace of sugar that may be left in the wine cannot be perceived by the taste buds. Consequently, what sometimes makes one red wine taste "drier" than another is the amount of tannin or acids present. Some well-known red wines are slightly sweet, however: *sangría* from Spain and Lambrusco from Italy are the best-known examples. There are also a number of inexpensive California red wines that are not completely dry. They are slightly sweetened before bottling, which rounds out their taste and makes them more appealing to many consumers.

After fermentation is complete, the wine is transferred to small barrels, large casks, or even larger tanks to age and to rid itself of its natural impurities. Depending on local custom, aging can take anywhere from a few weeks to three years or more.

The wine that drains freely from the fermentation tank is called free-run; that which is recovered from the remaining solids by pressing is classified as press wine. Generally speaking, press wine tends to have more color and body than free-run wine, and is harsher and more tannic as well. Sometimes a wine producer will sell off the press wine, sometimes it is blended with a free-run juice to intensify its flavor and add to its longevity.

Because the ferments are naturally present on grape skins at harvest time, winemaking is a natural process, but it must nevertheless be controlled very carefully at every step. If the fermenting juice, called must, gets too cold (an early frost in Germany) or too hot (a late summer in Spain), fermentation will stop and is extremely difficult to start again. What's more, if the new wine were just left exposed to air in its fermentation vat, another natural process would soon take place—through the presence of the vinegar bacteria—that would transform the wine into an acetic acid solution, i.e., into *vin aigre,* or sour wine.

There is another fermentation technique, called carbonic maceration, that is used to some extent in the Beaujolais and Rhône regions of France, and by some California wineries, to produce fruity, light-bodied red wines that can be consumed within months of the vintage. In conventional red-wine fermentation the grapes are crushed and fermentation takes place in the presence of air. When carbonic maceration is practiced, the grapes, which are not crushed at all, are loaded into a closed container that is filled with carbon-dioxide gas. Fermentation occurs within each grape in the absence of air, and color, but not much tannin, is extracted from the skins. Eventually, the grapes are removed from the closed container, pressed, and the must continues its fermentation in the normal way. In California, carbonic maceration is sometimes referred to as whole-berry fermentation.

White wines are made by a somewhat different method. Because they do not need to pick up color from their skins, the grapes are pressed immediately, and the juice ferments away from the skins. As a result, white wines have less tannin than reds, as tannin is derived primarily from the skins. Tannin is an important constituent of fine red wines and gives young red wines an astringent, puckerish taste. Its comparative absence from white wines constitutes the principal taste difference between red and white wines.

Perhaps the most significant technological achievement of the past twenty years in the production of white wines in California and throughout the world has been the increasing use of temperature-controlled fermentation tanks, which permits white wines to be fermented slowly at relatively low temperatures. Slow, cool fermentation retains the fruit and freshness that are the principal attributes of most white wines. If such wines are bottled within a few months instead of being aged in wood for a year or more, as is traditional in many wine regions, they will display a youthful appeal rather than the dull, woody, and even oxidized tastes so prevalent in the past.

There are certain naturally sweet white wines, notably Sauternes and Barsac from Bordeaux, some Auslese and Beerenauslese wines of Germany, and certain Late Harvest wines from California, which are produced by stopping the fermentation while residual sugar remains in the wine.

Besides normal alcoholic fermentation, many wines also undergo malolactic fermentation, by which malic acid is converted into lactic acid with carbon-dioxide gas as a by-product. This process is of interest to the winemaker because it decreases the acidity in a wine. It is also of interest to the consumer because if malolactic fermentation takes place after the wine is bottled, the carbon-dioxide gas will be trapped in the wine. The resulting delicate sparkle, more noticeable to the tongue than to the eye, is undesirable in a red wine, but can be delightful in certain white wines if the microorganisms that cause malolactic fermentation have not also produced off flavors.

One element of winemaking that is sometimes referred to, and that can affect the quality of wines, is chaptalization. The process is named after Chaptal, one of Napoleon's ministers, who encouraged the idea of adding sugar to the must during fermentation. After a cold or rainy summer, when grapes have not ripened sufficiently, their lack of natural sugar would result in a wine without enough alcohol to make it healthy and stable. Chaptalization is permitted in several countries, notably France and Germany, in order to raise the alcohol content of a wine to its normal level as determined by good vintages. Chaptalization can be overdone, producing unbalanced wines that are too high in alcohol, but without it many famous wine districts would be unable to produce much drinkable wine in certain years.

The wine laws of Italy and California do not permit chaptalization, but they do permit the use of concentrate, which is boiled-down grape juice. The effect is basically the same—the concentrate contains a high proportion of sugar, which is converted into alcohol—but other elements present in the juice, notably acid, are also concentrated. Consequently, many winemakers believe that chaptalization is a more effective way to compensate for a lack of natural sugar than is the use of concentrate. In some wine regions, notably in New York State, it is permitted to add both sugar and water to the must, the water having the effect of reducing high acidity by diluting it. Of course, the water dilutes the wine as well and permits the winemaker to produce more wine from a given amount of grapes.

At some point before a wine is bottled it is fined, or clarified, to remove any impurities that may be suspended in it. A primitive form of fining is used by campers when they throw crushed eggshells into coffee that has been made by boiling water and coffee together in a pot. Suspended coffee grounds will cling to the shells as they fall to the bottom of the pot; as a matter of fact, a traditional fining method that is still used is to mix beaten egg whites into red wine. Gelatin is more widely used today for red wines, and certain clays for white wines.

Just before bottling, wines are filtered to remove any remaining impurities. Because American consumers have traditionally rejected wines that are not completely bright and clear in appearance, many American wineries favor rather severe fining and filtering, which may also diminish a wine's character and depth of flavor. Today, a number of smaller wineries bottle their wines without fining or filtering because they believe the wines will retain more character and develop greater complexity. Not all winemakers agree with this view, but it explains why you may come across bottles of California wine labeled unfined or unfiltered.

Historically, many inexpensive wines were pasteurized to kill any microorganisms that may spoil the wine after it is bottled. Unfortunately, pasteurization may effectively stop a wine from developing in the bottle, and the exposure to heat may also give the wine a slightly cooked taste. An alternative to pasteurization that has been adopted by many California wineries and a number of European firms, is microfiltration—the use of an extremely fine membrane filter that removes most of the microorganisms that pasteurization would have killed.

Wine continues to age after it has been bottled, as the various pigments, acids, tannins, and other elements present in minute quantities combine and alter the characteristics of the wine. Age alone is no guarantee of quality, however, and it is only the best wines that are sturdy and complex enough to improve for several years. The life cycle of each wine is different, and some wines are at their best when they are bottled, or within six months. All rosés and white wines are best consumed within two or three years of the vintage, as are many light red wines. Some dry white wines, such as the best Burgundies and California Chardonnays, achieve additional richness and complexity with bottle age, as do the finest sweet white wines from Sauternes, Germany, and California. The best reds from Bordeaux, Burgundy, northern Italy, Rioja, and California will only begin to reveal their qualities after four or five years, and it is by no means unusual to discover that a red wine from a top vineyard is only coming into its own after ten or fifteen years in the bottle.

A note about bottle sizes: fine wines develop more slowly and sometimes more completely in larger bottles. For that reason connoisseurs ideally prefer an old red wine that has been matured in a magnum, which holds two bottles. Although half-bottles provide the opportunity of experimenting at less expense, remember that wine ages more quickly in a half-bottle and that a fine red wine may never fully develop its qualities in such a small container.

As to the contents of wine bottles, both American and imported bottles now conform to metric sizes and contain the same amount of wine, which was not previously the case. The standard bottle of 750 milliliters is equivalent to 25.4 ounces; the half-bottle contains 375 milliliters, or 12.7 ounces; a 1-liter bottle contains 33.8 ounces; the metric magnum holds 1.5 liters, or 50.7 ounces; and the 3-liter jeroboam is equivalent to 101.4 ounces. The familiar gallon and half-gallon sizes in which inexpensive jug wines were marketed are no longer permitted, and have been replaced by the metric magnum and jeroboam.

WINE
TASTING

For a professional wine buyer, wine tasting is a skill requiring a long apprenticeship and rather delicate judgment. For the person who enjoys wine with his or her meals, tasting is a most agreeable pastime. Unfortunately, many people imagine wine tasting to be a complex and mysterious art, dominated by snobs and dilettantes using a stylized and farfetched vocabulary.

On the simplest level, tasting wines is an inescapable part of drinking them, and there are many people who are content merely to determine whether a wine is "good" or "not good." Sooner or later the casual wine drinker will experiment with new wines, and at that point he or she begins to taste wine. Unlike most pursuits, such as golf or playing the piano, tasting wines is enjoyable from the very start and becomes increasingly fascinating and rewarding with experience.

The principal difference between the professional taster and everyone else is that he (and, increasingly, she) has a greater opportunity to taste many different wines, and thus his perspective is wider and his palate more developed. Furthermore, because a buyer tastes wine soon after the vintage, and months or years before the wine is even bottled, he has the additional opportunity of following the development of various wines from the cradle, so to speak. This is especially important as it is his role to judge young wines long before they are ready to be consumed, and he can do this precisely because he has tasted wines of previous vintages at a similar stage of their evolution.

However, there is another aspect of wine tasting that is most important, and that is concentration. We can't all spend days on end going in and out of wine cellars in Burgundy, the Rheingau, or the Napa Valley, but we can at least devote ten seconds or so to a wine when we first taste it with dinner. Different wines and different occasions call for a flexible approach. A bottle of Château Lafite-Rothschild 1961 served at a formal dinner demands more attention (and appreciative remarks) than does a Valpolicella served with pasta. But in each case a few moments' attention to the wine before you is the only way to build your knowledge and increase your pleasure. Look at the label and note where the wine comes from in general terms, and if it's a special wine, note the specific district or vineyard that produced it, as well as the vintage. As you sip the wine, try to place it geographically in your mind, and compare it to other wines you've tasted from the same place. Only in this way will you develop your palate; otherwise you will simply have tasted, in time, a blur of individual bottles that you can neither recall nor repurchase.

It's often assumed, by the way, that wine experts are people who can taste wines whose labels have been covered up and then name the vineyard and vintage. Although some members of the wine trade amuse themselves by putting their colleagues through such blind tastings, the real skill of a wine buyer is demonstrated in exactly the opposite manner. He stands in a particular cellar, tasting a specific wine, and has even noted the barrel from which it was drawn. He must now determine how good it is, how good it will be six months or six years later, and what it is worth. It is precisely this ability to concentrate on the wine at hand—in order to judge its value, not guess its origin—that is the primary attribute of his expertise.

When professional tasters are at work, they always spit out the wines they are judging—either onto the floor of a cellar or into a special bucket in a tasting room. For one thing, it's not a pleasant experience to swallow very young red wines starting at eight or nine in the morning. For another, a taster in the vineyard region may sample fifty or seventy-five wines in a day, and if he swallowed each wine, his judgment would soon become impaired, to say the least.

Whatever our specific knowledge about wine, each of us prefers to drink what he or she likes. As you taste different wines, it's interesting to try to determine why one wine is more pleasant than another, what attributes makes one cost three times as much as another, and why one wine might suit a particular dish more than another at the same price: in short, to taste a wine critically and to sort out your impressions. Wine tasters generally approach a wine in three successive steps—color, bouquet (or smell), and taste. These will be examined in some detail, but remember that when it comes to tasting a specific wine, all of these considerations can be reviewed mentally in just a few seconds of concentration.

The first attribute of a wine is its color. Just as we anticipate a dish even more when it's attractively presented on the serving plate, so our enjoyment of a fine wine can be heightened by a look at its color. For this reason, wine is served in clear, uncut glasses. There are two aspects of a wine's color that deserve attention. The first is its appearance in the glass. Whether red or white, a healthy wine should be bright—that is, free of any cloudiness or suspension. If a wine appears dull or hazy, it may be unsound in some way, and its unattractive appearance is your first warning signal. This cloudiness is not to be confused with sediment, which is harmless and will fall to the bottom of the glass. Sediment is a natural by-product of age in older red wines, and such wines should be decanted whenever possible (as described elsewhere). Very occasionally you will come across crystals in a white wine; these are harmless (although admittedly unattractive) tartrates that have been precipitated by excessive cold. Sometimes small crystals are found stuck to the bottom of a cork, even in red wines. Again, these are tartrates, not, as some people imagine, sugar crystals.

The second aspect of color is the actual hue of the wine. Moselles are pale gold with a touch of green, white Burgundies a richer gold, Beaujolais purple-red, and so on. It happens that red wines get lighter as they age, and white wines get darker. Thus a fine old Bordeaux will be pale brick-red in hue, and an older white wine will take on a deeper gold. This change in color is a good indication of how well—or how badly—the wine is aging. A three-year-old red Bordeaux that is already pale red-orange, or a young white wine that has taken on a brownish tinge, would immediately be suspect. To judge the hue of a wine, don't look into the glass, as the depth of wine in the glass will affect its color. Tip the glass away from you and look at the outer edge of the wine against a white cloth or backdrop. An indication of just how important color is in judging wines is evidenced by the design of the traditional Burgundian *tastevin*, used to taste new wines still in barrels. It is a shallow silver cup—often used as a decorative ashtray here—with dimpled sides. Those dimples are there specifically to refract light through the wine, so that its color and appearance can be closely examined, even in a dimly lit cellar.

The second step in judging wine is to smell it, and wineglasses are tapered to focus and retain a wine's bouquet. You may ask, Why bother to smell a wine when I'm about to taste it? About 80 percent of what we imagine to be taste is actually based on our sense of smell. When we taste a roast beef or a peach, it is in fact the olfactory nerves that are doing most of the work. You know that when you have a head cold, you can't taste a thing, and yet it's your nose, not your palate, that is affected by the cold. The reason that wineglasses should be big (at least eight ounces) is that they are meant to be filled only halfway, so that a wine can easily be swirled in the glass. It is this gentle swirling that releases the wine's bouquet through evaporation.

A wine's bouquet gives you a strong first impression of the wine itself: if a wine has any serious faults, they can be discerned by smell, and you can avoid tasting bad wine. Occasionally, a wine may be corky, which is revealed by a pronounced smell of cork, rather than of wine. This occurs much less frequently than many people suppose. When tasting minor or inexpensive wines, you should look primarily for the absence of any faults, as such wines are unlikely to have great virtues. Cheap white wines, for example, often cause an unpleasant prickly sensation in the nose, a sign of an excess of sulfur dioxide, used to stabilize wines. Sometimes a wine that has just been opened will smell musty, and swirling the glass to aerate the wine will usually dissipate this smell. From time to time you may come across a white wine that has a suspiciously brown color and a bouquet reminiscent of Madeira or dry Sherry without any of the fruit of a good wine. Such a wine is described as maderized (*maderisé*). Maderization is the result of excessive oxidation, and it may have been caused by overlong aging in wood, a faulty cork that let air into the bottle, or it may be the natural evolution and decay of a white wine that is just too old. Another warning signal is a sour, vinegary smell, which indicates that the wine contains an excess of acetic acid, the vinegar acid. If you leave out a glass of wine overnight, what you smell and taste the next day is just such an excess of acetic acid.

When tasting better wines, especially those made from one of the classic grape varieties, you should look for a bouquet that is typical of the wine's origins. A Moselle will be flowery and fragrant, a Beaujolais will also have quite a bit of fruit to it, a red Bordeaux or California Cabernet Sauvignon will have a deeper, more complex bouquet. In general, young wines have more fruit in their bouquet (more of the smell of the grape), whereas older wines exhibit a more refined and subtle character. The sense of smell is probably the most evocative of all the senses (as the perfume manufacturers discovered long ago), and many of us have a greater sense memory of smells than for taste, so make the most of it.

Finally, you taste the wine. (Remember that judging a wine takes less time than reading about it. Your impressions of color and bouquet should have taken you only a few moments.) The tongue is covered with taste buds that can distinguish only salt, sour, bitter, and sweet, and they are located on different parts of the tongue. You must let the wine rest on your tongue for a few moments, so that you can separate the different taste sensations. At this point some professional tasters chew the wine to make sure that it comes into contact with all their taste buds. Others will "whistle in," drawing air into their mouths and through the wine, to help release its flavor. The slurping sound is an accepted part of serious tastings, but it can be dispensed with at dinner parties.

Although there are certain chemical salts in wine, picked up from the soil in which the vines are planted, they are rarely discernible to the taste. Sweetness will, of course, be more easily discernible, and is found in many white wines and rosés, and a few red wines as well. Most red wines are vinified so as to retain no sugar, and if a Beaujolais or dry red wine seems slightly sweet, it may simply denote the presence of glycerin or other elements that round out a wine and give it a certain richness. It's worth noting that not everyone's palate reacts the same way to sweetness: someone who drinks coffee with three spoonfuls of sugar may describe a dry red wine as "sour," and a medium-sweet white wine or rosé as "dry."

Bitterness usually indicates the presence of tannin in wine. Tannin—perhaps the most important component of fine red wines—gives wine an astringent, puckerish quality that you will also taste, for example, in very strong tea. Tannin acts as the spine or skeleton of a wine, and its presence enables a wine to evolve and mature in the bottle for several years. Tannin comes from grape skins, and its presence is a result of the vinification method used. In Beaujolais, where wines are to be drunk early while they retain their freshness, a short vatting (the time the skins are in contact with the juice) is the rule so that relatively little of the astringent tannin enters the wine. In Bordeaux, where red wines of good vintages are expected to last for ten years or more, vatting may take as long as two weeks, and the resulting wine will be harsh and bitter at first, and unpleasant to drink before it is at least five years old. An important change in vinification in vineyards around the world, and especially in France during the past twenty years, is a trend toward shorter vatting, so that red wines can be consumed more quickly by a public that no longer cellars wine away for years of maturation.

The tannic bitterness in red wine is softened by foods that contain protein. For example, if you eat cheese while tasting red wines, the protein in the cheese combines with the tannin in the wine and reduces its bitter taste. It's the same effect that occurs when you add milk to strong tea: the protein in the milk combines with and diminishes the tannin in the tea. For this reason, young red wines are usually more appealing when drunk with food than when they are tasted on their own.

As a wine ages in bottle, the tannin combines chemically with the coloring matter to form a harmless deposit. That is why older red wines are both paler in color and less harsh to the palate. The amount of tannin you detect in a red wine tells you whether or not it is ready to drink, or rather, whether or not the wine has evolved sufficiently to make it attractive to you. Unfortunately, many consumers make the mistake of assuming that there is a particular point at which each bottle of fine wine is at its best. In fact, it is difficult to project the evolution of the wines of a region in any given vintage, even more so to determine when a specific wine from a particular vineyard or winery will be fully developed. Furthermore, different people enjoy wines at different stages of development. Some enjoy the vigor and intensity of young wines, others prefer a red wine that has lost virtually all its tannin and displays softness and harmony at the expense of a more positive character.

Acidity is essential to wine, especially to white wines, where it performs the same function—aiding longevity—as does tannin for reds. A certain amount of acidity is always necessary to give a white wine liveliness and a fresh taste. Very hot summers may produce wines with too little acidity, as the sun burns away the natural tartaric and malic acids in the grapes. Such wines tend to be flabby and short-lived. Too little sun results in grapes that are not fully ripe and contain too much acidity. Such wines are tart, sour, and unpleasant.

If you concentrate on a wine for the few moments that it's in your mouth, you should be able to isolate the elements that make up its taste, since it is not difficult to be aware of two or three taste sensations simultaneously. For example, lemonade is a simple combination of sweetness and acidity that most people have no trouble adjusting to suit their own preferences. Red vermouth is quite sweet, but it also contains bitter extracts, so that the initial impression of sweetness, which would be too cloying by itself, is balanced by a bitter aftertaste. Strong tea is a bitter solution dominated by tannin; if you put in a slice of lemon, you add acidity, and if you then add sugar to mask the first two elements, you have created a simple combination of bitter, sour, and sweet.

Besides the impression made on your taste buds, you will also get an overall sense of the weight of the wine in your mouth. Some wines are light and delicate, such as a Muscadet or a Moselle; others are rather big and full, such as a Châteauneuf-du-Pape or a California Petite Sirah. An unattractive wine may strike you as thin, another as too heavy. It is harmony and balance that is desired in wine, whatever its price. An inexpensive wine with no faults and a pleasant taste may be very good value. An expensive wine from a famous vineyard may be bigger and richer and, in many ways, more interesting, but may nevertheless lack the harmony that would make it a pleasure to drink.

Let me state again that the only way to learn about wines is to try different bottles and to be aware of what you are drinking. A good way to define your impressions more accurately is to compare two or three wines at a time: have two half-bottles for dinner, or invite like-minded friends over for an informal tasting. If you compare a Bordeaux to a Rioja, or a Beaujolais to a California Gamay, or a Moselle to an Alsatian Riesling—the possibilities are endless—you will soon learn to distinguish between the major wine-producing regions of the world. More important still, you will discover new wines to enjoy, and good values from each region.

You will soon realize that one of the great pleasures of drinking wines is to talk about them and to compare impressions. Trying to describe the color, bouquet, and taste of a wine is much less difficult when you are talking to someone who is drinking the same wine. The vocabulary of wine tasting may seem vague or precious, at first, but you will discover that its terms are fairly specific and easily understood by anyone who has tasted a number of wines. Although professionals may use technical terms to pinpoint certain impressions, a tasting vocabulary need not be complex. A good wine may be described as delicate, subtle, fresh, lively, mature, positive, spicy, deep, robust, complex, balanced, sturdy, clean, rounded, or crisp. An unattractive wine may be astringent, dull, heavy, harsh, small, thin, hard, ordinary, bland, musty, cloying, or coarse. It's fascinating to realize that although a wine chemist can easily spot a defective wine, he cannot distinguish by chemical analysis between, say, an inexpensive but soundly made Bordeaux Rouge and a considerably more expensive wine from one of the great châteaux of the Médoc. He must eventually taste each wine to determine its character, intensity of flavor, complexity, subtlety, and true value.

One habit that will help to clarify your own taste, and

will also help your wine buying considerably, is to keep some sort of record of the wines you drink both at your own table and away from home. Some hobbyists use a specially printed cellar book that has room for various entries. Many people simply use a pocket notebook, others prefer individual index cards. Whatever method you decide on, write down the name of the wine, who made it, and the vintage; when and where you bought it and the price; when you drank the bottle and, of course, what you thought of it. If you look back at this record every few months you'll be amazed at the number of wines listed that you might otherwise have forgotten. You may also detect a change in your wine preferences and the evolution of a more precise tasting vocabulary.

Another way to keep track of what you drink is to soak off the label and record your comments on the back. The simplest method is to get an itemized bill from the store and to jot down your reactions to each wine as you drink it, if only to separate the wines you enjoyed most from those you found less to your taste.

As to smoking, a great many wine buyers and winemakers are smokers, and experiments indicate that people who smoke can taste as well as those who don't. Anyone who doesn't smoke, however, is quickly thrown off by smoke in the air, and for that reason it is common courtesy not to smoke during a tasting or when fine wines are served.

THE WINES OF FRANCE

France is traditionally considered the greatest wine-producing country in the world, and its annual output of nearly two billion gallons accounts for about one-quarter of the world's wines. Although France does not always make the most wine (in many years Italy's total production is greater), it probably produces a greater variety of fine wines than any other country. The red wines of Bordeaux, the red and white wines of Burgundy, the sweet wines of Sauternes and Barsac, and the sparkling wines of Champagne attest to the quality and diversity of French wines, and the wines of the Charente region are distilled to make Cognac, the most famous of all brandies.

The first French vineyards were planted about twenty-five hundred years ago near what is now Marseilles, and viticulture soon spread to the north and the west. There are now three million acres of vines in France, and of course, the great bulk of the wine produced is undistinguished. This is the *vin ordinaire* that the French drink every day, which is available in every grocery store, just as milk and soda are here. Only the top 15 to 18 percent of French wines are bound by the *Appellation Contrôlée* laws, but most of the wines shipped here come from this strictly defined category.

The *Appellation Contrôlée* laws, established in the 1930s, are the key to understanding most French wine labels. The words mean controlled place-name, and they constitute a guarantee by the government that the place-

24

name on the label is in fact just where the wine comes from. There are now about 250 individually defined *Appellation Contrôlée* wines, of which perhaps two hundred can be found here. When you have a bottle of French wine in front of you, look for the word directly above *Appellation Contrôlée* or actually between *Appellation* and *Contrôlée*. This will indicate the origin of the wine. It may be a region (Bordeaux, Côtes du Rhône), a district (Graves, Anjou), a village (Saint-Julien, Pommard), or even an individual vineyard, as in Burgundy (Chambertin, Montrachet). As the place-name becomes increasingly specific, the *Appellation Contrôlée* laws become increasingly strict, for they legislate not only the actual geographical limits of a particular place-name, but several other quality-control factors as well. Because certain soils are best suited to certain grape varieties, the law specifies which varieties are permitted. Minimum alcoholic content is another factor, not because the best wines have the most alcohol, but because too little alcohol in a wine will render it unstable. This prevents the use of an established place-name for certain wines produced there in a very poor year, when the worst of them will be too thin and washed-out to be typical. Perhaps the most important control of all, however, is that of quantity. It's been observed that most of the world's best wine regions do not, in fact, contain the best or most fertile soil: the vine seems to thrive in difficult terrain. In Bordeaux, for example, the richest soil, known as *palus,* lies along the riverbanks; wines produced there cannot be sold as Bordeaux, only as *vin ordinaire.* Furthermore, the best grape varieties rarely give a high yield, and should not be permitted to overproduce. An individual vine nourishes its fruit by sending roots down into the soil, as does any plant. If the vine is not pruned back in the winter to limit the number of bunches it can produce, the same root will have to nourish a lot more bunches, and the resulting wine will lack intensity of flavor and a clearly defined character.

Since the *Appellation Contrôlée* laws were first established, however, modern viticultural practices have enabled vineyard owners to produce somewhat more wine per acre while still maintaining the style and quality for which each appellation is noted. Although very abundant vintages generally produce lighter and less-intense wines, there have also been some recent vintages in which excellent wines were produced in relatively large quantities. The *Appellation Contrôlée* laws are now flexible enough to permit some variation from year to year concerning maximum permissible yields. Nevertheless, in any given region the limits set for village appellations are always stricter than for a regional one, and those for individual vineyards strictest of all.

The *Appellation Contrôlée* laws were based on earlier attempts to control the authenticity and quality of French wines, which were in turn made necessary by the confusion resulting from the complete replanting of the French vineyards after their destruction by phylloxera toward the end of the nineteenth century. Phylloxera, a plant louse, was unwittingly brought over from the United States on American rootstocks, and began to infest the European vineyards about one hundred years ago. Various methods were proposed to combat the phylloxera epidemic, which was devastating the vineyards of one country after another, but the technique that finally worked was to graft European *Vitis vinifera* vines to native American rootstocks from the eastern United States that were resistant to this insect. Eventually just about every single vine in Europe (and many of those in California) was grafted onto an American rootstock.

There is another category of French wines, created in 1949, known as V.D.Q.S.—*Vins Delimités de Qualité Supérieure,* or Delimited Wines of Superior Quality. These wines rank below those of *Appellation Contrôlée* status because their quality is not quite as good or as consistent, and in a few instances, because the quantities produced are rather limited. There are about fifty V.D.Q.S. wines, and their total production is about one-quarter that of the *Appellation Contrôlée* category. A few V.D.Q.S. wines have been elevated to *Appellation Contrôlée* status in the past few years, notably Cahors, Côtes de Provence, and Côtes du Ventoux, and it is likely that others will be as well. The labels of V.D.Q.S. wines, which include Corbières, Côteaux du Languedoc, Sauvignon de Saint-Bris, and Côteaux d'Aix, are imprinted with an emblem that resembles a small postage stamp; it contains the appropriate words and an illustration of a hand holding a wineglass.

For many years a number of French wines were entitled to label themselves *Appellation d'Origine Simple.* The phrase misled some consumers into thinking that these wines, which rank somewhere between *vin ordinaire* and V.D.Q.S., were somehow associated with *Appellation Contrôlée* wines. In 1973, the name of this category of wines was changed to *Vins de Pays,* and there are now nearly a hundred defined areas whose wines are entitled to use this phrase on their labels. Three-quarters of the *Vins de Pays* come from the Midi region, and 98 percent of the total are reds and rosés. It is likely that as quality improves, some *Vins de Pays* will become V.D.Q.S., just as several V.D.Q.S. wines have been raised to *Appellation Contrôlée* status. *Vin de Pays* now has a specific meaning, but the phrase *vin du pays* is still used informally to refer to the wine of the region—that is, to whatever local wine is being discussed.

In addition to the various appellation wines described above, there are an increasing number of wines being shipped here that are simply blends of red or white wines produced anywhere in France. Some of them, sold in magnums and labeled only with proprietary names, are meant to provide an alternative to jug wines from California. Others may confuse consumers as to what they really are, because they are marketed by well-known firms in Bordeaux, Burgundy, the Rhône, and elsewhere whose names are traditionally associated with *Appellation Contrôlée* wines. Although these wines were created as a less-expensive alternative to *Appellation Contrôlée* wines, consumers who recognize the shipper's name may imagine that they are buying wines of a higher class than is actually the case. In fact, these nonappallation wines, which fall into the Common Market category *Vin de Table*, are usually no better than an anonymous *vin ordinaire*, despite the prices at which some of them are sold. The labels of such wines obviously do not show the words *Appellation Contrôlée*, and that is the simplest way to determine what they are, but at one time the shipper's name could be followed by the place in which the firm was located, such as Bordeaux, Beaune, Nuits-Saint-Georges, and so on. New regulations forbid the use, on a label of nonappellation wine, of a city or village whose name is associated with an *Appellation Contrôlée* wine, such as Bordeaux or Beaune, nor can such blends show a vintage date. The shipper's name can now be followed only by the French equivalent of a zip code, to avoid misleading the consumer as to the origin of the wine in the bottle.

BORDEAUX

Bordeaux has long been considered one of the centers of the world's fine wines, and is unmatched within France for both quantity and variety. Red, white, and some rosé is produced, and the whites include both dry and sweet wines. Although the thirty to fifty million cases produced annually in Bordeaux amount to less than 5 percent of the wines of France, they account for about one-quarter of all wines entitled to *Appellation Contrôlée* status.

Bordeaux was shipping its wines to England as early as the twelfth century, when Henry II married Eleanor of

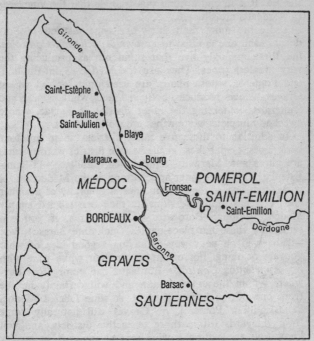

Aquitaine and thus annexed the region of Bordeaux as part of his empire. At that time, thousands of barrels were shipped annually of a pale red wine called *clairet*. The word evolved into claret, and properly refers only to red wine from Bordeaux, although it is often used to describe any dry red wine. It's only since the early nineteenth century, when the use of corks and cylindrical bottles became more common, making it possible for bottled wines to be stored on their sides for additional maturation, that claret as we know it today began to be produced: a deep-colored red wine that improves with age and that, in fact, needs years in barrel and in bottle to develop its best qualities.

The Bordeaux wine region lies within the *département* of the Gironde, and its principal city is, of course, Bordeaux itself, with a population of over 250,000. Two rivers, the Garonne and the Dordogne, meet just north of Bordeaux and form the Gironde estuary, which flows into the sea. It is in and around this triangle that the vineyards of Bordeaux are situated.

There are more than thirty-five wine districts in Bordeaux, each one entitled to its own *Appellation Contrôlée*, but there are only five that stand out as producing the very greatest wines. They are the Médoc, Saint-Emilion, and Pomerol, whose names are used only for red wines; Graves, which produces both red and white wines; and Sauternes, containing the inner district of Barsac, whose sweet and luscious white wines are world famous.

In addition to these five main districts, there are four communes, or parishes, in the Médoc district whose names are important: Margaux, Saint-Julien, Pauillac, and Saint-Estèphe. These are inner appellations of the Médoc, and a wine from one of these communes is generally of a higher class and has more individuality than one labeled simply Médoc. Although Bordeaux is a vast area, if you can remember these ten place-names (including Barsac), you will be well on your way to having a good idea of what you are drinking. For example, a red or white wine with the *Appellation Contrôlée* Bordeaux can come from anywhere within the entire region and will certainly not be from one of the better districts. A wine labeled Médoc, Saint-Emilion, Pomerol, or Graves will naturally come from vineyards within those respective districts, and you know you are getting a wine several steps up in quality from just a plain Bordeaux. If the label bears the name of one of the four communes in the Médoc, you are at a very high level within the hierarchy of Bordeaux appellations. This doesn't mean that a commune wine will always be better than a Médoc, but at least this provides a useful and fairly consistent ranking of relative quality.

Knowing these few names is also useful in reverse: that is, if a bottle of Bordeaux bears an unfamiliar *Appellation Contrôlée*, you know by the process of elimination that it must come from one of the many lesser districts. You may see names such as Côtes de Fronsac, Entre-Deux-Mers, Côtes de Bourg, Premières Côtes de Bordeaux, and the like, and while such wines can be very agreeable indeed, they should cost less than wines from the major appellations.

When you are confronted with the label of an individual vineyard, traditionally called a château in Bordeaux, looking for its *Appellation Contrôlée* is the simplest way to place it geographically. Let's say you are served a bottle of Château Trotanoy, and having enjoyed it, decide to buy a bottle for yourself. You may discover that the wine from this particular vineyard is not so easy to find, but if you noted its *Appellation Contrôlée*, you would have seen that it's a Pomerol. The chances are, then, that another Pomerol will have more of the general characteristics of Château Trotanoy than, say, a Médoc or a plain Bordeaux. If you try to memorize a vineyard name or the general appearance of a label, you will just be searching for one label among hundreds. Instead, you should place each wine you drink in its proper geographical context by noting its appellation of origin. Individual vineyard wines from Bordeaux are available in a wide range of prices. By paying attention to the *Appellation Contrôlée* of each wine you drink, you will not only be able to determine its relative rank among the appellations of Bordeaux, but you will also learn to distinguish the overall styles of wines from each major district. With the major appellations in mind, it becomes much easier to compare wines of different prices within an appellation, or to contrast wines of similar price from different appellations.

Although an individual vineyard in Bordeaux is called a château, there are very few homes that actually merit this description. Most properties consist of just a country house, some have more elaborate buildings dating from the late eighteenth or the early nineteenth century, and a few properties have no more than a large *chai*, or ground-level storage area, where the wines are made and stored. Nevertheless, labels for individual Bordeaux vineyards almost all contain the word *château* (a very few describe themselves as *domaine* or *clos*), and while there are a few properties elsewhere in France that also call themselves by a château name, when you see this word on a label, you can be pretty sure that the wine is from Bordeaux.

One way to approach the wines of Bordeaux is to divide them into two main categories: château wines, which are the product of an individual vineyard; and regional wines, which are marketed by their appellation or origin—Médoc, Saint-Emilion, Sauternes, and so on—rather than with the name of a specific property. The regional wines make up the backbone of the Bordeaux wine trade, and they probably account for three-quarters of all sales. The *négociants,* or shippers, of Bordeaux buy wines from a great many properties within a particular appellation of origin, as well as from the many cooperative cellars in the region, and blend them together to produce a wine of consistent quality and style. Most of the region's wines are shipped under two basic appellations, Bordeaux Rouge and Bordeaux Blanc, but the wines most frequently seen here are Médoc, Saint-Emilion, Graves, Sauternes, and Barsac. Margaux and Saint-Julien are also available, but it is rare to find regional wines from Pauillac, Saint-Estèphe, or Pomerol, as almost all the wines from these districts are bottled and sold by the vineyard proprietors as château wines. Since regional wines are blended, they do not express the characteristics of a particular vintage as clearly as do the wines of a single property. Nevertheless, there are vintage variations among regional wines, and it's always worth looking for the best recent vintages. Regional wines are meant to be consumed without much additional aging and the best of them are consistent and dependable wines, although many lack the distinction and individuality of château wines selling for the same price. Some of the Bordeaux shippers whose names are featured on labels of regional wines are Barton & Guestier, Calvet, Cordier, Cruse, Eschenauer, Ginestet, Nathaniel Johnston, Jouvet, De Luze, and Sichel.

In addition to the traditional range of regional wines, there are an increasing number of Bordeaux wines marketed with proprietary labels—names created and owned by individual shippers and promoted as individual branded wines. Mouton-Cadet, Grande Marque, Maître d'Estournel, Prince Noir, and La Cour Pavillon are some examples. These, too, are regional blends, but their labels emphasize the brand name rather than the appellation of origin or the name of the shipper.

Although regional and branded wines make up the most important part of the Bordeaux market, it is the great château wines of Bordeaux that have established the reputation of this region among connoisseurs. Of the more than two thousand individually named properties in Bordeaux, there are approximately a hundred châteaux whose wines are considered the finest of all, and which most fully display the characteristics that have made the wines of Bordeaux famous. Most of these wines have been officially classified at one time or another and are, therefore, referred to as *crus classés*, or classed growths (*cru* is synonymous with vineyard). Not all of these châteaux are readily available here, but there are probably fifty or sixty red wines and perhaps fifteen white wines whose names continually reappear in retail catalogs and on the wine lists of fine restaurants. Although the *crus classés* represent perhaps 3 percent of the wines of Bordeaux, this amounts to more than a million cases of very fine wine, and any discussion of Bordeaux wines will almost invariably turn to the classed growths. The classifications are explained and the wines listed district by district further on.

The great châteaux of Bordeaux are comparatively easy to learn about because the properties are fairly large—150 acres is not uncommon—and they are traditionally under a single ownership. All of the wines from a specific vineyard that are to be sold under the château name are blended together in the January following the vintage before being put into oak casks for maturation. As a result of this *assemblage*, each property bottles only one wine bearing the château label in any vintage. In contrast, most Burgundy vineyards are much smaller and almost all have several owners, each of whom makes a slightly different wine according to his skills and intentions. In Germany, also, the vineyards are small and under multiple ownership. In addition, each grower produces several different wines from the same vineyard in a good vintage, and these vary considerably in quality, taste, and price. By comparison with these other two great European wine regions, Bordeaux is relatively easy to understand, and the wines of the top châteaux are produced in sufficient quantities so that they are not difficult to acquire and compare. Many connoisseurs can discuss Bordeaux châteaux with great knowledge and enthusiasm, while remaining mystified about the wines of Burgundy or the Rhine.

It is possible to make comparisons among the wines of the many famous châteaux of Bordeaux because each of them has its own distinct characteristics. It may seem hard to believe, but each parcel of soil will produce a wine that is not only different from parcels nearby, but that is also consistently better or less good than those of its neighbors. A case in point is Château Latour and Château Léoville-Las-Cases: these two vineyards are contiguous, and it is impossible for a visitor to determine, unaided, where one vineyard ends and the other begins. Yet the first is a Pauillac, the second a Saint-Julien, and a bottle of Latour costs two or three times as much as a bottle of the (nevertheless excellent) Léoville-Las-Cases. Although the potential quality of a vineyard is determined by its soil and subsoil, its exposure to the elements and to the sun, there are other factors that enter into the quality and personality of the wine of a particular château. The grape varieties that are permitted for red Bordeaux are primarily the Cabernet Sauvignon, Cabernet Franc, and Merlot, plus small quantities of the Malbec and Petit-Verdot, and for whites the Sémillon and Sauvignon Blanc. The Cabernet Sauvignon brings finesse and depth of flavor to a red wine, the classic qualities of a claret; the Merlot is known for its suppleness and charm. Since many consumers are now drinking even the finest red Bordeaux within a few years of the vintage, before the wines have fully developed their qualities, a number of Médoc proprietors have replanted their vineyards with a higher proportion of Merlot than previously. The resulting wine is softer and sooner ready to drink. To achieve a similar goal, another proprietor may decide on a shorter vatting—the time during which the grapes are in contact with the fermenting must—and thus produce a somewhat lighter and quicker-maturing wine. At some châteaux the new wine is always put into new barrels, which gives the wines greater tannic complexity but which also represents a considerable investment if, say, eight hundred barrels have to be purchased every year. A proprietor who decides not to prune back his vines severely will produce a large crop of somewhat light wines; his neighbor may deliberately make less wine per acre, but that wine will be more intense and concentrated in flavor. In lesser vintages, some proprietors bottle only the best part of the crop and sell the rest off in bulk; others may bottle the entire crop. These are just some of the factors that can affect the personality of a wine, and comparing various châteaux in various vintages provides an endless source of pleasure to drinkers of Bordeaux.

Some years ago the best châteaux of Bordeaux began to bottle their wines themselves in their own cellars—rather than shipping them in barrels—as insurance that the wines bearing their labels are in no way tampered with. A branded cork bearing the name of the château and the vintage is used as well. The labels of such wines bear the words *mis en bouteille au château*, that is, bottled at the château. Just about every important château wine imported into this country is now château-bottled. In recent years, as Americans have learned to look for *mis en bouteille au château* on a Bordeaux label, a number of smaller properties have taken to château-bottling their wines as well. Wines of these *petits châteaux*, or lesser properties, as they are called, have become very popular here, and are now an important part of the Bordeaux trade. Their quality will vary considerably, and it is well to remember that if a wine is château-bottled you are guaranteed of its authenticity, but not necessarily of its quality. It's perfectly possible to bottle a second-rate wine at the property, and this is being done to take advantage of the momentum for château-bottled wines. There are, of course, a number of large, carefully tended properties in various districts that consistently produce good wines, and it's worth experimenting with the selection of *petits châteaux* available in local shops.

In the châteaux of Bordeaux, wines are stored in *barriques*, small oak barrels that hold about fifty-five gallons, or twenty-four cases of wine. At the best properties, the red wines mature in barrel for eighteen to twenty-four months, and this aging contributes greatly to their complexity, depth of flavor, and distinctive character. The traditional measure of trade in Bordeaux when new wines are being bought is the *tonneau*, an imaginary measure equivalent to four *barriques*, or ninety-six cases. Today, a *tonneau* actually consists of a hundred cases.

The word *supérieur*, as in Bordeaux Supérieur, only means that wines so labeled contain 1 percent more alcohol than those labeled simply Bordeaux. It is by no means an indication of superior quality, and in fact, many châteaux that could legally add *supérieur* to their appellations don't bother to do so. The word *monopole* on a shipper's label simply indicates that the firm has a monopoly, or exclusivity, on the particular brand name being used. *Grand vin* doesn't have any meaning, although *grand cru* does.

The Médoc district contains some of the most famous vineyards in the world, and most of its wines are on a very high level indeed. The wines of the Médoc have become well-known only in the last two hundred years or so. The wines shipped to England in the Middle Ages, for example, were mostly from Graves. The Médoc, which begins a few miles from the city of Bordeaux and extends for sixty miles, remained a dangerous and unprotected place in which to travel, and it was not until the seventeenth century that important vineyards began to be established there.

The Médoc is actually divided into two parts, originally known as the Haut-Médoc and the Bas-Médoc. These references to high and low are based simply on the position of each district relative to the Gironde, but the proprietors in the Bas-Médoc, which is the part farthest from Bordeaux, objected to its possible connotations on a label, and their appellation is now simply Médoc. The famous communes of Saint-Estèphe, Pauillac, Saint-Julien, and Margaux are all situated in the Haut-Médoc, but this district is usually referred to simply as the Médoc. Sometimes a lesser château will use the appellation Haut-Médoc on its label.

Perhaps the best way to approach the wines of the Médoc is from the top, which is to say, with the Classification of 1855. In conjunction with the Paris Exhibition of that year, representatives of the Bordeaux wine trade were asked to draw up a list of the best vineyards of the Médoc and of Sauternes, which will be discussed separately. By this time the Médoc has become considerably more famous than Graves, and Saint-Emilion and Pomerol were not yet widely known. The resulting classification grouped the wines on five levels of excellence, from *premiers crus* to *cinquièmes crus*. (Although Château Haut-Brion is located in the Graves district, it was already too important to leave out.) A fifth growth was by no means only one-fifth as good as a first growth—the ranking was gradual—and in any case all the classed growths represented the very best that Bordeaux had to offer.

THE CLASSIFICATION OF 1855
FOR THE MÉDOC

Premiers Crus—First Growths

VINEYARD	COMMUNE
Château Lafite-Rothschild	Pauillac
Château Margaux	Margaux
Château Latour	Pauillac
Château Haut-Brion	Pessac

Deuxièmes Crus—Second Growths

Château Mouton-Rothschild*	Pauillac
Château Rausan-Ségla	Margaux
Château Rauzan-Gassies	Margaux
Château Léoville-Las-Cases	Saint-Julien
Château Léoville-Poyferré	Saint-Julien
Château Léoville-Barton	Saint-Julien
Château Durfort-Vivens	Margaux
Château Lascombes	Margaux
Château Gruaud-Larose	Saint-Julien
Château Brane-Cantenac	Cantenac-Margaux
Château Pichon-Longueville	Pauillac
Château Pichon-Longueville-Lalande	Pauillac
Château Ducru-Beaucaillou	Saint-Julien
Château Cos d'Estournel	Saint-Estèphe
Château Montrose	Saint-Estèphe

Troisièmes Crus—Third Growths

Château Kirwan	Cantenac-Margaux
Château d'Issan	Cantenac-Margaux
Château Lagrange	Saint-Julien
Château Langoa-Barton	Saint-Julien
Château Giscours	Labarde-Margaux
Château Malescot-Saint-Exupéry	Margaux
Château Cantenac-Brown	Cantenac-Margaux
Château Palmer	Cantenac-Margaux
Château La Lagune	Ludon
Château Desmirail	Margaux
Château Calon-Ségur	Saint-Estèphe

* Reclassified as a *premier cru* in 1973.

Château Ferrière	Margaux
Château Marquis-d'Alesme-Becker	Margaux
Château Boyd-Cantenac	Cantenac-Margaux

Quatrièmes Crus—Fourth Growths

Château Saint-Pierre	Saint-Julien
Château Branaire-Ducru	Saint-Julien
Château Talbot	Saint-Julien
Château Duhart-Milon	Pauillac
Château Pouget	Cantenac-Margaux
Château La Tour-Carnet	Saint-Laurent
Château Lafon-Rochet	Saint-Estèphe
Château Beychevelle	Saint-Julien
Château Prieuré-Lichine	Cantenac-Margaux
Château Marquis-de-Terme	Margaux

Cinquièmes Crus—Fifth Growths

Château Pontet-Canet	Pauillac
Château Batailley	Pauillac
Château Haut-Batailley	Pauillac
Château Grand-Puy-Lacoste	Pauillac
Château Grand-Puy-Ducasse	Pauillac
Château Lynch-Bages	Pauillac
Château Lynch-Moussas	Pauillac
Château Dauzac	Labarde
Château Mouton-Baron-Philippe*	Pauillac
Château du Tertre	Arsac
Château Haut-Bages-Libéral	Pauillac
Château Pédesclaux	Pauillac
Château Belgrave	Saint-Laurent
Château Camensac	Saint-Laurent
Château Cos Labory	Saint-Estèphe
Château Clerc-Milon	Pauillac
Château Croizet-Bages	Pauillac
Château Cantemerle	Macau

* Formerly Château Mouton d'Armailhacq, now Château Mouton-Baronne-Philippe.

Over 120 years have gone by, but this classification remains virtually unchanged to this day, and the names and ratings are more or less familiar to all lovers of claret. Most of the châteaux on the list continue to indicate on their labels that they are a *cru classé* or *grand cru classé*, and any discussion of the vineyards of the Médoc will always revolve around these wines. The classification remains valid in many ways, and many of these wines are still among the best produced in Bordeaux, but this listing must be approached with a certain perspective. For one thing, a number of châteaux no longer exist—Desmirail has been absorbed by Palmer, Ferrière by Lascombes. Some have become run-down and produce only small quantities of undistinguished wine; others have been purchased by proprietors determined to increase the quality of a château's wines and to expand its production as well. Since the classification was drawn up, many of the *crus classés* no longer have the same boundaries as they did in 1855. A proprietor is legally permitted to buy vineyards anywhere within the appellation of his property—Margaux, Saint-Julien, Pauillac, or Saint-Estèphe—and sell that wine under the château label. Certain properties have doubled or tripled their production in the past twenty years by acquiring land from their neighbors.

The classification gave such prominence to the châteaux of the Médoc that the excellent vineyards of Graves, Saint-Emilion, and Pomerol were neglected until fairly recently. It must be added, however, that the vineyards of the Médoc are much bigger, on the average, than those of the other districts. A château producing twenty or thirty thousand cases is not unusual in the Médoc, whereas there are few châteaux producing even ten thousand cases in Saint-Emilion, Pomerol, and Graves.

Perhaps the most interesting development within the classification itself is that there has been so much attention focused on the four first growths, Lafite-Rothschild, Latour, Margaux, and Haut-Brion, that their prices are now two or three times that of almost any other classified wine. At the time of the classification, a second growth sold for only 10 or 15 percent less than a first, and a fifth growth cost about half as much as a first. To the four first growths of 1855 must be added Mouton-Rothschild, which never accepted its status as "first of the seconds." In recent years its wines have always been as expensive as those of the first growths, and in 1973 it was officially reclassified as a first growth.

This leads to the important point that the classification was, in fact, based on the prices that each wine had sold for in a number of previous vintages. This pragmatic approach to the value of a property is the one still in use today among the brokers and shippers of Bordeaux. In the Bordeaux wine trade, the wines of the classification are referred to simply as the first growths and the classed growths, the latter category including all but the five most expensive wines. Among the classed growths are a number of wines officially rated as third, fourth, or fifth growths, such as Palmer, Talbot, Beychevelle, and Lynch-Bages, that consistently achieve the same prices as the classified seconds, and in some cases, a bit more. To use the classification effectively look over the list from time to time so that you will know when you are drinking the wine of one of the more famous châteaux of Bordeaux. What you should not do is to pay undue attention to the exact rating of every wine, because a wine's relative price on an extensive retail listing of Bordeaux châteaux will give you a better indication of the way the Bordeaux wine merchants themselves rate the wine today.

There were also a number of other châteaux rated just below the *grands crus classés* as *crus exceptionnels* and *crus bourgeois*. Although the term *cru bourgeois* is often used informally to describe a property that sets high standards for itself, there is now an association of *crus bourgeois* organized by a number of proprietors in Médoc. Their most recent listing, published at the end of 1977, includes 123 châteaux. Three additional châteaux —Angludet, Gloria, and de Pez—are generally acknowledged to produce wines that are comparable to those of the classed growths. Some of the best-known *crus bourgeois* are listed below.

Château d'Agassac
Château Beau-Site
Château Bel-Air-Marquis-d'Aligre
Château Capbern
Château Castera
Château Chasse-Spleen
Château Citran
Château Coufran
Château Dutruch Grand Poujeaux
Château Fourcas-Dupré

Château Fourcas Hosten
Château du Glana
Château Gressier Grand Poujeaux
Château Greysac
Château Haut Marbuzet
Château La Bécade
Château Labégorce
Château La Cardonne
Château Lanessan
Château Larose Trintaudon
Château La Tour de By
Château La Tour-de-Mons
Château La Tour St.-Bonnet
Château Lestage
Château Liversan
Château Livran
Château Loudenne
Château Marbuzet
Château Maucaillou
Château Meyney
Château Les Ormes de Pez
Château Patache d'Aux
Château Paveil de Luze
Château Peyrabon
Château Phélan Ségur
Château Potensac
Château Poujeaux-Theil
Château Siran
Château du Taillan
Château Tronquoy-Lalande
Château Verdignan
Château Vieux Robin

The wines of the Médoc are known especially for their breed and finesse, and are the most elegant of all Bordeaux. In good vintages, the best châteaux need several years of bottle age to reveal their distinctive qualities, and a wine that is still improving after twenty or thirty years in the bottle is not exceptional, although finding such a wine may be.

One way to tour the Médoc is to drive straight out to Saint-Estèphe, the village farthest from Bordeaux, and then to visit the principal properties in turn. There are three châteaux in Saint-Estèphe whose wines are very familiar here—Cos d'Estournel, Montrose, and Calon-Ségur—and many other châteaux are found here as well, as Saint-Estèphe is by far the biggest wine-producing village in the Médoc. Saint-Estèphe wines are quite firm and tannic when young, and develop slowly: they are among the least supple of all clarets.

Pauillac probably has the highest average quality of wine of any village in France. Three *premier cru* châteaux are located there—Lafite-Rothschild, Latour, and Mouton-Rothschild—as well as a number of other properties whose wines are justifiably popular. Château Lafite-Rothschild is one of the few properties whose house actually resembles a château, and few sights are more impressive than the first view of its *chai* for the new wine. In a spacious and high-ceilinged ground-level warehouse, more than a thousand barrels are lined up in several rows, representing perhaps four million dollars' worth of maturing wine. Until 1967 a second wine was also made at the property, Carruades de Château Lafite-Rothschild, which came entirely from the Lafite vineyard, but was made up primarily of lighter and quicker-maturing wines from young vines. In 1974, Lafite began once again to market a second wine as Moulin des Carruades. In 1962, the proprietors of Lafite purchased Duhart-Milon, another Pauillac vineyard, and have since renamed it Duhart-Milon-Rothschild.

Château Mouton-Rothschild has been in the hands of Baron Philippe de Rothschild since the 1920s, and he gradually transformed the château into one of the showplaces of the Médoc. Apart from the dramatically lit cellars and the beautifully furnished main house, there is also a fascinating wine museum on the property that attracts a great many visitors every year. Since 1945, the labels of Château Mouton-Rothschild have incorporated a design by a different artist every year. These have included Jean Cocteau (1947), Salvador Dali (1958), Henry Moore (1964), Joan Miró (1969), Marc Chagall (1970), and Pablo Picasso (1973). In 1933, Baron Philippe acquired Château Mouton d'Armailhacq, which he renamed Mouton-Baron-Philippe in 1956. Beginning with the 1975 vintage, the label was changed to Mouton-Baronne-Philippe, in honor of the baron's late wife. Baron Philippe also purchased 'Château Clerc-Milon in 1970. The firm that markets the wines of Mouton-Rothschild also ships a very successful red and white regional Bordeaux called Mouton-Cadet.

Château Latour encompasses little more than modest living quarters, apart from its wine *chais*, although the ancient tower that gives the property its name and appears on its label still stands. Stainless-steel fermentation *cuves* were installed in time for the 1964 vintage (Château Haut-Brion had already been using similar *cuves*), and these innovations by first growths have encouraged other châteaux to adopt more modern methods of winemaking. Since the 1966 vintage, Château Latour has been bottling a second wine, which comes entirely from the Latour vineyards, as Les Forts de Latour. In some abundant years the château markets a third wine, also bottled at the château, labeled simply Pauillac. There are many Bordeaux vineyards that have incorporated the name Latour on their labels, but the one great château of this name is this one, in Pauillac.

Château Pichon-Longueville, a second growth of Pauillac, has long been divided into two parts, one labeled Baron Pichon-Longueville, the other, Comtesse de Lalande. The wines of the latter property are now labeled simply Chateau Pichon-Lalande.

Saint-Julien does not have any first growths, but it does have eleven classified châteaux within its borders. Just about all of them are available here, and they are excellent wines. Saint-Julien wines are somewhat softer and more supple than those of Saint-Estèphe and Pauillac, and mature more quickly. The three Léovilles are well-known—Châteaux Léoville-Las-Cases, Léoville-Poyferré, and Léoville-Barton—as is Château Beychevelle, whose seventeenth-century manor house is one of the sights of the Médoc. Château Talbot and Château Gruaud-Larose, owned by the Cordier firm, are both popular with American consumers, and many connoisseurs agree that Château Ducru-Beaucaillou produces wines that are consistently among the finest of the Médoc.

Margaux produces wines noted for their elegance and rich texture: they are often described as suave. Château Margaux, a first growth, is its most famous vineyard, and the fact that it bears the same name as the commune itself has often led to confusion. A blend of wines from various properties within the village can be labeled Margaux. But there is only one Château Margaux, and there could be only a general family resemblance between a regional Margaux and the wine of this outstanding property. In 1976, the Ginestet family sold Château Margaux for about sixteen million dollars. (Château Latour was bought by an English group in 1962 for about a million pounds, and in the 1930s another first growth, Château Haut-Brion, was acquired by an American, Clarence Dillon.) The wines of the nearby commune of Cantenac are now entitled to be sold as Margaux, and usually avail themselves of this better-known appellation. There are a number of excellent classed growths in Margaux, among them Château Prieuré-Lichine, greatly improved and expanded by its proprietor, Alexis Lichine. Château Palmer, classified as a third growth, now sells for more than any second growth, and Château Giscours, purchased by the Tari family in 1962, has considerably improved its reputation in recent years.

Two excellent classified vineyards that are not situated within the four main communes of the Médoc are Château La Lagune and Château Cantemerle. There are also two other communes—Listrac and Moulis—whose appellations are sometimes seen on château-bottled wines, and they are often reasonably priced.

There is no white Médoc as such, because the appellation applies only to red wines. There are, however, some attractive white wines made by a few châteaux in the district including Pavillon Blanc of Château Margaux and Caillou Blanc of Château Talbot. They are only entitled to the *Appellation Contrôlée* Bordeaux Supérieur.

Graves

The Graves district (whose name is derived from its gravely soil) begins just at the city limits of Bordeaux, and its most famous vineyard, Château Haut-Brion, can be reached by a local bus. As a matter of fact, land developers in Bordeaux have already bought up parcels of all but the best vineyards nearest the city and are turning them into housing projects. At one time the red wines of Graves were the most famous of all Bordeaux, but today the district is known mainly for its inexpensive white wines. A regional wine labeled simply Graves or Graves Supérieures will invariably be white, and it's often assumed that Graves makes only white wines; actually, half of its production is red. The red wines are usually sold under their individual château names, and are generally of a much higher class than the whites.

White Graves is usually a dry wine, but some regional bottlings are semi-dry or even noticeably sweet. Until recently, the relative sweetness of a Graves was rarely indicated on its label, but today dry wines are marketed as Graves, those with some sweetness as Graves Supérieures. The slightly earthy quality of Graves—and of white Bordeaux in general—plus the mellowness that one frequently encounters, have probably prevented the wine from being as popular as, say, Chablis or Pouilly-Fuissé. Furthermore, although it is accepted winemaking practice to stabilize white wines with a bit of sulfur dioxide, nowhere is this more evident than in the bouquet and taste of the cheapest Graves. The château wines are certainly more carefully made and a number of them are distinctive.

It is the red wines from individual châteaux, however, that are of the most interest, and some of them are among the best wines of France. If they lack the finesse of the best Médocs, they have instead a richer texture and are tremendously appealing clarets. Not only is Château Haut-Brion officially rated on a par with the first growths of the Médoc, but two other red Graves, Château La Mission-Haut-Brion and Domaine de Chevalier, consistently sell for more than any second growth of the Médoc.

The wines of Graves were classified in 1953 and again in 1959. Different levels of quality were not set up, as in the Médoc, and all of these wines are rated equally as *crus classés*. Naturally, Château Haut-Brion is considered to be in a class by itself.

Graves is the only important district in Bordeaux where many classified properties make both red and white wines.

GRAVES
Crus Classés—Classified Growths

Red Wines

Château Bouscaut
Château Carbonnieux
Domaine de Chevalier
Château de Fieuzal
Château Haut-Bailly
Château Haut-Brion
Château La Mission-Haut-Brion
Château La Tour-Haut-Brion
Château La Tour-Martillac
Château Malartic-Lagravière
Château Olivier
Château Pape Clément
Château Smith-Haut-Lafitte

White Wines

Château Bouscaut
Château Carbonnieux
Domaine de Chevalier
Château Couhins
Château Haut-Brion
Château La Tour-Martillac
Château Laville-Haut-Brion
Château Malartic-Lagravière
Château Olivier

Other good red and white wines from Graves include:

Château Baret	Château La Garde
Château Ferrande	Château La Louvière
Château Larrivet Haut-Brion	Château Magence
	Château Pontac-Monplaisir

Saint-Emilion

The picturesque village of Saint-Emilion is about twenty miles northeast of Bordeaux, and to drive there one must cross both the Dordogne and the Garonne rivers. Saint-Emilion is a medieval village whose winding streets are paved with cobblestones, and one of its main tourist attractions is a monolithic church whose chapel was carved out of a granite hillside a thousand years ago, arches, pillars, and all. The local restaurants feature a dish that visitors are always encouraged to try without necessarily being told what it contains: it is *lamproie*, the local eel, cooked in red wine and one of the few seafood dishes that is traditionally served with a red wine. The worldwide fame of Saint-Emilion, however, is its wine. Vineyards begin at the very edge of town and, unlike those of the Médoc and Graves, are to a large extent planted on slopes rather than flatlands. Saint-Emilion produces about two-thirds as much wine as the entire Médoc, but as its wines are not divided into inner appellations, the name Saint-Emilion is perhaps best known of all the Bordeaux appellations.

Saint-Emilion is often referred to as the Burgundy of Bordeaux because its wines are fuller and rounder than, say, those of the Médoc—the result of somewhat richer soil and a greater proportion of Merlot grapes. This comparison is misleading, however, as Saint-Emilions very much exhibit the classic qualities of Bordeaux, although they tend to mature more quickly than the wines of the Médoc and Graves. In 1955 the wines of this district were officially classified into a dozen *premiers grands crus classés*, and about seventy *grands crus classés*. The wines in the first group are considered on a par with the classed growths of the Médoc, and two châteaux, Cheval Blanc and Ausone, are generally recognized as being on a level with the first growths and are just as expensive. The larger second group, however, consists, for the most part, of small properties whose wines are often difficult to find.

Despite their *grand cru classé* ranking, most of these châteaux are at the quality level of bourgeois growths of the Médoc. Some Saint-Emilions display the words *grand cru* on their labels. These wines are not classified at all, and the phrase is permitted, on a vintage-by-vintage basis, to properties whose wines have passed a tasting test. The *grand cru* rating is usually achieved by about 150 châteaux in any given year.

Adjoining Saint-Emilion proper are five small *Appellation Contrôlée* communes to whose names Saint-Emilion has been affixed. The best-known are Montagne-Saint-Emilion, Saint-Georges-Saint-Emilion, and Puisseguin-Saint-Emilion, and each contains some châteaux whose wines can equal those of Saint-Emilion.

All of the *premiers grands crus classés* are listed here, as well as the better-known *grands cru classés*.

SAINT-EMILION

Premiers Grands Crus—First Great Growths

Château Ausone
Château Cheval Blanc
Château Beauséjour-Duffau-Lagarrosse
Château Beauséjour-Bécot*
Château Belair
Château Canon

Clos Fourtet
Château Figeac
Château La Gaffelière†
Château Magdelaine
Château Pavie
Château Trottevieille

Grands Crus Classés—Great Classified Growths

Château L'Angélus
Château Balestard-la-Tonnelle
Château Cadet-Piola
Château Canon-La-Gaffelière
Château Cap de Mourlin
Château Corbin
Château Corbin-Michotte
Château Curé-Bon
Château Dassault
Château Fonroque
Château Grand-Barrail-

Lamarzelle-Figeac
Château Grand-Corbin
Clos des Jacobins
Château La Clotte
Château La Dominique
Château Lamarzelle
Château Larcis-Ducasse
Château La Tour-Figeac
Château Pavie-Macquin
Château Ripeau
Château Soutard
Château Tertre-Daugey
Château Trimoulet

* Formerly Château Beauséjour-Fagouët
† Formerly Château La Gaffelière-Naudes

Château Troplong Mondot   Château Yon-Figeac
Château Villemaurine

Other Saint-Emilion châteaux include:
Château Ferrande   Château Monbousquet
Château Fombrauge   Château Puy-Blanquet
Château La Grace Dieu   Château Simard
Château Lapelletrie

Pomerol

Pomerol is the smallest of the top wine districts of Bordeaux, and produces only 15 percent as much wine as Saint-Emilion. Pomerol, in fact, adjoins the Saint-Emilion district, and for many years its wines were grouped with those of its better-known neighbor. About fifty years ago Pomerol was accorded a standing of its own, and its wines now have achieved the reputation they merit. As a matter of fact, a number of Pomerol vineyards consistently sell their wines for more than the second growths of the Médoc.

The vineyards of Pomerol are fairly small, and its most famous property, Château Petrus, produces only about four thousand cases a year. The comparatively small size of the Pomerol and Saint-Emilion vineyards probably accounts for their late-flowering reputations both in France and abroad. Vineyards were originally established in these two districts by members of the middle class. In contrast, the great vineyards of the Médoc were established in the early eighteenth century by an aristocratic class that was able to carve out much bigger estates in that undeveloped area. The greater production of the Médoc châteaux and the higher social standing of its owners gave this district a momentum from the very beginning. The Classification of 1855 did not even consider the vineyards of Saint-Emilion and Pomerol, and to this day, their limited production has prevented them from being as familiar to claret drinkers as the châteaux of the Médoc.

There is very little regional Pomerol available, as its wines are mostly sold under the names of individual châteaux. Pomerols are rich and full-flavored, with a distinctive earthy quality, and they generally mature more quickly than do the wines of Saint-Emilion. No classification has ever been established for Pomerol, but the following list indicates the best, and best known, of its vineyards. Château Petrus stands apart, on a level with the first growths of the Médoc.

POMEROL
Château Pétrus

Château Beauregard	Château Latour-Pomerol
Château Certan-de-May	Clos L'Eglise
Château Certan-Giraud	Domaine de L'Eglise
Château Clinet	Château L'Eglise-Clinet
Château Gazin	Château L'Enclos
Château La Conseillante	Château L'Evangile
Château La Croix	Château Nénin
Château La Croix-de-Gay	Château Petit-Village
Château Lafleur	Château Rouget
Château La Fleur Pétrus	Château Trotanoy
Château Lagrange	Vieux-Château Certan
Château La Pointe	

Other Pomerol properties include:
Château de Sales
Château Taillefer
Clos René

Sauternes

The luscious, sweet wines of Sauternes are among the most unusual in the world, and they are produced by a unique and expensive process that can take place only in certain years. The Sauternes district, which is about thirty miles from Bordeaux, is geographically contained within the southern part of Graves. Wines produced in the commune of Barsac are, technically speaking, Sauternes as well, but these wines are entitled to be marketed under their own *Appellation Contrôlée*. Some vineyards use the appellation Barsac, others use Sauternes, and a few use both names on their labels to make the most of the situation.

Sauternes is always a sweet wine. If a proprietor in Sauternes chooses to make a dry white wine, as some of them do to supplement their income, that wine can be sold only as Bordeaux Blanc. Although the name Sauternes is used (often without the final *s*) to label inexpensive white wines from other countries that range in taste from mellow to dry, they bear no resemblance to the wines made in Bordeaux in a rather special way. When the owners of vineyards producing red wines or dry white wines are already picking their grapes, the critical time has just begun for those who make Sauternes and Barsac. The proprietors must wait for their grapes—primarily Sémillon, with some Sauvignon Blanc and a little Muscadelle—to be affected by a beneficial mold called *pourriture noble,* or noble rot. The morning fog that rises from the Ciron River, which separates Barsac from the rest of the Sauternes region, provides the moisture necessary for the noble rot to appear. As the grapes become covered with the unattractive white mold *Botrytis cinerea,* they gradually shrivel up. And as water evaporates from the grape pulp, there is an increased concentration of sugar and flavor elements in the remaining juice. When the grapes are pressed and the rich juice is fermented, not all of the sugar is transformed into alcohol. The resulting wine is rich and sweet.

Although Sauternes can be made only when the right combination occurs—ripe grapes, alternating humidity and sunshine, and the absence of rain or frost in the fall—the finest Sauternes require even more care and risk. The vineyards must be harvested carefully so that only the fully botrytised, or "rotted," grapes are picked, and the rest are left to continue their transformation by the noble rot. This means not just one picking but several. It also means leaving part of the crop on the vines until late October or mid-November, in the hope that all the grapes will by then have been fully affected by the noble rot. Waiting those extra weeks involves risk, and sending harvesters through a vineyard six or eight times is expensive. In practice, much of the Sauternes region is harvested in only two or three pickings during late September or early October. As a result many wines produced in Sauternes are not much more than agreeable, sweet white wines that lack the intensity and concentration of the best Sauternes. Most important, they lack the distinctive botrytised taste, complex and honeyed, that distinguishes the finest wines, made from shriveled and rotted grapes, from those that are made primarily from ripe grapes only partly affected by *Botrytis cinerea*. Most of the wines from this region are blended and bottled by Bordeaux firms and sold as Sauternes or Barsac (or as Haut-Sauternes or Haut-Barsac, meaningless terms with no legal definition whatsoever). These regional bottlings almost invariably lack the character for which these wines are famous. Many are comparatively thin and weak sweet wines, and are likely to disappoint those who try them hoping to discover the qualities that make Sauternes unique. The finest Sauternes and Barsacs available here are château-bottled wines from about a dozen properties.

Sauternes is not as popular as it was in the last century, and although prices of château-bottled wines have increased in the past few years, these unique wines are still comparatively undervalued. Furthermore, some good château-bottled examples are not much more expensive than regional blends, most of which are lighter-bodied and less intense. At one time it was appropriate to serve a Sauternes or Barsac with a first course of fish, and this practice still exists today in Bordeaux to a limited extent. Although Sauternes is usually served with dessert, some connoisseurs feel that a sweet dessert tends to overwhelm the wine. Many who enjoy the distinctive taste of Sauternes have discovered that Roquefort cheese is one of the best accompaniments to this wine, since it provides an excellent contrast to the richness of the wine and brings out its qualities, instead of smothering them. Sauternes is not to everyone's taste, but you must not deny yourself the experience of tasting a bottle of this unique wine, preferably from one of the best châteaux.

There is one vineyard in Sauternes that is considerably more famous than all of the others, and that is Château d'Yquem. Its wines cost three or four times as much as those of other châteaux, and its 250 acres constitute one of the most famous vineyards in the world. A dry white wine is sometimes made at Château d'Yquem, primarily from Sauvignon Blanc grapes, and labeled "Y" (pronounced *ee-grek*).

The wines of Sauternes were classified in 1855 along with those of the Médoc and a great many of these château-bottled wines are imported into this country.

Grand Premier Cru—First Great Growth
Château d'Yquem

Premiers Crus—First Growths

Château La Tour-Blanche

Clos Haut-Peyraguey

Château Lafaurie-
    Peyraguey

Château de Rayne-Vigneau

Château de Suduiraut

Château Coutet

Château Climens

Château Guiraud

Château Rieussec

Château Rabaud-Promis

Château Sigalas-Rabaud

Deuxièmes Crus—Second Growths

Château Myrat

Château Doisy-Daëne

Château Doisy-Védrines

Château D'Arche

Château Filhot

Château Broustet

Château Nairac

Chéteau Caillou

Château Suau

Château de Malle

Château Romer

Château Lamothe

BURGUNDY

Burgundy, perhaps the most evocative of all wine names, conveys different impressions to different people. The historian knows Burgundy as an independent duchy that was annexed to France in the late fifteenth century. The decorator associates the name with a deep red color, although Burgundy produces white wines that are among the finest in the world. Many consumers recognize Burgundy as a name used in several countries other than France to label inexpensive red wines, although the province of Burgundy, situated in east-central France, is strictly delimited. And to many wine drinkers Burgundy means wines that are rich and heavy, although many of the finest Burgundies are noted for their delicacy, finesse, and refinement.

All of Burgundy produces about half as much wine as Bordeaux, but most of this comes from Beaujolais and the Mâconnais. Perhaps a more relevant comparison might be between Bordeaux and the heart of Burgundy—the Côte

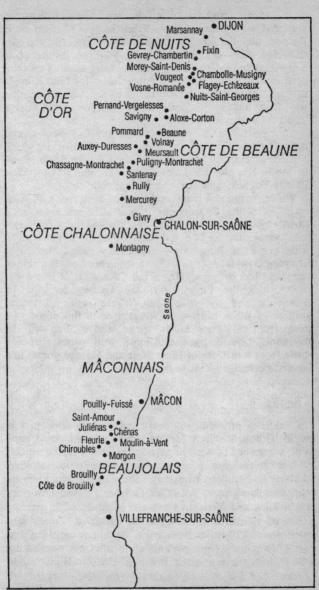

Marsannay • DIJON
CÔTE DE NUITS
Gevrey-Chambertin • • Fixin
Morey-Saint-Denis •
Vougeot • • Chambolle-Musigny
Vosne-Romanée • • Flagey-Echézeaux
• Nuits-Saint-Georges
CÔTE
D'OR
Pernand-Vergelesses •
Savigny • • Aloxe-Corton
Pommard • • Beaune
Auxey-Duresses • • Volnay
• Meursault *CÔTE DE BEAUNE*
Chassagne-Montrachet • • Puligny-Montrachet
• Santenay
• Rully
• Mercurey

• Givry • CHALON-SUR-SAÔNE
CÔTE CHALONNAISE
• Montagny

Saône

MÂCONNAIS

Pouilly-Fuissé • • MÂCON
Saint-Amour •
Juliénas • • Chénas
Fleurie • • Moulin-à-Vent
Chiroubles • • Morgon
Brouilly • *BEAUJOLAIS*
Côte de Brouilly •

• VILLEFRANCHE-SUR-SAÔNE

d'Or—which contains such famous wine villages as Gevrey-Chambertin, Nuits-Saint-Georges, Pommard, Beaune, and Puligny-Montrachet. There are only eighteen thousand acres of vines in the Côte d'Or, compared to 175,000 acres in Bordeaux, and the total amount of wine produced in the Côte d'Or is appreciably less than is made in the Médoc district of Bordeaux alone. This is another way of saying that the best wines of Burgundy will always be scarce and expensive.

The vineyards of Burgundy are divided into several main districts: Chablis, to the north; the Côte d'Or, which consists of the Côte de Nuits and the Côte de Beaune; and to the south, the Chalonnais, the Mâconnais (including Pouilly-Fuissé), and the vast Beaujolais district.

White Burgundy from any district must be made entirely from the Chardonnay grape, although there is a small amount of Pinot Blanc still planted in a few scattered vineyards. (It is now believed that the famous white wine grape of Burgundy—traditionally called the Pinot Chardonnay—is not actually a member of the Pinot family.) Red Burgundy from the Côte d'Or is made entirely from the Pinot Noir; the Gamay is used in Beaujolais and the Mâconnais. There is a substantial amount of white wine—rarely marketed in this country—made from the lesser Aligoté grape, and entitled only to the appellation Bourgogne Aligoté. Red wines that are made from a mixture of Pinot Noir and Gamay grapes are labeled Bourgogne-Passetoutgrain.

Chablis

Chablis is probably the best-known white wine in the world, although mainly for the wrong reasons. As it happens, a number of wine-producing countries, including the United States, are permitted to label any white wine Chablis, and millions of cases of inexpensive wines are so marketed every year. True Chablis from France, however, is a specific and distinctive wine. It is produced in strictly delimited vineyards that encircle the village of Chablis, situated about 110 miles from Paris. Although considered a part of Burgundy, the vineyards of Chablis, surrounded by wheatfields, are somewhat isolated: Chablis is 80 miles northwest of Beaune and 130 miles from the vineyards of

Pouilly-Fuissé, the wine with which Chablis is most often linked. Chablis is a comparatively big-bodied wine, bone dry and well defined, with a refreshing and distinctive touch of acidity. Years that are particularly hot and sunny produce Chablis that is not typical, and such wines tend to be heavy and lacking in crispness.

Considering the fame of Chablis, it's surprising to discover that, as recently as the early 1960s, the average production was only about 115,000 cases. Chablis, being so much farther north than the rest of Burgundy, is subject to spring frosts that, in the past, reduced the crop three years out of four. In 1957 the frost damage was so severe that fewer than ten thousand cases of this world-famous wine were produced. Since then, most vineyard proprietors have installed sophisticated frost-control equipment, and once they realized they could combat frost, they began to replant vineyards that had been abandoned since the nineteenth century. In 1957 there were fifteen hundred acres of vineyards in Chablis; today nearly four thousand acres are planted in vines. The average production now exceeds 600,000 cases, and in an abundant vintage Chablis can produce a million cases of wine.

The vineyards of Chablis, which are planted entirely in the Chardonnay grape, produce wines with four different appellations. The principal appellation seen on labels is, of course, Chablis, which accounts for about half the production. The highest appellation, Chablis *grand cru*, is limited to only seven vineyards: Les Clos, Valmur, Grenouille, Vaudésir, Les Preuses, Bougros, and Blanchot. *Grand cru* Chablis is always expensive, partly because the wine is produced in favored sites, but also because it is scarce. There are only 250 acres of *grand cru* vineyards, and no more can be planted. About thirty individual vineyards are entitled to the appellation Chablis *premier cru*, of which the ones most often seen here are Montée de Tonnerre, Fourchaume, Vaillons, La Forêt, Mont de Milieu, and Vaulorent. It's not necessary for the consumer to remember individual vineyard names, since the words *grand cru* and *premier cru* are always prominently displayed on the label. Petit Chablis is the least interesting of the Chablis appellations, as the wines come from vineyards on the outskirts of the district. These lighter-bodied wines are attractive when young, but few examples retain their appeal much beyond a year. What's more, the price of Petit Chablis in recent years has been almost as high as that of Chablis, so it is not often imported into this country.

Côte d'Or

The Côte d'Or, or Golden Slope, gets its name from the appearance of these hillside vineyards when they have taken on their autumn foliage. The vineyards of the Côte d'Or begin just below Dijon and continue, with a break midway, for about thirty miles down to Chagny. This strip of soil, never more than half a mile wide, produces only 15 percent of all the wines made in Burgundy, but it is here that are situated the famous villages and vineyards that most people associate with the name Burgundy. The northern half is the Côte de Nuits, and known primarily for its red wines. The Côte de Beaune, to the south, produces more red wine than white but is famous for its superb white wines.

Red Burgundies, which account for about 85 percent of the wines of the Côte d'Or, are considered easier to enjoy than Bordeaux, as they are softer, fuller, rounder wines. They have a more beguiling bouquet, generally discribed as more perfumed, and they seem to taste less austerely dry than claret. Unfortunately, many consumers think of red Burgundies as heavy, almost sweet wines, because of the many poor examples that are produced: such wines do not display the elegance and balance of the finest examples. The best white Burgundies have a richness and depth of flavor that justifies their reputation as one of the finest dry white wines in the world.

While good Burgundies may be very appealing to many wine drinkers, they are also considerably more difficult to understand than are the wines of Bordeaux. In the first place, there are more village names to remember in the Côte d'Or than in Bordeaux: fourteen or so that are important, several others that are less frequently encountered and that therefore provide some good values. Apart from these village names and two or three district names, there are thirty-one individual vineyards, officially rated as *grands crus*, which are legally entitled to their own *Appellation Contrôlée*. That is, the name of the vineyard appears by itself on a label (Chambertin, Montrachet, Musigny) without the name of its village of origin. In

Bordeaux, of course, even the best vineyards bear a commune or district appellation, which makes it considerably easier to place them geographically. Thus, Château Lafite-Rothschild has the *Appellation Contrôlée* Pauillac on its label, and Château Haut-Brion is identified as a Graves.

Not only is it necessary for the intelligent buyer of good Burgundy to know the wine villages and to have some familiarity with the *grands crus,* but one other important factor further complicates the choice of wine. Almost all of the vineyards in Burgundy, which are fairly small to begin with, are owned by several different growers. For example, Montrachet, only nineteen acres in size, has over a dozen owners. The twenty-three acres of Grands-Echézeaux are divided among ten owners; and Clos de Vougeot, whose 125 acres make it the biggest vineyard in Burgundy, has more than eighty owners today. This multiple ownership can be traced back to the French Revolution, when large domains owned by the Church and by members of the nobility were confiscated and sold in small parcels to the local farmers. The laws of inheritance in Burgundy have made these holdings even smaller, whereas in Bordeaux the large châteaux are maintained as corporate entities and have continued intact. Since each grower decides for himself when to replant old vines, how severely to limit his yield per acre, when to harvest, and exactly how to vinify his wines, the result is a number of different wines of different quality from the same vineyard. Two people can discuss the merits of Château Latour 1970, which they enjoyed separately, and be certain they are talking about the same wine. Two people comparing notes on previously consumed bottles of Chambertin 1969 or Volnay Caillerets 1971 must first establish who produced each wine.

There are three important levels of quality in the Côte d'Or: village wines, *premiers crus*, and *grands crus*. This rating system is incorporated into the official *Appellation Contrôlée* laws for Burgundy and was based on historical precedent and careful analysis of each vineyard. There has never been an official classification of the Côte d'Or vineyards similar in status to the 1855 classification for the Médoc, but an attempt was made in 1861. Each of the best vineyards was named a *Tête de Cuvée,* and this traditional distinction is still found on some labels, particularly for those vineyards that did not merit *grand cru* status under the *Appellation Contrôlée* laws. One indication of how difficult it must have been to rate each one of the small Burgundian vineyards is the fact that they are traditionally referred to as *climats*. In other words, it is understood that rain, for example, will affect each plot of land in a different way, depending on the ability of the subsoil to absorb water, that its exact position on a hillside will determine its exposure to the sun, and so forth. Perhaps a modern way of translating *climat* would be microclimate.

The principal wine villages are shown on the map, and will be discussed in detail. One confusing aspect of some of these villages names came about in the late nineteenth century when a number of villages appended to their names that of their most famous individual vineyard. Thus Gevrey became Gevrey-Chambertin, Chambolle became Chambolle-Musigny, Nuits changed to Nuits-Saint-Georges, and so on. As the great vineyard of Montrachet is partly situated in both Chassagne and Puligny, both of these villages added its name to their own. Consumers sometimes believe that they have drunk the wine of a specific great vineyard when in fact they have been served a village wine, which can come from vineyards anywhere in the named village. It must be remembered, however, that none of these villages produce a great deal of wine and their names on a label should by no means be thought of as a regional appellation. For example, Saint-Emilion produces twenty times as much wine as does Pommard, and there is a hundred times as much wine made in Beaujolais as in Nuits-Saint-Georges.

The *premier cru* vineyards of the Côte d'Or are not difficult to spot because their names always follow those of their respective villages. Thus, some *premier cru* wines from Volnay are Volnay Caillerets, Volnay Champans, Volnay Clos des Ducs, and so forth. Some *premier cru* wines from other villages include Gevrey-Chambertin, Clos Saint-Jacques; Pommard, Les Rugiens; Chassagne-Montrachet, Clos de la Boudriotte; and so on. Not infrequently you will see the words *premier cru* after a village name, without the name of a specific vineyard, such as Chassagne-Montrachet Premier Cru. This usually indicates that the wine comes from more than one *premier cru* vineyard or that the producer felt that the phrase by itself would make his wine more salable than the name of a specific, but unfamiliar, vineyard.

The highest rating in the Côte d'Or is that of *grand cru*, and the thirty-one wines so classed are listed below, vineyard by vineyard, along with some of the better-known *premiers crus*. If you recognize the village names, certain *grand cru* vineyards are easy to locate: Chambertin, Musigny, Montrachet, Romanée-Saint-Vivant, for example. Other *grand cru* names, however, bear no relation to that of their village of origin, and only homework will lead to familiarity: for example, Clos de la Roche, Richebourg, Bonnes Mares. *Grand cru* wines account for perhaps 5 percent of all the wines of the Côte de Nuits and Côte de Beaune, and they are always expensive. They are also among the greatest red and white wines in the world, and their study will be repaid by their excellence.

A grower in Burgundy does not produce a single wine, as does a Bordeaux château. He deliberately has vines in several vineyards, and often in two or three adjoining villages, so that he is protected to some extent from the hailstorms and frosts that occasionally occur and that often affect only a very small area at a time. Of course, another factor leading to scattered holdings is that domains in Burgundy are built up slowly as money is accumulated and vines become available for sale.

A visitor to a Bordeaux château will be taken on a tour of the *chai*, see hundreds of barrels of new wine aging in spacious surroundings, and then be offered a glass of one or perhaps two vintages currently in wood. Visiting a cellar in Burgundy means crowding in among barrels, called *pièces*, piled two or three high, and tasting will include as many as a dozen different wines from different villages and vineyards. A famous Bordeaux château may produce fifteen thousand to thirty thousand cases of a single wine in a year. A Burgundian grower whose domain is big enough to justify bottling his own wines at the property may produce only five hundred to one thousand cases, made up of several wines. His share of a *grand cru* vineyard may only be big enough to produce four barrels, or one hundred cases, a year. A domain that produces four or five thousand cases is considered quite large in the Côte d'Or.

It is evident, then, that whereas in Bordeaux a knowledge of the main districts and of a few major châteaux will get you off to a good start, knowing Burgundy is a bit more time-consuming. You must know the villages, at least a few *grand cru* vineyards, and then pay strict attention to the name of the shipper or grower whose wine you are drinking.

The relative merits of wines blended and bottled by shippers and those estate-bottled by individual growers is a subject that often provokes discussion among Burgundy drinkers. Most growers in Burgundy sell their wines in barrel to the big shipping firms, who blend together wines from each appellation to make what they hope will be a consistently dependable Beaune, Pommard, Nuits-Saint-Georges, and so on. A number of growers have traditionally preferred to bottle their wines themselves, as do the châteaux of Bordeaux. Such wines bear the words *mis en bouteille au domaine, mis au domaine,* or *mis en bouteille à la propriété,* and these estate-bottled wines are the Burgundian equivalent of the château-bottled wines of Bordeaux. The phrase *mis en bouteille dans nos caves,* bottled in our cellars, is often used by shippers and does not signify estate-bottling. The English words *Estate Bottled* sometimes appear on labels without the French equivalent. Although such wines may be authentic examples of estate-bottled wines, Common Market regulations specify that the phrase is not binding unless it also appears in the language of the producing country.

Those who prefer estate-bottled Burgundies suggest that the wines of each shipper tend to have a family resemblance that cuts across the individual appellations. Each shipper has certain ideas about what a good Burgundy should taste like and tries to maintain his standards and his style, sometimes at the expense of the particular characteristics of a village or vineyard. By comparison, the best of the growers produce wines that have more individuality and that define more clearly the style of each appellation. In reply, a shipper might point out that he is a specialist in the aging and bottling of fine wines, and that his judgment and experience in these matters are more reliable than that of many growers, especially those who have only recently decided to estate-bottle their wines. Furthermore, a shipper who buys from a great many growers is likely to have more perspective on the style of each appellation and greater flexibility in blending wines to a consistent style than a grower whose production and concerns are limited to wines from his own vineyards. Unfortunately, many estate-bottled wines today are of inferior quality, just as many shippers' wines are undistinguished and lack definition. Perhaps the most important element in this controversy is the reputation of the firm or person whose name is on the label. There are several dozen individual growers whose wines are recognized as outstanding examples of Burgundy, and a number of serious shippers who produce a wide range of excellent Burgundies.

There is another controversial issue concerning the style and quality of fine Burgundy. Many people who enjoy red Burgundies feel that the overall style of these wines has been gradually transformed over the past twenty years or so by what is often referred to as the new vinification. According to this view, the longer vatting practiced years ago to produce deep-colored, tannic, and long-lived red Burgundies has given way to shorter vatting and lighter wines that are sooner ready to drink, but often lack intensity and flavor. It is undoubtedly true that some Burgundian winemakers have responded to the demand from many wine drinkers for red wines that can be consumed within a few years of the vintage, but it is also true that many shippers and growers continue to make long-lived wines in more traditional ways. As it happens, a number of Burgundian producers believe that the most significant factor affecting the quality of Burgundy has been that of overproduction, not vinification. As the demand for red and white Burgundies has intensified, many growers have increased their production per acre, which usually results in weak, light wines without much character or depth. Although *Appellation Contrôlée* laws for Burgundy limit the amount of wine that can be produced for each appellation, the system of declassification permitted growers to market their excess production easily. For example, a grower who owned vines in the *grand cru* vineyard of Chambertin was not permitted to produce more than thirty hectoliters per hectare, which is about 133 cases per acre. (A hectoliter equals about eleven cases of wine, a hectare 2.47 acres.) However, if his production in a given vintage was greater than thirty hectoliters, he could simply declassify the excess and sell it with the village appellation Gevrey-Chambertin, whose limits were fixed at thirty-five hectoliters per hectare. Any excess beyond that could be further declassified and sold as Bourgogne Rouge, as the limits for that regional appellation were fifty hectoliters. In other words, a proprietor who owned a hectare in Chambertin could produce as much as fifty hectoliters and expect to sell all of it with one appellation or another. The *cascade des appellations*, as the declassification system was often referred to, meant that, in this example, the same barrel of wine was entitled to be sold under any one of three different appellations. Although growers who bottled their own wines may have had the incentive to produce a smaller quantity of finer wine, those who sold off their wine in barrel to local shippers had little reason to deprive themselves of additional income.

New legislation adopted in 1974 did away with the concept of declassification. Before each harvest, a committee of growers and legislators estimates the production for each village and *grand cru* vineyard appellation based on that year's growing conditions. After the harvest the estimates are confirmed and a maximum yield limit is established that also takes into account the quality of the vintage. The wine from each plot is then entitled to only one appellation. That is, a grower in Chambertin can declare his wine as Chambertin or Gevrey-Chambertin, but not as both; a grower in Gevrey-Chambertin can declare his wine as such or as Bourgogne Rouge, but not as both. A grower is permitted a leeway of 20 percent above the base limits established for that year, but the additional 20 percent is entitled to the appellation only if a sample of the wine is approved by a tasting panel. If a grower exceeds even the 20-percent allowance, then none of his wine is entitled to the appellation. Many observers feel that this new law, which effectively ends the *cascade des appellations*, will encourage growers in the Côte d'Or to limit their production. Winemakers can still choose to vinify their red wines in a lighter style rather than a tannic one, but the washed-out and insipid red and white wines that resulted from overproduction in recent years may eventually be replaced by wines with more flavor and complexity.

What this means to the consumer of good Burgundy, of course, is that good vintages in the Côte d'Or are likely to produce better wines than in the recent past. It also means that the concept of declassification and overproduction no longer exists. In the past, it was common practice for a retailer to tell a customer that a particular Bourgogne Blanc, for example, was really a declassified Meursault from a grower who overproduced, or that a Gevrey-Chambertin was really a declassified Chambertin. Anyone who makes such a claim today about a Burgundy is, at the very least, simply misinformed. It's also well to remember that even in the days when declassified wines were available, they still represented overproduction. If the Bourgogne Blanc and Gevrey-Chambertin cited above were values, then surely the wines sold as Meursault and Chambertin respectively, which were identical, must have been overpriced. Although the new system has been in effect for several years, it is still too soon to determine its overall effect on the wines of the Côte d'Or. It does indicate, however, how important quantity is in determining the quality of Burgundy, and of fine wines in general.

What follows is a closer look at the individual wine villages of the Côte d'Or, starting with the Côte de Nuits. With a few exceptions, which will be noted, all the wines of the Côte de Nuits are red.

Just below Dijon is the little village of Marsannay, whose wines are sometimes seen over here, especially the delightful Bourgogne Rosé de Marsannay (from the Pinot Noir grape) and the Pinot Noir de Marsannay.

Fixin, pronounced by its inhabitants as *fee-san*, produces less than a tenth as much wine as Nuits-Saint-Georges or Pommard, but good wines from its best vineyards can occasionally be found here.

The next village is world famous: Gevrey-Chambertin. Its two principal vineyards, Chambertin and Chambertin-Clos de Bèze, sit side by side and extend for about seventy acres. Vines were planted in Gevrey by the abbey of Bèze as early as the seventh century, and its wines soon achieved a high reputation. In the thirteenth century, the story goes, a farmer named Bertin planted vines in the adjacent field, which was known as *champ de Bertin*, or Bertin's field. Although these two vineyards are now known for their outstanding red wines, it's interesting to note that at one time there was also a white Chambertin, an early example of trial and error. Most of the proprietors of one vineyard own vines in the other, so it's hard to distinguish between the two plots. Moreover, whereas Chambertin can only be labeled as such, wines from Chambertin-Clos de Bèze can also be sold as Chambertin.

There are, in addition to these two vineyards, seven other vineyards of *grand cru* stature bearing the name Chambertin, including Chapelle-Chambertin, Charmes-Chambertin, Latricières-Chambertin, Ruchottes-Chambertin, Mazys-Chambertin, Mazoyères-Chambertin, and Griotte-Chambertin. The wines of Mazoyères-Chambertin may be sold as Charmes-Chambertin, and almost always are. The two great vineyards produce about ten thousand cases a year, the other seven together about twenty thousand cases. Gevrey-Chambertin produces more wine than any other village in the Côte d'Or and the best of them are the biggest-bodied of all Burgundies.

The village of Morey-Saint-Denis lies between the considerably more famous ones of Gevrey-Chambertin and Chambolle-Musigny. Its name is not often seen on wine labels here partly because many of its growers, who own vines in the adjoining towns, market their wines under the name of those better-known villages; and also because one-third of the wine produced in Morey comes from *grand cru* vineyards and is sold without reference to the village. These vineyards are Clos de la Roche, Clos Saint-Denis, Clos de Tart, and a small part of Bonnes Mares. Clos de la Roche is by far the biggest vineyard; Clos de Tart is one of the few vineyards in Burgundy under single ownership.

Chambolle-Musigny is known for its elegant and distinguished wines, and its two *grand cru* vineyards, Musigny and most of Bonnes Mares, are in the top rank of all Burgundies. A very small amount of white wine, Musigny Blanc, is also produced in that vineyard.

The little hamlet of Vougeot produces some attractive red wines sold as such, but its fame is derived from its single great vineyard, Clos de Vougeot. First planted in vines by the Cistercian monks in the twelfth century, its 125 acres have been maintained as a single vineyard throughout the centuries. The vineyard is so extensive, however, that some parcels are much better situated than others. Moreover, there are so many proprietors who own vines in this vineyard—some of them producing only one or two barrels a year—that quality varies considerably from bottle to bottle. The Clos de Vougeot itself is now the headquarters of the Chevaliers du Tastevin, an organization founded in the 1930s to promote the wines of Burgundy, and the large hall is frequently the scene of convivial dinners. A white wine from Vougeot, Clos Blanc de Vougeot, is produced in limited quantities.

Flagey-Echézeaux does not have its own village appellation because its wines can be sold as Vosne-Romanée, but it does contain two *grand cru* vineyards. Grands-Echézeaux, which adjoins Clos de Vougeot, is divided among several proprietors. Wines from the eleven vineyards entitled to the Echézeaux appellation can also be sold as Vosne-Romanée Premier Cru. The production of Echézeaux is three times that of Grands-Echézeaux.

Vosne-Romanée produces village wines of a very high level, and its best vineyards are among the most famous and most expensive in the world. The village includes the four-acre vineyard of Romanée-Conti, the most expensive of all Burgundies. The property is owned by the Domaine de la Romanée-Conti, which also owns all of La Tâche and parts of Richebourg, Grands-Echézeaux, Echézeaux, and Montrachet. The Domaine also makes and markets the wine from that part of the Romanée-Saint-Vivant vineyard originally owned by General Marey-Monge. A three-acre vineyard that does not have official *grand cru* status but that is on a par with the best of Burgundy, is La Grande Rue, situated between Romanée-Conti and La Tâche. The *grand cru* wines of Vosne-Romanée are all expensive, but a number of *premiers crus* produce excellent wines as well.

Nuits-Saints-Georges, with its five thousand inhabitants, is the biggest village in the Côte de Nuits, and its wines are among the best known of all Burgundies. Nuits-Saint-Georges and Gevrey-Chambertin produce between them about half the wines of the Côte de Nuits sold with village appellations, but this is not nearly enough to satisfy world demand. The wines of Prémeaux, which adjoins Nuits-Saint-Georges, can be marketed as Nuits-Saint-Georges. Its best-known vineyard is Clos de la Maréchale.

The appellation Côte de Nuits-Villages is a regional one for the whole district, and such wines come from the less important towns of the Côte de Nuits, such as Corgoloin, Comblanchien, and Brochon, not from Nuits-Saint-Georges itself. The lesser appellation Bourgogne-Hautes Côtes de Nuits applies to wines produced in the hills behind the Côtes de Nuits.

At this point, the Golden Slope disappears for a few

miles and, when it reappears, it becomes the Côte de Beaune. The first important village is Aloxe-Corton, dominated by the impressive hill of Corton, on whose slopes lie the best vineyards. Aloxe-Corton (locally pronounced *ah-loss*) makes some very agreeable red wines, but the best of its wines are labeled Corton, often with a supplementary plot name. In other words. Aloxe-Corton is a village appellation, and its *grand cru*, logically enough, is Corton, but there are several vineyards on the hill of Corton, such as Corton Clos du Roi, Corton Bressandes, Corton Renardes, and Corton Maréchaudes, whose *grand cru* wines can be sold either with the specific vineyard designation or simply as Corton.

Until now, all of the wines discussed have been red, but in Aloxe-Corton we encounter the first of the important white wine vineyards, Corton-Charlemagne. In the Côte de Beaune the only *grand cru* vineyard producing red wines is Corton; all the others produce white wines. Corton-Charlemagne bears testimony to the influence of the Emperor Charlemagne, who owned vineyards in Burgundy in the eighth century. At its best, it is a superlative wine of great power and breed. The vineyard actually produces more wine than any other *grand cru* except Clos de Vougeot and Corton. The best known of Corton-Charlemagne's several owners is the firm of Louis Latour, which also markets red wines from their holdings in Corton under the proprietary name Château Corton Grancey. The wines from most of the Corton-Charlemagne vineyards can also be sold simply as Charlemagne, but this *grand cru* appellation is very rarely used.

Pernand-Vergelesses lies behind Aloxe-Corton, and adjoins it: Ile-des-Vergelesses is its best vineyard. Savigny-les-Beaune is one of the biggest wine-producing villages of the entire slope, and almost all of its wines are red. Being less familiar, this excellent wine is usually less expensive than those of its more illustrious neighbors.

Beaune is not only the center of the Côte de Beaune, but of Burgundy itself. It is the biggest town of all, and most of the shippers have their offices here. Beaune is also the scene of one of the world's most famous wine events. Every year, on the third Sunday in November, the wines of the Hospices de Beaune are auctioned off, and buyers from several countries arrive to participate in the auction and in the general festivity that prevails for three days.

The Hospices de Beaune is a charitable hospital built in the fifteenth century by Nicolas Rolin and his wife, Guigone de Salins. Over the years vineyard parcels have been bequeathed to the Hospices, and the money obtained from the sale by auction of their wine is used to support the institution. The wines are generally considered to be overpriced, but the sums they fetch often affect the general price levels of the year's crop throughout the Côte d'Or.

The Hospices de Beaune now owns about 130 acres in several villages, and produces about fifteen thousand cases a year. The wines are auctioned in lots identified for the most part by the name of the donor rather than that of an individual vineyard. One cannot simply refer to a bottle of Hospices de Beaune wine, but must properly identify it with the village and the specific parcel, or *cuvée*, among the thirty-odd that make up the Hospices' holdings. What's more, the wines are aged and bottled by the buyer, not by the Hospices, so that if the many barrels that make up a particular *cuvée* are auctioned off to several buyers, as is usually the case, there will be variations among the different bottlings of that *cuvée*. Among the most famous red ones are Beaune, *Cuvée* Nicolas Rolin; Beaune, *Cuvée* Guigone de Salins; Corton, *Cuvée* Docteur Peste; and Pommard, *Cuvée* Dames de la Charité. The Hospices' white wines are almost all from Meursault and include Mersault-Charmes, *Cuvée* Albert Grivault, and Meursault Genevrières, *Cuvée* Baudot.

Beaune is one of the three or four largest wine-producing villages along the Côte d'Or, and almost all of its wines are red. Perhaps the best known of its white wines is Beaune Clos des Mouches of Joseph Drouhin. A wine labeled Côte de Beaune-Villages, often a good value, does not come from Beaune, but from any one of sixteen other villages, including such unfamiliar ones as Saint-Aubin, Saint-Romain, and Chorey-les-Beaune. Bourgogne-Hautes Côtes de Beaune is an appellation used for wines produced in the hills behind the Côte de Beaune.

Pommard is probably the most famous name in Burgundy and there can be no doubt, unfortunately, that some of the red wine sold as Pommard doesn't even bear a nodding acquaintance with the village itself. Good examples display a distinctive *terroir*, or undertaste, that characterizes the wines from this village. Although there are no *grands crus* in Pommard, most experts agree that the *têtes de cuvées* of the 1861 classification, Rugiens and Epenots, deserve the same status today.

Volnay, despite its simple name, has not achieved the same popularity in this country as Pommard and Nuits-Saints-Georges. Its elegant red wines, at best, display a delicacy and finesse that belie the popular misconception of Burgundy as a heavy wine.

Meursault is the first of the white-wine villages. Its vineyards, along with those of Chassagne-Montrachet and Puligny-Montrachet, produce almost all of the greatest white wines of Burgundy. Meursault actually produces more wine than the other two villages combined, and its wines are characterized by a certain texture and tangy dryness that set them apart. Although there are no *grand cru* vineyard in this village. Perrières and Genevrières are considered its best sites. Some red wine is produced in Meursault, notably Meursault-Blagny. Part of the Santenots vineyard is also planted in Pinot Noir: the whites are sold as Meursault-Santenots, the reds as Volnay-Santenots.

Set back from the main highway are the two villages of Monthélie and Auxey-Duresses. Monthélie produces red wines with the lightness of its neighbor, Volnay. Auxey-Duresses makes both red and white wines, and both are very agreeable. Wines from less-commercialized villages such as these are worth looking for.

Chassagne-Montrachet is famous for its white wines, but in fact two-thirds of its production is red. The white wines of Chassagne are, of course, outstanding, and within the village are parts of two great vineyards, Montrachet and Bâtard-Montrachet, as well as all four acres of Criots-Bâtard-Montrachet.

Puligny-Montrachet makes white wines only and of a very high quality. The rest of Montrachet and Bâtard-Montrachet are situated within its borders, as well as all of Chevalier-Montrachet and Bienvenue-Bâtard-Montrachet.

Montrachet, whose production varies between two and three thousand cases a year, is considered to be the best vineyard in the world for dry white wines, and it can indeed produce superlative wines. It's also true that not all of its several owners are equally conscientious, and the high price that Montrachet commands is often due as much to its fame and scarcity as to the quality of its wine. The adjoining *grand cru* vineyards should not be overlooked, nor should the many excellent village and *premier cru* wines of Chassagne-Montrachet and Puligny-Montrachet from good sources.

Santenay is the southernmost village of note in the Côte de Beaune, and its agreeable wines, almost all red, are well worth trying.

CÔTE DE NUITS: *Red Wines*

Village	Grands Crus	Premiers Crus
Fixin		Clos de la Perrière
		Clos du Chapitre
		Les Hervelets
		Les Arvelets
Gevrey-Chambertin	Chambertin	Clos Saint-Jacques
	Chambertin-Clos de Bèze	Varoilles
	Latricières-Chambertin	Les Cazetiers
	Mazys-Chambertin	Combe-au-Moine
	Mazoyères-Chambertin	
	Ruchottes-Chambertin	
	Chapelle-Chambertin	
	Charmes-Chambertin	
	Griotte-Chambertin	
Morey-Saint-Denis	Clos de Tart	Clos des Lambrays
	Clos Saint-Denis	Clos Bussière
	Clos de la Roche	
	Bonnes Mares (part)	
Chambolle-Musigny	Musigny	Les Amoureuses
	Bonnes Mares (part)	Les Charmes
Vougeot	Clos de Vougeot	
Flagey-Echézeaux	Grands-Echézeaux	
	Echézeaux	
Vosne-Romanée	Romanée-Conti	La Grande Rue
	La Romanée	Les Gaudichots
	La Tâche	Les Beaumonts
	Richebourg	Les Malconsorts
	Romanée-Saint-Vivant	Les Suchots
		Aux Brûlées
		Clos des Réas
Nuits-Saint-Georges (including Prémeaux).		Les Saint-Georges
		Les Vaucrains
		Les Cailles
		Les Pruliers
		Les Porrets
		Aux Boudots
		La Richemone

Village	Grands Crus	Premiers Crus
		Clos de la Maréchale
		Clos des Corvées
		Aux Perdrix
		Les Didiers
		Aux Thorey

The Côte de Nuits produces very little white wine, but the following can be found here: Musigny Blanc, Clos Blanc de Vougeot, and Nuits-Saint-Georges Les Perrières.

CÔTE DE BEAUNE: *Red Wines*

Village	Grands Crus	Premiers Crus
Aloxe-Corton	Le Corton	Corton Clos du Roi
		Corton Bressandes
		Corton Maréchaudes
		Corton Renardes
		Corton Les Meix
Pernand-Vergelesses		Ile des Vergelesses
Savigny-les-Beaune		Les Vergelesses
		Les Marconnets
		La Dominode
		Les Jarrons
		Les Lavières
Beaune		Les Grèves
		Les Fèves
		Les Marconnets
		Les Bressandes
		Les Clos des Mouches
		Les Cent Vignes
		Clos du Roi
		Les Avaux
Pommard		Les Epenots
		Les Rugiens
		Le Clos Blanc
		La Platière
		Les Pézerolles
		Les Chaponnières
Volnay		Clos des Ducs
		Les Caillerets
		Les Champans
		Les Fremiets
		Santenots
		Le Clos des Chênes
Monthélie		Les Champs Fuillots
Auxey-Duresses		Les Duresses
		Clos du Val

Chassagne-Montrachet	Clos Saint-Jean
	Clos de la Boudriotte
	Morgeot
	La Maltroie
	Les Caillerets
Santenay	Gravières
	Clos Tavannes

CÔTE DE BEAUNE: *White Wines*

Village	*Grands Crus*	*Premiers Crus*
Aloxe-Corton	Corton-Charlemagne	
	Charlemagne	
Beaune		Les Clos des Mouches
Meursault		Les Perrières
		Les Genevrières
		La Goutte d'Or
		Charmes
		Santenots
		Blagny
		Poruzot
Puligny-Montrachet	Montrachet (part)	Les Combettes
	Bâtard-Montrachet (part)	Le Champ Canet
		Les Caillerets
	Chevalier-Montrachet	Les Pucelles
	Bienvenue-Bâtard-Montrachet	Les Chalumeaux
		Les Folatières
		Clavoillon
		Les Referts
Chassagne-Montrachet	Montrachet (part)	Les Ruchottes
	Bâtard-Montrachet (part)	Morgeot
		Les Caillerets
	Criots-Bâtard-Montrachet	Les Chenevottes

Southern Burgundy

Southern Burgundy is made up of three districts, the Chalonnais, the Mâconnais, and Beaujolais. Beaujolais is well known for its red wines, and the Mâconnais contains the inner appellation of Pouilly-Fuissé, but the Chalonnais wines are not established in world markets, despite their resemblance and proximity to the famous wines of Burgundy. The two most interesting villages in the Chalonnais, which takes its name from the city of Chalon-sur-Saône, are Givry and Mercurey, noted primarily for their red wines, although both produce some white wines as well. Made from the Pinot Noir, and governed by *Appellation Contrôlée* laws very similar to those in effect in the Côte d'Or, the red wines are, not surprisingly, quite similar to those of the Côte de Beaune, although a bit lighter in body. The best examples are good, well balanced, and often as attractive as wines from better-known villages of the Côte d'Or. Givry doesn't produce very much wine, but Mercurey makes about as much red wine as does Gevrey-Chambertin or Pommard. The village of Montagny produces only white wine, Rully produces a limited amount of red and white wine in about equal quantities.

The Mâcon district produces red and white wine as well as some rosé, and the wines have long been available here. The red, made from the Gamay, lacks the style of the best wines of Beaujolais. The whites, from the Chardonnay, are generally better wines, and have become a popular alternative to the more expensive white Burgundies of the Côte de Beaune. In recent years some shippers have been marketing the white wines of Mâcon by their traditional varietal name—Pinot Chardonnay—in imitation of the approach used by California wineries. If a wine so labeled is from Burgundy, its label will also indicate its *Appellation Contrôlée*, usually Mâcon or Mâcon-Villages, sometimes Bourgogne.

The most famous wine of the Mâconnais is Pouilly-Fuissé. The appellation is limited to wines coming from the four hamlets of Solutré-Pouilly, Fuissé, Chaintré, and Vergisson. Although this wine is extremely popular and is ubiquitous on all restaurant wine lists, there is actually not much of it made. An abundant year will produce perhaps 350,000 cases and many vintages produce considerably less. As a result of continually increasing demand, especially from consumers in the United States, this wine, which is really not much more than a good Mâcon Blanc, now costs almost as much as wines from the villages of Meursault, Chassagne-Montrachet, and Puligny-Montrachet.

Close to the four communes of Pouilly-Fuissé are those of Loché and Vinzelles, which produce about one-tenth as much wine. They are marketed as Pouilly-Loché and Pouilly-Vinzelles, and are similar in style to those of Pouilly-Fuissé. Saint-Véran, a new appellation that went into effect with the 1971 vintage, comes from several communes that were formerly entitled to the appellation Beaujolais Blanc and Mâcon Blanc.

BEAUJOLAIS

Beaujolais is one of the best known of all red wines, and in this country it probably outsells those from any other French district. Unfortunately, Beaujolais is no longer an inexpensive wine, but the best of them are among the most enjoyable wines produced anywhere. Many people think that all Beaujolais is alike and are willing to settle for the cheapest example when they are looking for a pleasant red wine. Compared to the best wines of Bordeaux and the Côte d'Or, those of Beaujolais are not as exciting, as scarce, or as difficult to understand, but there is actually quite a variation in price, quality, and taste available from this extensive district in southern Burgundy. Poor examples lack the charm and distinctive flavor that makes Beaujolais almost unique among red wines, and given its increasing price, bottles of this popular wine should be chosen with some attention.

The Beaujolais district begins near Mâcon (about sixty miles south of Beaune) and stretches down to the outskirts of Lyons, forty-five miles farther south. The vineyard district stretches about ten miles across, along the western bank of the Saône River. The region takes its name from the village of Beaujeu, originally a barony established more than a thousand years ago. Beaujeu is no longer an important town, and the center of the Beaujolais wine trade now is Villefranche, which lies about halfway between Mâcon and Lyons. The hills and valleys of Beaujolais make up one of the most picturesque and agreeable vineyard districts in France, and the landscape has charmed many tourists who have come to the area in search of Roman ruins or to visit the remains of the monastery of Cluny with its gigantic twelfth-century church.

In an abundant vintage, the Beaujolais district produces about ten million cases of wine. (A certain amount of agreeable white and rosé wines are also produced, but more than 99 percent of Beaujolais is red.) Beaujolais is made from the Gamay grape. Although this variety is scorned in the vineyards of the Côte d'Or, the Gamay comes into its own in the granitic soil of southern Burgundy and produces wines much more charming and agreeable than would be produced from the Pinot Noir. The wines of Beaujolais are at their best when consumed young, before they are three years old, and the wines are vinified with this in mind. Vatting is limited to three days or less so that a minimum of tannin is imparted to the wine. The wines are then bottled—and often consumed—within six months of the vintage, so that they retain the freshness and fruit that make Beaujolais so agreeable.

For many years bistros in Paris and Lyons have featured Beaujolais *nouveau* or *primeur* (the names are interchangeable), which are specially selected light and delicate wines that can be released for sale as early as mid-November, just weeks after the harvest. In the past ten years or so, these fresh and charming wines have become popular in England and the United States as well, and it is no longer unusual to find new Beaujolais on sale here well before Christmas. In fact, the popularity of this wine is such that in some years as much as one-quarter of the entire crop is sold as *nouveau* or *primeur*. These wines are not meant to last, and are best consumed by the following March or April. (*Beaujolais de l'année* is used informally to refer to wine from the most recent vintage.) New Beaujolais accounts for a negligible proportion of the wines shipped here, which are rarely quite as delicate, since light-bodied wines don't keep very well. Wines chosen to be bottled for export are generally fuller-flavored and sturdier, although the best examples will naturally display the grace and charm typical of Beaujolais.

The Beaujolais district can be divided into three parts: Beaujolais, Beaujolais-Villages, and the nine *crus* of Beaujolais. The southern portion produces somewhat lighter wines entitled to call themselves simply Beaujolais. The appellation Beaujolais Supérieur differs from Beaujolais only in that this wine requires an extra degree of alcohol and production per acre is slightly less. Actually, most of the wine sold by its producers as Beaujolais could equally well be sold as Beaujolais Supérieur, yet only 10 percent is so declared, because it is really the same sort of wine. What this means to the consumer is that there is essentially no difference in quality between wines labeled Beaujolais and Beaujolais Supérieur.

The next step up the ladder of *Appellation Contrôlée* laws for the Beaujolais district is Beaujolais-Villages. Wines so labeled come from about thirty-five towns in the center of the region, whose vineyards consistently produce better wines than those farther south. Occasionally, the actual village name will appear on the label, but as these are not at all known here, the wines are usually labeled simply as Beaujolais-Villages. About 25 percent of all Beaujolais is entitled to be called Beaujolais-Villages.

The finest of all Beaujolais comes from nine communes, or *crus*, in the northernmost part of the region: Moulin-à-Vent, Fleurie, Brouilly, Côte de Brouilly, Morgon, Saint-Amour, Chénas, Juliénas, and Chiroubles. These communes produce the wines with the most distinction, they are longer-lived, and the price is somewhat higher than for a simple Beaujolais. As these wines are often labeled with only the name of the *cru*, without the word Beaujolais, it pays to remember their names if you are looking for something special from the district. Each wine has its special characteristics and its devotees, and these *crus* are among the most agreeable wines found anywhere.

The Beaujolais *crus* account for about one-quarter of all Beaujolais in an average year, and of the nine *crus*, Brouilly, Morgon, Moulin-à-Vent, and Fleurie alone produce 75 percent of the total. Moulin-à-Vent is probably the best known of them all, and is usually the most expensive, as its wines are considered the sturdiest and longest-lived. Although Moulin-à-Vent doesn't have the power or depth of a wine from the Côte de Nuits, it does have considerably more character than the typical Beaujolais and can be served with more robust foods. One of the reasons that there is so much Moulin-à-Vent produced is that most of the wines of the neighboring villages of Chénas and Romanêche-Thorins are also entitled to be sold as Moulin-à-Vent.

Fleurie and Brouilly produce lighter and more elegant wines, with an enchanting perfumed bouquet. Although it might be imagined that Côte de Brouilly is a lesser appellation than Brouilly (as is the case with Beaune and Côte de Beaune), the opposite is in fact the case. Côte de

Brouilly is an inner appellation reserved for vineyards on the slopes of Mont Brouilly. Morgon produces a very sturdy wine that needs some bottle age before it's ready to drink. Although the crop is comparatively large, the wine is not often seen in this country.

Juliénas and Chénas both have a rather distinctive *goût de terroir*, or taste of the soil, that sets them apart from their neighbors. Juliénas can be found here, but most of the production of Chénas is legally sold as Moulin-à-Vent. The wines of Saint-Amour, despite its romantic name, are not often exported to the United States, nor are those of Chiroubles. Of the two, Chiroubles is generally a more attractive and distinctive wine.

Beaujolais is made by thousands of small producers, most of whom sell their wine in barrel to local shippers. About one-third of all the Beaujolais produced, from the simplest wines to the best *crus*, come from the eighteen cooperative cellars in the region. There are also a number of larger domains that produce hundreds of barrels annually from their extensive vineyards. Occasionally, the name of a particular vineyard appears on a Beaujolais label—and some of these are quite good—but Beaujolais is a region where individual vineyards are not nearly as important a guide to quality as in Bordeaux or Burgundy, for example.

In sum, the wines of Beaujolais vary from rather light and fragile wines to the richer and fuller wines of some of the *crus*. There is naturally a tremendous choice, but it is a sad fact that there is much more Beaujolais drunk than is produced in the vineyards themselves. A cheap Beaujolais will rarely have the delightful characteristics of a true Beaujolais, and unfortunately, many consumers have formed their opinion of Beaujolias on disappointing examples. As it happens, if you shop around you can often find a wine from one of the *crus* for only a little more money than one labeled simply Beaujolais or Beaujolais-Villages, and the difference in quality can be considerable. Remember that when you taste Beaujolais you are looking for fruit rather than for the depth of flavor and complexity that are the characteristics of a fine Bordeaux or Burgundy. Beaujolais tastes best at cellar temperature (55 to 60°F) and you might try putting a bottle in the refrigerator for twenty or thirty minutes to cool it down slightly. The wine tastes all the fresher and seems more delightful.

THE RHÔNE VALLEY

The Rhône River joins the Saône at Lyons and continues south, reaching the sea near Marseilles. The wines of the Côtes du Rhône come from vineyards planted on both banks of the Rhône, starting about twenty miles south of Lyons at Vienne and continuing 120 miles to Avignon. About 95 percent of Rhône wines are red, but the region includes a famous rosé—Tavel—and some unusual white wines.

The hot and sunny climate typical of the Rhône Valley produces red wines that are generally more robust and fuller-flavored than those of Burgundy. The growing conditions along this part of the Rhône are more dependable than in most parts of France, and consequently, the best vintages for Rhône wines do not always correspond, for example, to those for Bordeaux and Burgundy. The intense heat here produces wines that contain more alcohol—and hence more body—than in more northerly vineyards, and this is reflected in the minimums set by the *Appellation Contrôlée* laws. Whereas 9 percent is required for Beaujolais and only 10 percent for a Beaujolias *cru* such as Moulin-à-Vent, the minimum for Côtes du Rhône is 10.5 percent and for Châteauneuf-du-Pape, 12.5 percent.

Although Rhône wines are usually all grouped together, there are actually two distinct districts within this region: the southern Rhône, near Avignon, whose best-known wines are Châteauneuf-du-Pape, Tavel, and the regional Côtes du Rhône; and the northern Rhône, between Vienne and Valance, which includes Côte Rotie, Hermitage, and Crozes-Hermitage.

Châteauneuf-du-Pape, a village located about ten miles from Avignon, produces about a million cases a year of what is surely the most famous of all Rhône wines. Although several thousand cases a year of white Châteauneuf-du-Pape are produced—the wine is distinctive and full-flavored—it is for its red wines that the village is world famous. The name comes from a now-ruined castle, built in the fourteenth century as a summer house for Pope Clement V. During most of the fourteenth century the popes were French, and Avignon replaced Rome as the papal seat. The summer residence was called Châteauneuf, or new castle, to distinguish it from the existing papal fortress in Avignon. It was at this time that vines were first planted in the district. When the castle was destroyed two centuries later, the vineyards went untended until the nineteenth century. At that time the wines of Châteauneuf-du-Pape were reintroduced to Parisian society, and the wine has now established itself as one of the best-known red wines in the world.

Winemakers have discovered over the years that the intense heat of the Rhône Valley does not favor the growth of any of the finest grape varieties. Instead, a number of different varieties are used, each one contributing a particular characteristic to the finished wine. In Châteauneuf-du-Pape, a dozen grape varieties are permitted, including the Grenache, which produces wines high in alcohol; the Syrah, which contributes character, tannin, and longevity; and the Cinsault, noted for its aroma. Each grower plants his vineyards in somewhat different proportions, so that the wines of Châteauneuf-du-Pape vary from domain to domain. This variation in wine is further affected by the different vinification methods used in the district. Châteauneuf-du-Pape has long been known as a wine that needs several years of bottle age to reach maturity, and a number of growers continue to employ the long vatting and long maturation in barrel that produce long-lived wines. At the same time, the increasing demand for well-known wines throughout the world and the eagerness of the consumer to drink good vintages as soon as they are available have caused a number of domains to vinify their Châteauneuf-du-Pape to produce a full-bodied but relatively fast-maturing wine that will be ready to drink sooner. You should, therefore, be prepared to experiment among the different shippers and domains to find the style you prefer. Although Châteauneuf-du-Pape is rarely an exceptional wine, it is usually dependable and widely available.

About eight miles on the other side of Avignon is Tavel, which produces what many people consider the finest rosé of France. Made primarily from the Grenache grape, the wine is dry, has a most attractive and distinctive pink-orange hue, and is certainly the rosé with the most character and balance. About 300,000 cases are made annually, and a great deal of that comes from the Cooperative of

Tavel, although it goes to market under various names. There are, as well, a number of large domains producing estate-bottled Tavel.

Close to Tavel is the village of Lirac, which produces red and rosé wines. The rosé is similar in style to that of Tavel, but less well known.

Most of the wines of the southern Rhône are sold simply as Côtes du Rhône. Production is abundant—about fifteen million cases are produced, virtually all of it red. Côtes du Rhône is made from a number of different grape varieties, primarily Grenache and Carignan. Although many examples of Côtes du Rhône lack character or distinction, there are an increasing number of well-made, fuller-flavored wines to be found as well. More than a dozen villages within the region are entitled to label their wines Côtes du Rhône-Villages, and this appellation is generally of a higher quality: Cairanne, Chusclan, and Vacqueyras are perhaps the best known. The village of Gigondas, which was granted its own *Appellation Contrôlée* in 1971, produces wines that are bigger and more distinguished than regional Côtes du Rhône, and more expensive.

Côtes du Ventoux and Côteaux du Tricastin, both situated just east of the Côtes du Rhône region, achieved *Appellation Contrôlée* status in 1973. They produce large quantities of relatively inexpensive wines, primarily red, which are similar in taste to a lighter Côtes du Rhône. A small amount of sweet, intensely flavored Muscat wine is made in the Rhône village of Beaumes-de-Venise, and marketed as Muscat de Beaumes-de-Venise.

Although Châteauneuf-du-Pape, Tavel, and the regional appellation Côtes du Rhône account for almost all the shipments to this country of Rhône Valley wines, most connoisseurs agree that the finest wines of the Rhône come from the northern part of the region. Côte Rotie and Hermitage are both powerful, deeply flavored red wines made from a single grape variety, the Syrah. (The vineyards of Côte Rotie also produce a very limited amount of white Viognier grapes that are traditionally vinified along with the Syrah.) These two appellations produce about fifty thousand cases of distinguished, long-lasting red wine. Hermitage is usually described as richer and more solid, Côte Rotie as having perhaps more finesse. Crozes-Hermitage comes from vineyards that encircle those of Hermitage and that produce nearly ten times as much wine. The soil and exposure are different, production per acre is bigger, and the wines generally lighter-bodied as well as less expensive. The villages of Cornas and Saint-Joseph, on opposite banks of the Rhône, produce good red wines in limited quantities, with those of Cornas generally longer-lived.

A soft and flowery white wine, with a ripe, fruity bouquet, is made at Condrieu from the Viognier grape. More famous is the little vineyard of Château Grillet, which produces less than a thousand cases a year of an expensive wine similar to Condrieu. Much more readily available here are the flavorful dry white wines of Hermitage and Crozes-Hermitage made primarily from the Marsanne grape.

THE LOIRE VALLEY

The Loire is famous to tourists for its historic châteaux and for a variety of agreeable wines produced along its banks. But although the châteaux of the Loire are centered around Tours, the wines of the Loire Valley are produced along most of its 650-mile course. About three-quarters of the wines produced along the Loire are white, and a certain amount of agreeable and popular rosé is made. A small amount of red wine is also produced, although the red wines are not so easily found in this country. If the Loire Valley produces no great wines (with the possible exception of some sweet wines that are rarely exported), it does produce quite a variety of delightful wines that can be—and should be—consumed young.

Starting at Nantes at the mouth of the Loire, the first wine district is Muscadet. This appellation is atypical of French wine names as it is not the name of a place, but the grape variety used to make the dry white wines of the region. The Muscadet grape, brought from Burgundy in the sixteenth century, was extensively planted and ultimately gave its name to the vineyard region around Nantes. American wine drinkers may have been put off at first by its name, similar to that of the sweet Muscatel wines produced from the Muscat grape, to which Muscadet bears no relationship whatsoever. In the past a good deal of Muscadet was sold as Chablis, which gives you some indication of its taste, although this refreshing wine is usually lighter-bodied and somewhat more acid. Nantes is the capital of Brittany, a region famous for its shellfish, and Muscadet is a perfect accompaniment to seafood, a first course, or lighter foods in general.

The best examples of Muscadet come from the Sèvre-et-Maine district, and these words will be found on the label. Rather than being an inner appellation, however, Sèvre-et-Maine actually produces about 85 percent of all Muscadet, so most of the wines imported here come from this district. You will also find bottles labeled Muscadet *sur lie*, or on the lees. This indicates that the wine was bottled directly from the barrel or vat while still resting on its lees, or natural deposits, without first being transferred to another container. Muscadet *sur lie* must now be bottled no later than the spring after the vintage, and the best of them have a distinctive crispness and yeasty freshness; unfortunately, many wines labeled *sur lie* lack these characteristics.

Another light, dry white wine produced in this region is Gros Plant du Pays Nantais. Gros Plant is the local name for Folle Blanche, and this V.D.Q.S. wine, occasionally shipped here, is at its best within a year or so of the harvest.

The next wine city up the Loire is Angers, which has given its name to the district of Anjou. The best known of the Anjou wines is, of course, Rosé d'Anjou. This light, mellow, and agreeable wine is made from a lesser grape variety, the Groslot. The relative sweetness of the wine depends on the shipper's specifications, although none of the Anjou rosés on the market is dry. Another rosé, labeled Cabernet d'Anjou, is made from the Cabernet Franc grape of Bordeaux. This wine is generally less sweet and has somewhat more character than does Rosé d'Anjou.

The Anjou district also produces white wines ranging in character from fairly dry to quite sweet and rich. The wines are made from the Chenin Blanc grape, known locally along the Loire as the Pineau de la Loire, although it is not related to the Pinot Blanc of Burgundy. The three main producing areas are the Côteaux de la Loire, the Côteaux de l'Aubance, and the Côteaux du Layon, the Aubance and the Layon being tributaries of the Loire. The Côteaux du Layon produces by far the most wine—mellow and rounded in character—but it is hard to find here. The wines produced in Quarts de Chaume and Bonnezeaux are especially rich and luscious wines that are considered by local partisans to rival the best châteaux of Sauternes.

The village of Saumur produces white wines from the Chenin Blanc and rosés and red from the Cabernet Franc. The reds are attractive, especially those from the village of Champigny, which are labeled Saumur-Champigny to distinguish them from the white wines of Saumur.

The city of Tours is the one most familiar to tourists, as it is here that most of the historic châteaux are found. Chambord, Azay-le-Rideau, Chenonceaux, and Amboise (where Leonardo da Vinci is buried) are among the most famous. Unfortunately, most of the Touraine wines are of minor interest and consumed locally. The most-famous exception is the wine of Vouvray, a village ten miles from Tours. The town is noted for its chalk hills, and its inhabitants have dug caves into the slopes that are used both as wine cellars and as homes. A number of the houses built along the slopes are mere facades with the greater part of these homes situated within the hillsides themselves.

We know Vouvray in the United States as a pleasant and fairly dry white wine, but if you visit the local cellars, you'll discover that Vouvray can be very dry, mellow, or quite sweet, and that it can be still, *pétillant*—that is, slightly sparkling—or fully sparkling like Champagne. The Chenin Blanc grape is used to make Vouvray and in sunny years it produces a most attractive mellow wine; when there is less sunshine, the wine will be drier in taste. In recent years, however, the trend here and elsewhere toward drier wines has encouraged the Vouvray winemakers to alter their vinification so that their wines are, more often than not, fairly dry. As for the rich dessert wines, they are carefully produced in exceptionally sunny years, and a visit to a local shipper or grower will often end with a bottle of ten- or twenty-year-old sweet Vouvray.

Vouvray is also known for its *mousseux*, or sparkling wines, made by the Champagne process. The *pétillant* wines are those that are bottled before fermentation is complete, so that a certain amount of sparkle is produced in the corked bottle, giving the wine a pleasant crackling quality.

Across the river from Vouvray is Mountlouis, whose wines are similar to those of Vouvray, though perhaps not quite as good.

The Touraine also produces two red wines in the villages of Chinon and Bourgueil. Rabelais was born in Chinon, and he often sang the praises of wine in general and of his local wine in particular. Made from the Cabernet grape, these two wines combine the tannic character of a light Bordeaux with an appealing fruitiness. Adjoining Bourgueil is the village of Saint-Nicolas-de-Bourgueil, whose light and elegant wines are so labeled.

Up the Loire past Orléans and just before Nevers are two villages that produce the best white wines of the Loire Valley—Sancerre and Pouilly-sur-Loire. Although we know the hamlet of Sancerre for its wines, it is as famous to the French for its goat cheese. Many of the winegrowers also maintain a herd of goats, and they serve their homemade cheeses with as much pride as their wines. The wines of Sancerre are not abundant, but they have a distinctive character that has established their reputation in Paris and, now, in this country. The wine is made from the Sauvignon Blanc grape that is used to make the dry white wines of Bordeaux, but it takes on a completely different character in Sancerre—very dry, full-flavored, and with an attractive tang. For this reason Sancerre is a good wine to serve with full-flavored dishes that call for a white wine.

The growers of Sancerre have also planted part of their vineyards with the Pinot Noir grape, and they make very agreeable rosé and red wines as well.

The village of Pouilly-sur-Loire produces two wines. The Chasselas grape (well-known in Switzerland as the Fendant) produces a wine labeled appropriately enough, Pouilly-sur-Loire. This is an agreeable country wine that is not often seen here and that is at its best within a year of the vintage. The village also produces in greater quantity a wine from the Sauvignon Blanc grape, locally known as the Blanc Fumé, or Smoky White (there are various explanations, none of them definitive). The correct name of this wine is Blanc Fumé de Pouilly-sur-Loire, to distinguish it from a Pouilly-sur-Loire. As it happens, a number of potential customers here and elsewhere, seeing the words Pouilly-sur-Loire on the label, incorrectly assumed that the lesser wine was being palmed off on them. The name was thus shortened to Pouilly-Fumé, an unusual appellation for France, as the village and grape name are combined. This, in turn, has led many people to confuse

Pouilly-Fumé from the Loire with Pouilly-Fuissé from southern Burgundy, made from the Chardonnay grape. In any event, Pouilly-Fumé is readily found here, and its rich flavor makes it a good all-purpose accompaniment to food.

The white wines of Quincy and Reuilly are also considered Loire wines, although these towns actually situated along the Cher, a tributary of the Loire. The wines have a crisp, dry taste similar to those of Sancerre and Pouilly-Fumé.

ALSACE, PROVENCE, AND OTHER WINES

Alsace

The hillside vineyards of Alsace are among the most beautiful in all of France, and the area is dotted with delightful little villages of the kind that are used as illustrations in children's storybooks. France is separated from Germany here by the Rhine, but the vineyards of Alsace are set back from the river's edge and extend for about seventy miles along the slopes of the Vosges Mountains. Alsace often produces ten or eleven million cases of white wine a year, which makes it the biggest producer of *Appellation Contrôlée* white wines after Bordeaux and Champagne. Their flavorful and refreshing qualities complement perfectly the rich cuisine of the region, with its *foie gras*, sauerkraut dishes, and sausages.

Between 1870 and 1918 Alsace and the neighboring province of Lorraine were part of Germany. At the time, Germany did not want Alsatian wines to compete with her own Rhine and Moselle wines and encouraged the production of cheap, inferior wines, much of which was used for blending or in the manufacture of Sekt, German sparkling wine. After World War I, the growers of Alsace realized that their best chance for commercial success would be with finer wines, and they set about replanting their vineyards with better grape varieties. Today, nearly 70 percent of the vineyards of Alsace are planted in three varieties—Riesling, Gewürztraminer, and Sylvaner. The rest is made up of Pinot Blanc (also known as Klevner), Pinot Gris (also marketed as Tokay d'Alsace, although it bears no relation to the Tokay of Hungary), Muscat, Chasselas, and Pinot Noir. The last is used to make a small quantity of Pinot rosé—98 percent of Alsatian wines are white.

The wines of Alsace were finally granted the *Appellation Contrôlée* Vin d'Alsace in 1962, but the wines themselves are traditionally labeled and marketed with the name of a specific grape variety. Riesling, Gewürztraminer, and Sylvaner are the best known, and each is made entirely from the named grape. The *Appellation Contrôlée* laws also permit a blend of several grapes—usually the Chasselas, Sylvaner, and Pinot Blanc—to be sold as *Edelzwicker*, or noble blend, but this name is rarely seen here.

The wines of Alsace are fermented until they are dry, and this is what distinguishes them from German wines, with which they are sometimes confused. Whereas German Rieslings, Sylvaners, and Gewürztraminers are fragrant and sweet, those made in Alsace are fuller-flavored, with more body and alcohol, and austerely dry. The Sylvaner produces comparatively light, agreeable wines without much distinction. The Alsatians consider the Riesling to be their finest wine, and many customers agree that the dry Rieslings of Alsace are more appropriate with food than the sweeter wines produced in Germany. It is the Gewürztraminer, however, that most people associate with Alsace. The wine has an intense, spicy bouquet and a unique, pungent taste that makes it one of the most unusual and readily indentifiable white wines in the world. The wine was originally made from the Traminer grape. *Gewürz* means spicy, and Alsatian shippers used to select the most intensely flavored lots of Traminer and market them as Gewürztraminer. As a result, one shipper's Traminer might turn out to be spicier than another one's Gewürztraminer. To simplify matters, a new wine law that went into effect at the beginning of 1973 prohibited the use of Traminer on an Alsatian label—all the wines made from this variety must now be sold as Gewürztraminer. Actually, some Alsatian shippers believe that a natural clonal selection has occurred over the years so that there is now a Gewürztraminer grape that has replaced the Traminer orginally planted in the vineyards.

Some wines shipped from Alsace are labeled *grand cru*. In the past these simply contained a higher minimum-alcohol content and had to conform to stricter quality controls. Since the 1978 vintage, *grand cru* applies only to wines from certain specific sites within Alsace made from the Riesling, Gewürztraminer, Pinot Gris, or Muscat. Words such as *Réserve* or *Réserve Personnelle* are not legally defined and their significance depends on the standards of the individual shipper.

Alsatian shipping firms—Hugel, Trimbach, Willm, and Dopff & Irion are the best-known here—market about half of the wines of the region, a third are produced by the many cooperative wine cellars, and the rest is estate-bottled and sold by individual growers. Unlike their counterparts in Bordeaux and Burgundy, who buy only wine, many Alsatian shippers also buy grapes and make the wines in their own cellars. This gives the shippers greater control over the style and quality of wines they market. The wines are generally bottled within six months or a year of the harvest, and since 1972, all Alsatian wines must be bottled within the region—none are permitted to be shipped in bulk and bottled elsewhere.

Provence

The region of Provence extends along the Mediterranean coast from Marseilles east to Nice. This 120-mile stretch is dotted with fishing villages and with such famous resorts as Saint-Tropez, Cannes, Antibes, and Juan-les-Pins. A holiday mood and a *salade niçoise* on a terrace overlooking the water can add a great deal of enchantment to the agreeable rosés of Provence, and it is disappointing to discover that these wines rarely taste quite the same when consumed at home. It's true that many of these delicate and charming wines served in carafes do not travel well, but then neither does the mood in which they were first enjoyed. Of the vast amount of wine produced in this part of France, mostly for local consumption, there is a certain amount that stands out from the rest. The best-known wines are labeled Côtes de Provence, and they account for about one-tenth of all the wines of Provence. They were elevated from V.D.Q.S. status to *Appelation Contrôlée* with the 1977 vintage. About eight million cases are produced within the appellation, two-thirds of it rosé. An increasing amount of red wine is also made, as well as a limited amount of white wine. Côteaux d'Aix is a

V.D.Q.S. wine that includes reds, whites, and rosés produced near the town of Aix-en-Provence.

The seacoast villages of Bandol and Cassis each produce red, white, and rosé wines that are entitled to *Appellation Contrôlée* status. Bandol produces mostly reds and rosés—they are dry wines with a fairly well-defined character. Cassis is known primarily for its white wine, full-flavored and a favorite accompaniment to the local *bouillabaisse*. The wines of Cassis bear no relation to the *crème de cassis* made in Dijon. The latter is a black-currant syrup used on desserts and to flavor certain drinks, notably Kir, a popular aperitif that is a mixture of white wine and *crème de cassis*.

Other Wines

Near the Swiss border, not far from Geneva, two white wines are produced that are occasionally seen in this country. Crépy, made a few miles from the lake of Geneva, is a light, dry wine made from the Chasselas grape. Being a wine made in the mountains near Switzerland and from a grape widely grown there, it's no surprise that Crépy resembles Swiss white wines. Seyssel is a dry white wine from the Haute-Savoie, and much of its production is transformed, by the Champagne process, into a sparkling wine. Seyssel *mousseux* is well known to skiers at nearby Mégève and Chamonix, and is shipped to this country as well.

The vast area of the south of France produces tremendous amounts of ordinary wine and is by far the largest viticultural area in the country. Most of this wine is totally anonymous and is used to make the commercial blends sold within France. There are a few districts, however, that produce more distinctive wines, and these are entitled to the V.D.Q.S. appellation. Few of these wines are shipped here, but you may come across Corbières. Minervois, Costières du Gard, Faugères, and Côteaux du Languedoc. Fitou, also from the Midi, is an *Appellation Contrôlée* wine. About 98 percent of the wines are red, and they are similar in taste to a Côtes du Rhône.

In the Dordogne region just east of Bordeaux, a number of relatively unfamiliar *Appellation Contrôlée* wines are produced from the same grape varieties as in Bordeaux. Among the wines that occasionally find their way here are the red and white wines of Bergerac, and the white wines of Montravel and Monbazillac.

The vineyards around Cahors, a city about 120 miles east of Bordeaux, produce deep-colored, full-bodied red wines made from the Malbec grape. For many years this wine, greatly admired by those who were able to find it, was produced in limited quantities. In 1971, Cahors was elevated from V.D.Q.S. to *Appellation Contrôlée* rank, production has increased to about half a million cases, and many examples today are no longer as dark, tannic, and intense as in the past. More than half the production comes from a cooperative cellar at Parnac.

The Jura district, east of Burgundy, produces a limited amount of red, white and rosé wines of which Arbois rosé is the most often seen in Paris. There are also several thousand cases a year produced of a very special white wine, Château-Chalon, made in a rather unusual way. After fermentation, the wine is aged for at least six years in small barrels that are not completely filled, thus exposing the wine to air. The resulting oxidation causes a yeast film to form, similar to that produced in certain Sherries by a similar exposure, and the finished wine is known as a *vin jaune,* or yellow wine. Château-Chalon (which is the name of a village, not a vineyard) is a most curious white wine; although not fortified, it is similar to a dry Sherry, but perhaps less complex.

THE WINES OF GERMANY

Germany produces only 2 or 3 percent of the world's wines, and its vineyards—situated within a relatively small area in the southwestern part of the country—amount to only a tenth that of France or Italy. Nor is wine the national beverage, as it is in those two countries; beer is the German's daily drink. Nevertheless, Germany makes what are acknowledged to be among the very greatest white wines in the world. The classic Riesling grape, when planted in the best sites along the Rhine and Moselle, produces a truly superb wine with an incomparable bouquet and with extraordinary elegance and breed.

Until the eighteenth century most German wines were red, but today more than 85 percent of Germany's vineyards produce white wine. Red wines are still made—primarily from Blauer Spätburgunder (Pinot Noir), Portugieser, and Trollinger grapes—in Baden and Württemberg, in the Rheinpfalz, along the Ahr, and in the villages of Assmannshausen in the Rheingau and Ingelheim in the Rheinhessen, but they are almost always too light to compare favorably with red wines available from other countries. All of Germany's white wines, with the possible exception of the Steinweins from Franconia, bear a family resemblance: a distinctive, flowery bouquet, and a taste characterized by a more-or-less harmonious balance of sweetness and acidity that gives them a distinctive piquancy. There are many consumers who willingly try wines from different countries, but who reject all German

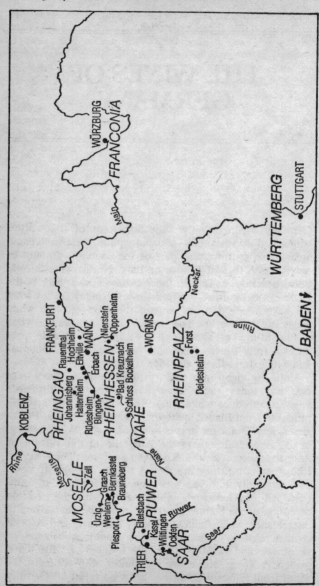

wines as too sweet. It's true that even the driest examples of Rhines and Moselles do not have the full-bodied dryness of, say, a good white Burgundy. But German wines have instead a charm and appeal unequaled by any other wines, and the best of them have an extraordinary richness of bouquet and ripeness of flavor that has established their outstanding reputation.

Unfortunately, many people are put off by German wine labels, with their unfamiliar and seemingly unpronounceable names, often made even less comprehensible by the use of Gothic script. Admittedly, understanding these labels requires more knowledge than many people care to acquire, even if they recognize that the style of these wines cannot be matched in any other wine region. There are a much greater number of important wine villages in Germany than in Burgundy, for example, and more individual vineyards of note than in Bordeaux. Furthermore, most German vineyards are split up among several owners, each of whom will make a somewhat different wine than his neighbor. To complicate matters even more, in a good vintage German winemakers produce not one but several different wines from the same vineyard by successive pickings of increasingly ripe grapes.

As a result of this discouraging complexity, German wine shippers and most consumers have limited their attention to just a few regional appellations such as Liebfraumilch, Bereich Bernkastel, Bereich Johannisberg, Bereich Nierstein, Piesporter Michelsberg, and Zeller Schwartze Katz; and wines so labeled account for more than 80 percent of the German wines sold here. Such wines exist at all prices, and most of them can only hint at the aromatic bouquet and opulence of taste that characterizes the best German wines, without in any way suggesting their refinement and complexity. Many consumers who have tasted, at least on occasion, fine wines from other countries remain unaware of Germany's best wines. My own experience suggests that anyone who is offered a good German wine for the first time will almost invariably express amazement and delight that wines of this style and caliber exist.

The German vineyards extend up to, and even slightly beyond, what is known as the northern limit of the vine. Farther north, excessively cold winters will kill the vines, and summers lacking in adequate sunshine would prevent grapes from properly ripening. The best wines are made on slopes and steep hillsides facing south, where their height and direction enable the grapes to catch the maximum amount of sunshine. The poor soil that characterizes these vineyards is unsuitable for any other crop, and the steep incline of many vineyards makes it impossible to use modern machinery. It is by the hand labor of thousands of growers that these vines are tended, and it's only because the wines produced can be so remarkable—and expensive—that it is still commercially worthwhile for these vineyards to be cultivated. There are over 100,000 growers tending their own vines in Germany, and 90 percent of them own less than five acres. Only three hundred or so estates consist of more than twenty-five acres, but it is among these larger domains that most of the famous wine-producing names are found.

The Rhine is the informing river of German viticulture, and all German wines are produced either along the Rhine or along the banks of its many tributaries. The principal wine regions along the Rhine itself are the Rheinpfalz, or Palatinate, known for its soft, full, rounded wines; the Rheinhessen, which produces a tremendous quantity of agreeable wines (it is the home of Liebfraumilch); and the Rheingau, a comparatively small district that produces the very finest of the Rhine wines—elegant, rich, and well balanced. The Moselle (spelled Mosel in German) joins the Rhine at Koblenz. Its wines, and those of its two tributaries, the Saar and the Ruwer, are light-bodied, fragrant, and possess a refreshing crispness derived from their acidity. The Nahe joins the Rhine at Bingen, and despite its geographical position halfway between the Rhine and Moselle, its wines have the richness and style of Rhine wines.

The vineyards of Franconia, along the Main, produce wines quite different from those of the Rhine and Moselle, and less often seen here. These drier wines have less bouquet and more body, and a distinctive earthy taste. Franconia wines, sometimes referred to generically as Steinweins after its most famous single vineyard, are easy to spot because they are always shipped in the distinctive *Bocksbeutel*, a squat, flat-sided, gourdlike bottle.

The two German states of Baden and Württemberg produce about 25 percent of Germany's wines, and a third of that is red. Stuttgart is the principal city of Württemberg, whose wine villages are spread out on both sides of the Neckar River. Baden is the southernmost of the German wine regions, and part of its vineyards extend between the Black Forest and the Rhine, opposite the Alsace region of France.

Except for the wines of Franconia, just about all German wines are sold in slender tapering bottles—Rhine wines in brown bottles, Moselles in pale green. This distinction can be of help in remembering their general characteristics: the rich, full, deep flavor of the Rhines, and the pale, fresh, delicate, and graceful wines of the Moselle.

Virtually all of Germany's fine wines are made from the Riesling, and it is along the Rhine and Moselle that this grape has most successfully demonstrated why it is considered one of the world's half-dozen classic varieties. The Riesling needs a long growing season, however, and does not ripen fully every year, so that despite the quality of its wines, it accounts for only 20 percent of the acreage in Germany. It is the principal variety in the Mosel-Saar-Ruwer and the Rheingau, but is planted in less than 15 percent of the Rheinpfalz vineyards, and only 5 percent of those in the Rheinhessen. Until quite recently it could be assumed that the finest wines of the Rheingau and the Mosel-Saar-Ruwer—those from individual vineyards and top estates—were made from the Riesling, whether or not the variety was named on the label. Because of increased plantings of other varieties in recent years that assumption can no longer be made, and with few exceptions producers whose wines are made from the Riesling now indicate that on their labels.

The Riesling is widely planted throughout the world, and although it sometimes retains its name, as in France's Alsace region, the true Riesling of Germany is often identified by a somewhat different name in other countries—Johannisberg Riesling or White Riesling in California, Rheinriesling in Austria, Riesling Renano in Italy, Rjanski Rizling in Yugoslavia, Rhine Riesling in Australia, and so on. More often than not, wines from other European countries that are simply labeled Riesling are made from a variety known as the Welsch Riesling or Italian Riesling, and are rather neutral in taste. A California wine labeled

Riesling is actually made from the Sylvaner, and wines marketed as Riesling from South America, where very little Riesling is planted, are more likely to be made from Sauvignon Blanc or Sémillon. It would therefore be a mistake to expect any of the so-called Rieslings produced around the world to have any similarity whatsoever to those of Germany. With few exceptions, even wines made from the true Riesling in other countries lack the elegance, distinctive aroma, and particular combination of fruit and acidity of German Rieslings.

The Sylvaner (spelled Silvaner in German) was once the most widely cultivated variety, and accounted for almost a third of all plantings. Today, it covers only 15 percent of the vineyards, but is still widely found in the Rheinhessen, Rheinpfalz, and Franconia, where it is sometimes called the Franken Riesling. The Sylvaner produces wines without much finesse or distinction, neutral and low in acid, which makes them useful for blending. Nevertheless, the best examples from good vintages, especially from vineyards in the Rheinhessen, can be very good.

The Müller-Thurgau, now the most extensively planted variety in Germany, was developed about a hundred years ago by Professor Müller, who came from Thurgau in Switzerland. It was long assumed to have been a cross of Riesling and Sylvaner, but some ampelographers now believe that it was produced from two clones of Riesling. It has the advantage of being adaptable to a wide variety of soils and ripening early, making it a good all-pupose variety. It produces wines that are mild, neutral, and low in acid, which makes them useful in blending, although when bottled on their own they age rather quickly.

The Traminer, famous in Alsace for its spicy, aromatic wines, is not widely planted in Germany. The Ruländer, known as the Pinot Gris in France, and the Weisser Burgunder, or Pinot Blanc, are both cultivated to some extent, primarily in Baden. The most significant recent development has been the increased plantings of new varieties. Some, such as the Morio-Muskat and the Scheurebe, have been known for some time. Others, including the Optima, Ortega, Bacchus, Kerner, and Ehrenfelser, have been registered only in the past ten or fifteen years, and these new varieties are now found in some of the best-known estates along the Rhine and Moselle. Each has particular attributes that make it worth cultivating—resistance to frost, early ripening, higher sugar contents, low acidity—and they are useful for blending with Riesling in lesser years. Some of them are also bottled individually, and marketed with their own names.

Curiously enough, although grapes do not fully ripen every year in the northerly vineyards of Germany, the yield is relatively high. On the average, Germany produces half again as much wine per acre as do France and Italy, and it is not unusual for the Riesling to produce the equivalent of more than four hundred cases of wine per acre, which is about twice the yield of the best vineyards of Bordeaux and Burgundy, and more than the Johannisberg Riesling produces in California. Other varieties may produce six or seven hundred cases per acre in an abundant vintage.

In most of the world's vineyard districts, a good vintage is one in which the grapes ripen fully and the resulting wine is dry, balanced, and complete, with a proper degree of alcohol. In Germany, the best vintages are those in which the grapes are not only ripe, but overripe, so that the grape sugar and natural flavor extracts present in the grapes will produce wines that are sweet, intense, and complex. These considerations are the basis of the new German wine regulations that went into effect in 1971. The new laws established three basic categories for German wines based not simply on geographical origin, but also on the ripeness of the grapes at the time of picking as expressed by their natural sugar content.

The lowest category of wine is *Deutscher Tafelwein*, German table wine. These wines, which rarely account for more than 10 percent of Germany's total production, can be labeled with only the broadest regional appellations of origin—Rhein, Mosel, Main, Neckar, and Oberrhein—and only if at least 75 percent of the wine was produced in the named region. A wine labeled simply *Tafelwein* can be blended from wines produced outside Germany. Relatively little *Deutscher Tafelwein* is shipped to this country, even though the category includes the once popular regional wine Moselblümchen.

The most important category of German wines, in terms of volume, is *Qualitätswein bestimmter Anbaugebiete*, quality wines from specified regions, also known as *Q.b.A.*

or simply as *Qualitätswein*. There are eleven delimited regions within the *Qualitätswein* category—Mosel-Saar-Ruwer, Rheingau, Rheinhessen, Rheinpfalz, Nahe, Franconia, Württemberg, Baden, Ahr, Hessische Bergstrasse, and Mittelrhein. Virtually all of the wines shipped to this country come from the first five regions listed; wines from the last three, which produce about 1 percent of Germany's wines, are almost never seen here. The name of one or another of these regions must appear on the label of every *Qualitätswein*, which gives the consumer at least a general idea of where the wine comes from, no matter how puzzling or unfamiliar the rest of the label may be.

The third and highest category of German wines is *Qualitätswein mit Prädikat*, or quality wine with a special attribute. The special attribute—designated on the label by the word *Kabinett, Spätlese, Auslese, Beerenauslese,* or *Trockenbeerenauslese*—does not reflect the origin of the wine but the ripeness of the grapes when they were picked. Chaptalization, adding sugar to the must, is permitted for *Tafelwein* and *Qualitätswein*, but is prohibited for *Prädikat* wines. Before 1971, the word *Kabinett*—or *Cabinet*, as it could then be spelled—was used at a grower's discretion to indicate a wine of special quality. Kabinett is now clearly defined as the first level among *Prädikat* wines. *Spätlese* means late picked, and traditionally refers to wines made from grapes that have been left on the vines after the harvest has begun so that they will ripen more fully. Such wines are somewhat sweeter and richer than a Kabinett wine from the same vineyard. A wine labeled *Auslese*, selected picking, is made from especially ripe bunches of grapes that are fermented separately. Auslese wines are even sweeter and richer in taste than those labeled Spätlese, and have a more concentrated flavor. *Beerenauslese*, selected berry picking, is several steps higher in quality and scarcity: grapes that are unusually ripe are picked individually and set aside to make a particularly sweet and intense wine. The very scarcest and most highly prized wines of all are called *Trockenbeerenauslese*, which means selected picking of dried berries. They are made from overripe grapes that have been attacked by *Botrytis cinerea*, the noble rot called *pourriture noble* in Sauternes and *Edelfäule* in Germany. The juice that remains in these shriveled grapes has a very high proportion of natural sugar, and its flavor is intensified to a remarkable degree. The resulting wine, which ferments very slowly and with great difficulty, is the rarest and most extraordinary wine that a German vineyard can produce. It is very sweet, of course, but has a balancing acidity that makes it harmonious rather than cloying.

Beerenauslese and Trockenbeerenauslese wines are made only in exceptionally fine years, and then only in minute quantities. A large estate that produces, say, 300,-000 bottles of wine altogether might harvest a thousand bottles of Trockenbeerenauslese and perhaps three times that amount of Beerenauslese. The prices for these rare wines are correspondingly high—$50 to $75 a bottle for a Beerenauslese, $150 to $300 or even more for á bottle of Trockenbeerenauslese.

There is one other designation that occasionally appears on a label of *Prädikat* wine—*Eiswein,* or ice wine. An Eiswein is made late in the year from fully ripe grapes that have frozen on the vine when the temperature has dropped to 20°F or less. The grapes are gathered in the early-morning hours, before the sun appears, and are carefully crushed to obtain only the rich unfrozen juice. The Eiswein designation may now appear on a label only in conjunction with one of the special attributes, such as Spätlese or Auslese. The particular conditions required to produce an Eiswein are not the same as those for a Beerenauslese, for example, and consequently Eiswein is not usually made in what are considered the finest vintages. Because the unfrozen juice from which this rare wine is made concentrates not only the sugar in the grapes but also the acid, Eiswein is characterized by a relatively high acidity that gives it a distinctive elegance and finesse.

Before the new wine laws went into effect, each producer was allowed a certain amount of leeway in determining which of the special designations to put on his labels. Now the minimum requirements for a *Prädikat* wine, and for each additional level of ripeness up to Trockenbeerenauslese, are determined by the wine's Oeschsle degree. The Oechsle scale, named after the scientist who invented it in the early nineteenth century, measures the sugar content of unfermented juice. For example, to qualify for the category *Qualitätswein mit Prädikat,* a Rhine wine made from the Riesling must have a minimum natural sugar content of 73° Oechsle; a Moselle, 70° (which is equivalent to a potential alcohol content of about 9 percent). Such a wine could be labeled Kabinett, the driest and least-expensive level of *Prädikat* wines. The Oechsle degree required for each of the special attributes varies from region to region and from one grape variety to another: the minimums established for a Riesling from the Rheingau are 85° for a Spätlese, 95° for an Auslese, 125° for a Beerenauslese, and 150° for a Trockenbeerenauslese.

Since the quality of German wines is to a large extent determined by the Oechsle scale, it is possible to make some interesting comparison among German vintages since the new laws went into effect. In 1975, for example, there was very little *Tafelwein* produced, and the rest of the crop was about evenly divided between *Qualitätswein* and *Prädikat* wines. Almost all the *Prädikat* wines were of Kabinett and Spätlese quality, however, with very little Auslese. In 1976, considered a remarkable year, no *Tafelwein* was made, and more than 80 percent of the harvest consisted of *Prädikat* wines. Spätlese and Auslese wines actually accounted for more than 80 percent of the wines made in the Mosel-Saar-Ruwer, 66 percent of the Rheingau wines. In 1977, a relatively unsuccessful year, *Tafelwein* accounted for 10 percent, *Qualitätswein* for 76 percent, and *Prädikat* wines for only 14 percent. Almost all of the *Prädikat* wines were at the Kabinett level, and virtually no Spätlese and Auslese wines were made at all.

Ripeness plays a role not simply in the quality, but also in the variety of German wines. In most wine regions around the world, a producer makes wine from the same vineyard or group of vineyards every year—the number of wines does not change, only their quality. In Germany, a large estate on the Rheingau may own vines in, say, thirty vineyards in half a dozen villages. In a fine year, when each vineyard yields a wide range of *Prädikat* wines, the estate may bottle more than a hundred different wines. In a lesser year, when few wines exceed the *Qualitätswein* category, the estate may produce only a third as many wines.

Grape juice that contains a high proportion of natural sugar will not be able to complete its fermentation, and it is the residual sugar remaining in the wine that has traditionally given German wines whatever degree of sweetness they possessed. About twenty years ago some German winemakers began to use *Süss-reserve,* or sweet reserve, and this technique has now been adopted by most producers. *Süss-reserve* is unfermented grape juice, rich in sugar, that is kept aside and then added to a wine just before bottling to increase its sugar content. This permits the winemaker to ferment his wines out until they are dry, since he will have the opportunity of adding sweetness back later on. The winemaker no longer has to arrest the fermentation of a Kabinett, Spätlese, or even Auslese when just the right amount of residual sugar remains in the wine, and he can control the exact degree of sweetness of the bottled wine. About 15 percent of a good crop is set aside as *Süss-reserve,* which may be used to sweeten the wines of a poor year as well. Not all producers use *Süss-reserve,* and in exceptionally ripe years, when very high Oechsle degrees are achieved, some producers prefer to arrest the fermentation in an Auslese wine while residual sugar remains, although they will probably permit Kabinett and Spätlese wines to ferment until they are dry.

By way of suggesting the relative sweetness of the different *Prädikat* wines, there might be 30 or 35 grams per liter—3 or 3.5 percent—of sugar in a Kabinett wine (compared to 25 grams or so in a typical Liebfraumilch); 40 or 50 grams in a Spätlese, 60 or 65 grams in an Auslese, 80 or 90 grams in a Beerenauslese, and 150 grams or more in a Trockenbeerenauslese. These are only general figures, however, because there are bound to be variations in the sugar content—and intensity of flavor—of wines labeled Spätlese or Auslese from different regions, different vintages, and different producers. The minimum sugar requirements expressed in Oechsle degrees apply to the unfermented juice when the grapes are picked, not to the wine when it is bottled.

Although the sweetness of one of these wines is the most obvious aspect of its taste, the winemakers consider that the amount of acidity present is just as important because it determines whether the wine is harmonious and well-balanced or simply sweet and clumsy. In addition, the presence of botrytised grapes, those affected by the noble rot, adds a distinctive, honeyed flavor and complexity of taste that sweetness alone cannot provide. Although the particular taste that comes from botrytised grapes is almost always found in Trockenbeerenauslese and Beerenauslese wines, there are years—such as 1976—in which the noble rot is so prevalent in the vineyards that even Auslese and Spätlese wines display the characteristically honeyed taste. Sometimes *Botrytis cinerea* does not occur even in a good vintage. In 1959, for example, grapes dried up on the vines without being affected by the noble rot. Even though Trockenbeerenauslese wines were produced, they completely lacked any botrytised character.

The presence of the noble rot also affects the sequence in which grapes are harvested in Germany. In a typical good vintage, each level of *Prädikat* wines is harvested in order of increasing ripeness. When there is a great deal of noble rot, however, growers may begin the harvest by picking the grapes for Auslese and Beerenauslese wines, and there are even instances when the first wines to be made were Trockenbeerenauslese. The usual dscription of the German winemaker consciously deciding whether or not to risk leaving his grapes on the vine for an additional two or three weeks of ripening is not always an accurate one. What the winemaker must decide in an outstanding year is just how much Trockenbeerenauslese and Beerenauslese wines to make, since the grapes he sets aside for these superb wines will, to some extent, diminish the richness and concentration of the rest of his crop. The one wine that is always produced by a conscious decision is Eiswein. Since a grower may have to wait until December or even January for the grapes to freeze on the vines, he can produce an Eiswein only by deliberately leaving a part of the crop unpicked and hoping that the necessary frost occurs before the fully ripe grapes simply spoil.

None of the wines described so far is dry, but there are two new types of wine that are now being made in Germany, Trocken, dry, and Halbtrocken, half-dry. In the past few years a number of producers have begun to market dry wines in an effort to provide the German consumer with a wine he or she could drink with meals. The maximum permissible sweetness of these wines is determined by a formula based on both sugar and acid. Basically, a Trocken wine cannot exceed 9 grams of sugar, and most have only 4 or 5 grams; a Halbtrocken cannot contain more than 18 grams of sugar, and most have about 14 grams. In a good vintage, a grower may decide to make Trocken and Halbtrocken wines of Spätlese and even Auslese quality by fermenting them out until they are dry, and such wines have noticeably more body and flavor. Because these wines are so different from traditional German wines and are likely to confuse many consumers, and because most countries have adequate sources of dry white wines, Trocken and Halbtrocken wines are not widely exported. Nevertheless, some of the most important estates along the Rhine and Moselle are producing these wines in limited quantities, and you may occasionally come across a bottle.

Although the success of a vintage and of individual wines in Germany is to a large extent measured in Oechsle degrees, the origin of each wine is still of prime importance, as it is throughout the world, in determining its particular style and personality. The new wine laws have established three increasingly specific appellations of origin within the eleven *Qualitätswein* regions: *Bereich*, or district; *Grosslage*, or collective vineyard site; and *Einzellage*, or individual vineyard site. There are thirty-two *Bereiche*, most of whose names are those of well-known wine villages. Since the average size of a *Bereich* is about 7,500 acres, these district appellations should not be confused with wines from the village whose name is used. For example, Bereich Johannisberg includes virtually all of the wine producing villages along the Rheingau. There are only four *Bereiche* for the Mosel-Saar-Ruwer, and the best-known, Bereich Bernkastel, encompasses sixteen thousand acres of vineyards and sixty villages. Bereich Nierstein in the Rheinhessen and Bereich Schloss Böckelheim in the Nahe are other examples of these rather extended regional appellations. It is under such names as these, plus Liebfraumilch, that most branded German wines are sold.

The most specific appellations of origin, as in most wine-producing countries, are those of individual vineyards, now called *Einzellagen*. German labels for individual vineyards almost always indicate the village of origin followed by the vineyard. Thus, a wine labeled Bernkasteler Graben comes from the Graben vineyard in the village of Bernkastel (which takes the possessive *er*, as a person from New York is called a New Yorker). Piesporter Treppchen, Rauenthaler Baiken, and Forster

Jesuitengarten are wines that come from individual vineyards, or *Einzellagen*, in the villages of Piesport, Rauenthal, and Forst respectively. Exceptions to this rule, vineyards so famous that their names may appear on a label without that of the village in which each is located, include Schloss Johannisberg, Schloss Vollrads, Steinberg, Scharzhofberg, and Maximin Grünhaus.

The new laws reduced the number of individual vineyards in Germany from more than thirty thousand to 2,600, and the minimum size of an *Einzellage* was set at five hectares, or a little more than twelve acres. Many small vineyards were combined, and even sizable vineyards were considerably expanded. Bernkasteler Bratenhöfchen was expanded from six acres to seventy-five, Piesporter Goldtröpfchen from eighty-six acres to nearly three hundred. The average size of the *Einzellagen* created by the new laws is over ninety acres.

Despite the dramatic reduction in the number of individual vineyard names, there are still quite a few for the consumer to keep in mind—120 in the Rheingau, for instance, and over five hundred in the Mosel-Saar-Ruwer. The new laws established an intermediate appellation called a *Grosslage,* which is made up of a number of neighboring *Einzellagen.* A *Grosslage* appellation consists of a village name followed by what seems to be an individual vineyard—Bernkasteler Kurfürstlay, Piesporter Michelsberg, Rauenthaler Steinmacher, Forster Mariengarten. In fact, Bernkasteler Kurfürstlay is a name that can be used for wines made in any one of eleven villages along the Moselle, and nine villages along the Rheingau can market their wines as Rauenthaler Steinmächer. There are 150 *Grosslagen* in Germany, including nineteen in the Mosel-Saar-Ruwer and ten in the Rheingau. The average size of a *Grosslagen* is fifteen hundred acres. A consumer who does not recognize the names of the principal *Grosslagen* is likely to confuse wines so labeled with those from individual vineyards, especially since many names now used for *Grosslagen,* such as Bernkasteler Badstube and Johannisberger Erntebringer, were actually those of individual vineyards before 1971. The names of the most important *Bereiche, Grosslagen,* and *Einzellagen* for the major wine regions are listed further on.

With few exceptions, each *Einzellage,* or vineyard site,

is divided among several owners. Consequently, the names of individual proprietors and domains, whose holdings may be scattered among a number of vineyards in several villages, must also be taken into consideration when choosing German wines. The label of an estate-bottled wine bears the word *Erzeugerabfüllung*, bottled by the producer, or *Aus eigenem Lesegut*, from the grower's own harvest, followed by the name of the producer. (Before 1971, *Originalabfüllung* was used to indicate an estate-bottled wine.) As in Burgundy, the consumer must have some familiarity with the names of the best producers as well as those of the best vineyards. Unlike Burgundy, however, where most growers bottle only a few thousand cases, there are quite a few large domains in Germany that produce twenty-five thousand to fifty thousand cases of wine a year, and their names consistently appear on any list of German wines. The owners of these large domains—which will be listed region by region further on—include noble families, religious orders, and the German state.

Many German winemakers traditionally bottle the contents of each cask separately, rather than blending them together. Before 1971, the number of the actual barrel from which a wine came was sometimes indicated on a label, preceded by *Fass* for Rhine wines, *Fuder* for Moselles. Also, *feine* or *feinste* (as in *feine* Auslese) was an indication by the producer that the wine was especially fine. These designations are no longer permitted, as they are considered too arbitrary. Nevertheless, some estates still bottle the contents of each cask separately, and may, therefore, market several different wines labeled Spätlese, Auslese, and so on from a given vintage. Today, the relative qualities of similarly labeled wines might be indicated by the use of different lot numbers on a producer's price list, or by the use of different colored capsules on the bottles. The consumer who has already made an effort to remember the names of the best vineyards and best estates may be discouraged to learn that two bottles of Auslese from a particular domain may not, in fact, be identical, but the winemaker's insistence on preserving the quality and individuality of each barrel of his wine must at least be recognized.

In addition to the vineyard proprietors who bottle their

own wines and those who sell their wines in bulk to the many German wine shippers, there are also thousands of growers who are members of cooperative wine cellars. Nearly four hundred cooperative cellars exist in Germany today, and they account for about a third of all the wines made. Cooperatives produce a relatively small proportion of wines in the Mosel-Saar-Ruwer and the Rheingau, but half the wines of Franconia come from cooperatives, and three-quarters of those from Baden and Württemberg. *Winzergenossenschaft* or *Winzerverein,* wine grower's co-operative, are the words you are most likely to see on the label of one of these wines.

Other German words that are useful to know are *Kellerei,* cellar; *Weingut,* wine domain; *Erben,* heirs; *Freiherr,* baron; *Graf,* count; and *Fürst,* prince. Weissherbst, not often seen here, is a rosé produced for the most part in Baden and Württemberg from Blauer Spätburgunder grapes.

One other indication that must appear on the labels of all *Qualitätswein* and *Prädikat* wines if the *Amtliche Prüfungsnummer,* or certification number. This is usually shortened to *A.P. Nr.* followed by a numbered code. To obtain a certification number, each lot of wine must undergo laboratory analysis and must be approved at a quality-control tasting.

Despite the exceptional quality of the best German wines, the branded regional wines marketed by a number of German shippers dominate the market here. Most consumers are put off by the diversity of German wine names, and in any case weather conditions do not permit individual producers to make fine wines every year. The simplified labeling and consistent quality of the leading brands, as well as their appealing taste, account for their popularity.

The single best-known wine of Germany is Liebfraumilch, which accounts for half of all the wines exported. The name may have originally referred to the wines produced in the small vineyard belonging to the Liebfrauenkirche in Worms (situated on the border between the Rheinhessen and Rheinpfalz), but the name can now be used for wines produced throughout the Rheinhessen, Rheinpfalz, Rheingau, and Nahe from Riesling, Sylvaner, or Müller-Thurgau grapes. In practice, most Liebfraumilch comes from the Rheinhessen and it is unlikely that much Riesling finds its way into the blend. Among the best-known brands are Sichel Blue Nun, Kendermann Black Tower, Deinhard Hanns Christof, Langenbach Meister Krone, Julius Kayser Glockenspiel, Valckenberg Madonna, and Madrigal.

Apart from Liebfraumilch, the most frequently seen regional appellations are Bereich Bernkastel, Bereich Johannisberg, and Bereich Nierstein. A number of *Grosslagen* wines are also readily available from several shippers, including Bernkasteler Kurfürstlay, Piesporter Michelsberg, Zeller Schwarze Katz, Johannisberger Ernte-bringer, and Niersteiner Gutes Domtal. At least 85 percent of a wine must come from the *Bereich* or *Grosslage* on the label, and at least 85 percent of a vintage-dated wine must come from that vintage. If a label also indicates the name of a specific grape variety, as in Bereich Bernkastel Riesling or Piesporter Michelsberg Riesling, 85 percent of the wine must be made from the named grape. These re-quirements apply not only to regional wines, but to estate-bottled wines from individual vineyards as well. In the case of *Prädikat* wines from the top estates, however, it is likely that the wine comes entirely from the vineyard, vin-tage, and variety shown on the label.

One problem that everyone who admires German wines must face is how to match them with food. *Qualitätswein,* which includes branded regional wines and Liebfraumilch, can certainly be drunk with a meal, especially in warm weather, as can many Kabinett wines. The finer *Prädikat* wines, Spätlese and up, are too sweet to accompany most foods, and not sweet enough to stand up to rich desserts, which tend to overwhelm them. The Germans themselves drink these wines on their own, in the afternoon or late in the evening. The delicate flavor and refreshing acidity of many German wines, especially Moselles, make them a de-lightful wine to serve as an aperitif before dinner. Since German wines are comparatively low in alcohol—few con-tain more than 10 percent—they can be drunk more casu-ally and copiously than many of the headier white wines produced elsewhere.

Although white wines are usually consumed young, the finest German whites—Auslese, Beerenauslese, and Trock-enbeerenauslese—will improve with a few years of bottle age. The initial sweetness and opulence will give way to a more harmonious and complex taste. Even Spätlese wines, especially those from the Rhine, will acquire added interest with bottle age.

German wine labels are considered the most specific in the world, especially for the finest wines, but a knowledge of German wines is not so easily acquired. There are nearly 1,400 wine villages and 2,600 vineyards whose names may appear on a label. Add to that the various levels of ripeness among *Prädikat* wines and the result is a truly awesome number of possibilities. Nevertheless, a rule of thumb can be formulated when selecting German wines: once you decide whether you want a Rhine or Moselle, if you choose a *Prädikat* wine of Spätlese or Auslese quality made from the Riesling in a good vintage, you will be well on your way toward a good bottle. If you then select a wine from one of the top estates, you will almost inevitably be getting a single vineyard wine as well. In time you can make your own evaluations of wines from different vineyards and from different estates, but by focusing on the vintage, special attribute, and the reputation of a major estate, you can drink fine wines without having to learn the names of villages and vineyards. Anyone who has enjoyed a few bottles of fine German wine, however, will want to know more about just where each wine comes from, and the following pages contain some basic information about the major regions.

THE GERMAN WINE REGIONS

Rheinpfalz

The Rheinpfalz usually produces more wine than any other region in Germany, and enjoys the warmest weather as well. Its wines are generally fuller, softer, and less acid than those of more northerly regions, and Auslese and Beerenauslese wines are not uncommon. The Pfalz vineyards are not actually situated along the Rhine, but extend for about fifty miles along the slopes of the Haardt Mountains, ten or fifteen miles west of the river. The Deutsche Weinstrasse, or German wine road, runs through the entire region almost to the northern end of Alsace.

About half the Pfalz wines are made from Müller-Thurgau and Sylvaner, and this region supplies much of Germany's carafe wines. The Riesling predominates in the Middle Haardt, however, the central section that contains the best wine-producing villages: Forst, Deidesheim, Ruppertsberg, Wachenheim, and Bad Dürkheim (whose wines are labeled simply Dürkheimer). When choosing wines from this district, it is helpful to remember that three producers in particular are famous for the high quality of their wines: von Bassermann-Jordan, Bürklin-Wolf, and von Buhl.

The two *Bereiche* names of the Pfalz are rarely seen, and of its twenty-six *Grosslagen*, the best-known are Forster Mariengarten and Deidesheimer Hofstück.

VILLAGE	IMPORTANT VINEYARDS
Forst	Kirchenstück, Jesuitengarten, Ungeheuer, Pechstein
Deidesheim	Leinhöhle, Hohenmorgen, Grainhübel, Nonnenstück
Ruppertsberg	Hoheburg, Nussbien, Reiterpfad
Wachenheim	Goldbächel, Rechbächel, Gerümpel
Dürkheim	Spielberg, Herrenmorgen, Steinberg

Rheinhessen

The Rheinhessen begins where the Rheinpfalz ends, at Worms, and these two regions account for almost half the vineyard acreage in Germany. The Rheinhessen is not an elongated region, but triangular, with Worms, Mainz, and Bingen as its three points. Müller-Thurgau and Sylvaner are the principal varieties here, and a certain amount of full, ripe Spätlese and Auslese wines are made from these grapes. The bulk of Rheinhessen wines are used to make up shippers' regional blends, however, notably Liebfraumilch.

The best wines of the region come from a number of villages situated along the Rhine as it flows north toward Mainz. The Riesling is extensively planted in this section, whose best-known villages are Nierstein, Nackenheim, and

Oppenheim. To this group must be added the village of Bingen, situated some miles away opposite the Rheingau village of Rüdesheim; Scharlachberg is Bingen's best-known vineyard. The estates of Franz Karl Schmitt and Anton Balbach, both located in Nierstein, produce some of the region's best wines.

Bereich Nierstein is the best-known of the region's three *Bereiche*. Of the twenty-four *Grosslagen*, the ones most frequently seen are Niersteiner Rehbach, Niersteiner Spiegelberg, Niersteiner Gutes Domtal, and Oppenheimer Krötenbrunnen.

VILLAGE	IMPORTANT VINEYARDS
Nierstein	Hipping, Orbel, Pettenthal, Hölle
Oppenheim	Sackträger, Herrenberg, Daubhaus

Rheingau

The Rheingau accounts for only 3 percent of Germany's vineyards, but it has a higher proportion of Riesling—about 75 percent—than any other region. Its best wines are, with the very best of the Moselle, the finest wines of Germany. Rheingau wines have more body and depth, and perhaps more character, than those of the Moselle, which impress more with their grace and delicacy. Spätlese and Auslese wines from the Rheingau are richer and more opulent than those of the Moselle, and generally longer-lived as well.

The Rheingau extends along the Rhine for about twenty-five miles as it flows from east to west. The vineyards face south, which enables them to obtain the maximum amount of sunshine, and they are protected from cold winds by the Taunus Mountains to the north. There are two villages that are not situated along this stretch of the Rhine, but that are considered as part of the Rheingau: Hochheim, which is actually on the Main River just before it joins the Rhine; and Assmannshausen, known primarily for its red wines. The English traditionally refer to all Rhine wines as Hocks, derived from the village of Hochheim, from which the wines of this region were originally shipped to England. To this day, many English wine lists divide German wines into Hocks and Moselles.

There are many outstanding vineyards in the Rheingau, but three of them are so famous that each of their names may appear alone on a label, without being preceded by that of a village: Schloss Johannisberg, Schloss Vollrads, and Steinberg. These vineyards are unusual because they are quite large, eighty acres or more, and because each has a single owner. Steinberg is owned by the Hessian state, and at one time its wines were made at Kloster Eberbach, a twelfth-century monastery located in Hattenheim. The Hessian state is actually the largest single owner of vineyards along the Rheingau with more than four hundred acres in several villages. Its simple label, with a stylized black-and-gold eagle and the identification *Staatsweingüter,* is a familiar one.

Schloss Vollrads belongs to the Matuschka-Greiffenclau family, who built the imposing castle in the fourteenth century. A distinctive feature in the presentation of the wines of Schloss Vollrads is that a different colored capsule is used for each category—green for *Qualitätswein,* blue for Kabinett wines, pink for Spätlese, white for Auslese, and gold for Beerenauslese and Trockenbeerenauslese. In addition, specially selected lots within each of the first four categories are indicated by adding gold bands to the capsules. The present Graf Matuschka-Greiffenclau has taken a particular interest in Trocken and Halbtrocken wines, and such wines are identified by silver bands on the capsules.

Schloss Johannisberg is probably the single most famous vineyard in Germany, and its renown is such that the Riesling grape is known as the Johannisberger in Switzerland, and as the Johannisberg Riesling in California. The vineyard was given to the von Metternich family, its present owners, by the emperor of Austria more than 150 years ago, but it was famous long before that. The wines of Schloss Johannisberg are marketed with two different labels—one shows the family crest, the other a drawing of the castle. The label that depicts the castle is used for only a small proportion of the estate's wines, and only for *Prädikat* wines, never for *Qualitätswein.* Here again, different colored capsules are used for the various quality categories, but they simply conform to the label designation and have no further significance, as do the silver-and-gold-banded capsules used by Schloss Vollrads.

The interested consumer will enjoy comparing wines from each of the Rheingau villages and from the different estates, many of which are quite extensive. Langwerth von Simmern, Schloss Reinhartshausen, Schloss Groenesteyn, Schloss Eltz, and Schloss Schönborn are some of the most-respected names. The largest privately owned domain is that of Graf von Schönborn, whose 150 acres includes holdings in forty-five individual vineyard sites located in thirteen different villages. The wines are labeled Schloss Schönborn, with the village and vineyard designation appearing in smaller type. In fact, a number of estates have adopted this Schloss method of labeling, in which the estate name is more prominently displayed than that of each vineyard. Only the names Schloss Vollrads and Schloss Johannisberg, however, actually refer to a single vineyard. Since the 1977 vintage, the Schloss Eltz domain has been owned by the state.

Only one *Bereich* has been established for the Rheingau—Bereich Johannisberg. There are ten *Grosslagen*, the most familiar of which are Hochheimer Daubhaus, Rauenthaler Steinmächer, Eltviller Steinmächer, Hattenheimer Deutelsberg, Johannisberger Erntebringer, and Rüdesheimer Burgweg.

VILLAGE	IMPORTANT VINEYARDS
Hochheim	Domdechaney, Kirchenstück
Rauenthal	Baiken, Gehrn, Wülfen
Eltville	Taubenberg, Sonnenberg, Sandgrub
Kiedrich	Wasseros, Sandgrub
Erbach	Marcobrunn, Steinmorgen
Hattenheim	Steinberg, Nussbrunnen, Wisselbrunnen, Mannberg
Hallgarten	Schönhell, Hendelberg
Oestrich	Lenchen, Doosberg
Winkel	Schloss Vollrads, Hasensprung
Johannisberg	Schloss Johannisberg, Klaus, Hölle

Geisenheim	Rothenberg, Kläuserweg
Rüdesheim	Bischofsberg, Berg Rottland

Nahe

The wines of the Nahe are not very well-known in this country, and even German consumers are less familiar with its best sites. The best of the Nahe wines are very good indeed, and although they are said to combine the best characteristics of the two districts that adjoin it—the Rheingau and the Moselle—they are much closer in style to the best Rheingaus. The best wine-producing villages are Bad Kreuznach (which shortens its name on a label to Kreuznacher), Niederhausen, and Schloss Böckelheim. Although *Schloss*, or castle, is associated with two famous Rheingau vineyards—Schloss Johannisberg and Schloss Vollrads—Schloss Böckelheim is the name of a village, not a specific vineyard. When used in conjunction with a vineyard, it is contracted into one word, as in Schlossböckelheimer Kupfergrube.

There are two *Bereiche*, Bereich Kreuznach and Bereich Schloss Böckelheim, and seven *Grosslagen*, including Schlossböckelheimer Burgweg and Rüdesheimer Rosengarten (not to be confused with Rüdesheimer Rosengarten in the Rheingau).

VILLAGE	IMPORTANT VINEYARDS
Schlossböckelheimer	Kupfergrube, Felsenberg, Königsfels
Niederhausen	Hermannshöhle, Hermannsberg
Kreuznach	Hinkelstein, Krotenpfuhl, Narrenkappe

Moselle

Compared to the majestic flow of the Rhine, the erratic path of the Moselle seems frivolous and nowhere more so than in the section known as the Middle Moselle. Yet it is along these steep banks that are found the world-famous wine villages of Piesport, Bernkastel, Wehlen, Zeltingen, Ürzig, Graach, and a few others whose names, coupled with that of their best vineyards, identify some of the finest wines to be found anywhere. The Moselle zigzags here to such an extent that the greatest vineyards, always planted so as to face toward the south, are located first on one bank, then on the other. In some cases, the village itself is on the opposite bank, so that these choice slopes can be used entirely for the production of wine. During the vintage, the growers must keep crossing the river to bring the grapes back to their press houses.

Fifteen years ago, the Riesling accounted for 80 percent of the acreage along the Moselle; today, that figure has dropped to 65 percent. Furthermore, because the Riesling yields less wine per acre than do other varieties, it now accounts for only half the wine produced along the Moselle. The finest wines still come from the Riesling, but the consumer can no longer assume that a Moselle has been made from that grape unless its name appears on the label. The wines of the Moselle are noted for their flowery and fragrant bouquet, for their delicacy and elegance, and for a fruity acidity that gives them a lively and refreshing taste. They are light-bodied wines that are comparatively low in alcohol—8 or 9 percent is not uncommon—which makes them very appealing with many foods and also by themselves as an aperitif.

The most famous vineyard along the Moselle is Bernkasteler Doctor, which was expanded in 1971 from three to twelve acres by incorporating parts of the Badstube and Graben vineyards. Bernkasteler Doctor's three owners are the Dr. Thanisch and Lauerberg estates and the shipping firm of Deinhard. The Sonnenuhr, or sundial, vineyard of Wehlen, about one hundred acres in size, is also famous. The Joh. Jos. Prüm estate has the biggest share of this vineyard, and other branches of this family have holdings as well.

Some of the proprietors whose names are often found on the best bottles include Bergweiler, Berres, and von Kesselstatt, proprietor of the Josephshöfer vineyard. The Schorlemer name is now used by a cooperative cellar. There are also several hospitals, schools, and religious orders with extensive holdings along the Moselle (and the Saar and Ruwer as well): Vereinigte Hospitien, St. Nikolaus Hospital, Friedrich-Wilhelm-Gymnasium, Bischöfliches Konvikt, and Bischöfliches Priesterseminar. The last

two estates were combined with that of the Hohe Dom-
kirche in 1966 to form the Bischöfliche Weingüter, but the
wines are still labeled with the name of each estate.

The villages of Zell and Kröv have given their names to
two popular wines, Zeller Schwarze Katz, or Black Cat,
and Kröver Nacktarsch, or Bare Bottom, whose labels usually illustrate their names. Both these names are now
Grosslagen, but the new boundaries for Kröver Nacktarsch are so limited that this wine is not often seen anymore.

Along the Moselle, Bereich Bernkastel is by far the best
known, as it encompasses virtually the entire Middle
Moselle. Bernkasteler Kurfürstlay and Piesporter
Michelsberg are the most popular *Grosslagen*, and widely
used by shippers as regional wine appellations. Ürziger
Schwarzlay, Graacher Münzlay, and Bernkasteler Badstube are other *Grosslagen*, as are Zeller Schwarze Katz
and Kröver Nacktarsch, already referred to.

VILLAGE	IMPORTANT VINEYARDS
Trittenheim	Apotheke, Altärchen
Piesport	Goldtröpfchen, Günterslay, Falkenberg
Brauneberg	Juffer
Bernkastel	Doctor, Lay, Graben
Graach	Josephshöfer, Himmelreich, Domprobst
Wehlen	Sonnenuhr
Zeltingen	Sonnenuhr, Himmelreich
Ürzig	Würzgarten, Goldwingert
Erden	Treppchen

Saar

The Saar joins the Moselle just below Trier, the Ruwer
just above that historic city. Wines from these two districts
are labeled, as are those of the Moselle, with the overall
regional appellation Mosel-Saar-Ruwer. In fine years, Saar
and Ruwer wines are even more delicate and elegant than
those of the Moselle, and some connoisseurs prefer the
particular finesse of these wines to the softer and rounder
flavor of Moselles. In lesser years, however, Saar and
Ruwer wines are disappointingly thin and acid.

The most famous vineyard of the Saar is Scharzhofberg, whose name may appear by itself on a label, without that of Wiltingen, the village in which it is located. In 1971, the vineyard was expanded from forty-five acres to sixty-seven acres, and is now split up among ten owners, the most respected of which is Egon Müller. Scharzberg, which was the name of an individual vineyard prior to the new laws, has now been transformed into the *Grosslage* name Wiltinger Scharzberg, which can be used to label wines produced anywhere in the entire Saar region. Bereich Saar-Ruwer encompasses both regions. Dr. Fischer, Rheinart, and the State Domain are vineyard proprietors along the Saar.

VILLAGE	IMPORTANT VINEYARDS
Serrig	Kupp, Würzberg
Ayl	Herrenberg, Kupp
Ockfen	Bockstein, Geisberg, Herrenberg
Wiltingen	Scharzhofberg, Kupp
Oberemmel	Altenberg, Rosenberg
Kanzem	Altenberg, Sonnenberg

Ruwer

There are two particularly famous vineyards along the Ruwer, each with a single proprietor. Maximin Grünhaus, owned by von Schubert, is in Mertesdorf, but since 1971 its name has been treated as if it were that of a village, and may appear by itself on a label. The vineyard name is followed by that of a specific section of the property: Abtsberg is considered the best, followed by Herrenberg and Bruderberg. In Eitelsbach, the Karthäuserhofberg vineyard is divided into five sections, the biggest of which are Kronenberg, Sang, and Burgberg. Perhaps with a sense of irony, the proprietors have devised one of the smallest of all German wine labels to bear so many long names. The *Grosslage* Kaseler Römerlay is used for the entire Ruwer.

VILLAGE	IMPORTANT VINEYARDS
Avelsbach	Herrenberg, Altenberg
Waldrach	Laurentiusberg, Krone

Kasel	Nieschen, Kehrnagel, Hitzlay
Maximin Grünhaus	Abtsberg, Herrenberg, Bruderberg
Eitelsbach	Karthäuserhofberg

Franconia

The wines of Franconia, shipped in the distinctive *Bocksbeutel,* are comparatively dry, less typically German in flavor, and characterized by a *Bodengeschmak,* or taste of the earth, that sets them apart from the more fragrant wines of the Rhine and Moselle. In the past, the Sylvaner was the variety most typically associated with the wines of this region, but the Müller-Thurgau now accounts for half the plantings. Although Franconia is not a major wine district in terms of volume, its vineyards are rather extensively spread out along the Main River and its tributaries. Frankenwein and Steinwein are often used as regional names for these wines, but the latter should properly be used only for the wines from the Stein vineyard in Würzburg. The Staatliche Hofkellerei, Juliusspital, and Bürgerspital have extensive holdings in this region.

Franconia is divided into Bereich Mainviereck, Bereich Maindreieck, and Bereich Steigerwald, and two of its *Grosslagen* are Würzburger Himmelspforte and Randersacker Ewig Leben.

VILLAGE	IMPORTANT VINEYARDS
Würzburg	Stein, Innere Leiste, Schlossberg
Escherndorf	Lump, Berg
Randersacker	Teufelskeller, Sonnenstuhl

THE WINES OF
ITALY

In most years Italy is the biggest wine-producing country in the world, and Italy and France together account for nearly half of all the wines made. Not only does Italy make almost two billion gallons of wine in abundant vintages, but it can claim to be the most completely vinous nation of all, as vines are planted in just about every part of the country. Despite the tremendous variety of wines produced throughout Italy, the American consumer was for many years confined to a few well-known wines from a limited number of producers. Today, an interested wine drinker can find a much more varied selection of attractive and moderately priced wines from Italy, as well as an increasing number of that country's finest wines.

Although many appealing white wines are produced in Italy, especially in the northern part of the country, it is the red wines that have achieved a greater reputation. The best of them are characterized by a complex bouquet and maturity of taste that reflect the long barrel aging that many Italian red wines undergo before bottling. Even as the best Italian wines have become more widely available here, however, many consumers have been slow to recognize their merits. One reason may be that the wines of each region are not structured into a clear upward progression from district to village to vineyard, as is the case in France and Germany. Also, very few Italian wines are known by individual vineyard names, and consequently there exists no ranking of classified vineyards, as in Bor-

deaux, or listing of *grands crus* and *premiers crus,* as in Burgundy, that makes it easier for an informed consumer to recognize the best wines and their relative standing.

The consumer who wants to venture beyond the half-dozen best-known Italian wines faces a confusing array of names that do not seem to follow any specific pattern. Some wines are known by the grape from which they are made, some by their village or district of origin, others by a combination of both, and a few are marketed with colorful names such as Lacryma Christi or Est! Est!! Est!!! Since many Italian wine villages are not yet as familiar to consumers as are those of France and Germany, and since the grape varieties grown in Italy include many that are not readily found elsewhere, it's not always easy to recognize one or the other. Barolo and Barbaresco are villages, Barbera and Bonarda are grapes. Albana and Cortese are grapes, Lugana and Carema are villages. Verdicchio and Lambrusco are grapes. What's more, it's not unusual for a specific name to be used for a wine that can be made either dry or sweet, still or sparkling.

Italy has been producing wine for almost three thousand years, and even twenty centuries ago wine was the daily drink of the people. Italians have always taken wine for granted, and this casual attitude is reflected in the easygoing way in which some of Italy's vineyards are cultivated to this day. Rows of vines are interspersed between plantings of wheat, corn, and olive trees, and this system of mixed cultivation, called *coltura promiscua,* goes back to a time when wine was only one of the products of a particular property. Twenty years ago *coltura promiscua* accounted for 70 percent of Italy's vineyards. Nowadays, most of these vineyards have been uprooted and extensive new plantings make better use of available land as well as permitting the use of tractors and other mechanical aids. *Coltura promiscua* now amounts to only 30 percent of all vineyards, and in Soave, for example, less than 5 percent of the land is in mixed cultivation. There has been an evolution in winemaking techniques as well, as many small growers have banded together to form local cooperative cellars, which permits the purchase and use of modern equipment. There are now more than six hundred cooperative cellars in Italy, and they account for nearly half of that country's wine production.

The Italian's informal approach to winemaking, combined with his traditionally individualistic attitude, made it difficult in the past to establish quality controls similar to those enforced in many other countries. In a number of wine districts growers and shippers banded together to form a *consorzio*, or association, to establish certain minimum standards. This self-discipline varied in intensity from one *consorzio* to another, the most famous of which was established by the producers in Chianti Classico. In 1963 the Italian government—spurred on by Italy's entry into the Common Market—took an active role in establishing wine laws for the most important districts. These laws, which are in some ways more complete than the *Appellation Contrôlée* laws of France, are known as *Denominazione di Origine Controllata*, or DOC. The first decrees were issued in 1966 and the DOC laws went into effect in 1967, when fourteen DOC wines accounted for about eleven million cases of wine. There are now about two hundred DOC wines, and they account for sixty to eighty million cases of wine a year, which usually amounts to between 7 and 11 percent of Italy's total production. All these wines display the words *Denominazione di Origine Controllata* on their labels.

The DOC laws specify the geographical limits of each appellation, the grape varieties that can be used, the maximum amount of wine that can be produced per acre, and the minimum alcoholic content of the wine, among other details. Unlike the wine laws of France and Germany, the DOC laws also specify a minimum amount of aging for many wines, and this is sometimes as much as three or four years in cask. Reflecting the generally favorable climate that prevails throughout much of Italy, the DOC laws are more generous with regard to maximum production per acre than are the *Appellation Contrôlée* laws of France. For example, the production permitted in Chianti, Soave, and Valpolicella is about twice as much as in Saint-Emilion or Pommard, and more wine per acre can be made in Barolo than in Beaujolais. These limits are not usually achieved, of course, and furthermore, if the limits are exceeded in Italy, the entire production of a property is rejected, not just the excess. On the other hand, the addition of up to 15 percent of wine from outside the named district of origin is allowed for certain wines, including

Chianti, Valpolicella, Bardolino, and the Valtellina wines.

Although many Italian wines are labeled with the name of the grape variety from which each is made, every DOC wine comes from a specific region or district whose boundaries are strictly defined. Thus, wines labeled simply Barbera, Nebbiolo, Sangiovese, Lambrusco, Cabernet, or Pinot Grigio are not entitled to DOC status. If they are, the varietal name has to be combined with an appellation of origin—Barbera d'Asti, Nebbiolo d'Alba, Sangiovese di Romagna, Lambrusco di Sorbara, Cabernet del Trentino, or Pinot Grigio del Piave.

The DOC laws for many districts also specify that if a wine is made from grapes grown within an inner zone, it may be labeled *classico*. In some districts, such as Chianti and Soave, the Classico zone may account for less than a third of the wines produced; in others, such as Valpolicella, as much as 60 percent of the wines can be marketed as *classico*. A wine labeled *superiore* has a slightly higher minimum alcoholic content and must be aged somewhat longer, a few months for some white wines, perhaps a year for certain red wines.

Of the two hundred or so DOC wines, only a dozen appellations account for about 60 percent of the total DOC production, and four well-known wines—Chianti, Soave, Valpolicella, and Bardolino—make up nearly a third of that. The same four names also account for almost all the DOC wines shipped to this country, but more than sixty DOC appellations can now be found here.

Although the DOC laws have now been in effect for many years, many of the *consorzi* are still functioning and, in fact, a number of new ones were created after the advent of DOC. Their purpose is to provide an even stricter measure of self-regulation than the DOC laws to encourage the production of wines of a higher quality within each district. Each *consorzio* has its own seal—the best known is the black rooster used for Chianti Classico—and it appears on a strip attached to the neck of each bottle. A producer in any region who chooses not to join the local *consorzio* can nevertheless continue to sell his wine, but without the *consorzio* seal.

There is also a higher and even more select category of wines, *Denominazione di Origine Controllata e Garantita*, or DOCG. The first two wines entitled to this appellation were Barolo and Barbaresco from Piedmont, followed by two Tuscan wines, Brunello di Montalcino and Vino Nobile di Montepulciano.

Apart from a wine's appellation of origin and such supplementary indications as *classico* and *superiore*, there are a number of other words and phrases that you are likely to encounter on Italian wine labels. These include *rosso* (red), *bianco* (white), *rosato* (rosé), *secco, asciutto* (dry), *abboccato, amabile* (semi-sweet), *dolce* (sweet), *liquoroso* (intensely sweet), *spumante* (sparkling), *frizzante* (lightly sparkling), *cantina* (cellar), *cantina sociale* (cooperative cellar), *azienda vinicola* (wine company), *casa vinicola* (winery), *tenuta* (estate), *imbottigliato* (bottled), and *fattoria* (farm or estate).

What follows is a description of Italian wines, starting with the best-known and most popular ones, and then continuing with a number of less-familiar wines.

The region of Tuscany, with Florence as its capital, is the home of one of the most famous red wines in the world: Chianti. Fifty million cases of wine are produced in Tuscany, and Chianti accounts for about a quarter of this. Perhaps no wine is as closely associated with a particular bottle as Chianti is with the straw-covered *fiasco*, or flask (plural: *fiaschi*). Unfortunately, the familiar *fiasco* perpetuates the image of Chianti as an ordinary wine and obscures the fact that the best examples can be taken seriously and are worth the higher prices at which they must be sold. There is a difference between the lighter, younger wines most often found in *fiaschi*, and the more distinct and tannic wines usually shipped in the straight-shouldered Bordeaux bottle. Even if a producer uses the same quality of wine in bottles and in *fiaschi*, which is not always the case, the wine ages less well in *fiaschi*—corks are usually shorter and *fiaschi* cannot easily be stored on their sides. As it happens, these distinctive bottles are gradually disappearing, since the expensive hand labor required to weave the straw has driven the cost to up to fifty cents each, or six dollars a case for empty *fiaschi*. One effort to move away from straw was the creation, a few years ago, of the *misura chiantigiana*, a distinctively shaped 59-ounce bottle (since converted to a 50.7-ounce metric magnum) that was meant to replace the half-gallon *fiasco*. Some shippers have simply discontinued the *fiasco* in this country, and in the past few years total shipments of Chianti in *fiaschi* here have decreased from more than 80 percent to less than half that figure. Anyone who buys a cheap *fiasco* of Chianti today is likely to be paying more for the straw than for the wine.

Chianti producers generally divide Chianti into two basic categories. One is the young, fresh, light-bodied, and occasionally *frizzante* wine served in the trattorias of Florence as early as March following the vintage; the other is a bigger, more tannic wine that needs time to mature in cask and bottle. Both styles are made from the same four or five grape varieties. According to DOC law, Sangiovese must account for 50 to 80 percent, blended with 10 to 30 percent of Canaiolo, and 10 to 30 percent of two white grapes, Trebbiano and Malvasia. Up to 5 percent of Colorino may also be used. The Sangiovese contributes body and character, the Canaiolo delicacy and fruitiness, and the white grapes soften the wine. One of the problems facing Chianti today is that many producers use too high a proportion of white grapes, which makes Chianti lighter, quicker to age, and less typical of the appellation. When the DOC laws were established for Chianti, the name Chianti Bianco was discontinued, and the white wines of the region are now sold as Toscano Bianco or simply as Bianco. There has been some interest in creating a DOC for white Chianti, partly to take advantage of the increasing market for white wines, partly to improve the quality of Chianti by using more of the region's white grapes to make a white wine.

The traditional vinification of Chianti makes use of an unusual technique called *governo alla toscana.* Especially ripe grapes are dried for some weeks on trays so as to concentrate their sugar content. They are then crushed, and when they begin to ferment, they are added to the wine already made in the normal way. The *governo* system adds body, alcohol, and richness to the new wine, as well as a lightly sparkling taste, which makes it more palatable when young. This technique has traditionally been associated with wines meant to be consumed young, but in practice it has also been used for better wines that need longer barrel age. Today, what is still referred to as the *governo* system does not often make use of specially dried grapes, but most frequently of grape concentrate, or boiled-down must, which adds body and alcohol to the wines. This adaptation of the *governo* system is now used for almost all Chianti, especially in poor years, when the grapes lack adequate sugar.

Within the Chianti region is the inner Chianti Classico zone, which lies directly between Florence and Siena. Its boundaries were defined more than 250 years ago, and the producers within the zone claim that theirs is the only true Chianti. The best wines from the Chianti Classico zone are acknowledged to display more body, character, and longevity than most other Chianti, but since wine made in the surrounding area has been sold as Chianti for well over a hundred years, the vineyard proprietors in the original zone formed a Chianto Classico *consorzio* in 1924 to define the limits of the Classico zone and to regulate the quality and authenticity of its wines. The seal of the Chianti Classico *consorzio*, which appears on the neck of the bottle, is the *gallo nero*, or black rooster, on a gold ground surrounded by a red circle, which has become one of the best-known quality symbols in the world of wine. When the DOC laws for Chianti went into effect in 1967, they confirmed the geographical limits of the Classico zone as originally defined by the *consorzio*, so a wine may be entitled to the DOC Chianti Classico even if its producer is not a member of the *consorzio*. Consequently, the *consorzio* no longer promotes the *gallo nero* as a guarantee of a wine's appellation of origin, but of its superior quality, and continues to act as a self-regulating body with somewhat stricter standards than those established by the DOC laws. For example, the amount of wine that can be produced per acre is less than that permitted by the DOC law, and a certain proportion of Chianti Classico wines are rejected each year by a *consorzio* tasting panel as not being up to the higher standards of the *gallo nero* seal.

In the past ten years, the area planted in vines in the Classico zone has increased from less than four thousand acres to more than seventeen thousand acres, and production has more than doubled. About three million cases of Chianti Classico are produced today, which often account for as much as 30 percent of all the wine made in the Chianti region. Most proprietors within the Classico zone belong to the *consorzio*, but some shippers prefer to trade on their own reputations without benefit of the *gallo nero*. Ruffino was never a member of the *consorzio*, for example, and in the mid-1970s, Brolio, Antinori, and Nozzole resigned.

What this means to the consumer is that of the wines labeled with the DOC Chianti Classico (which account for about 40 percent of the Chianti shipped to this country), some also carry the black-rooster neck strip, others do not. Ruffino, Brolio (which also markets a Chianti under the name Ricasoli), Antinori, and Nozzole are the best-known firms that produce Chianti Classico without the *gallo nero;* Melini is now the biggest producer of Chianti Classico within the *consorzio*.

There are six delimited zones within the Chianti region in addition to the Classico zone, but their names are not often seen on bottles shipped here. In 1927, producers in the Colli Fiorentini zone formed their own *consorzio*, whose emblem consists of a pink cherub, or *putto*, on a blue ground. In the past few years this *consorzio* has expanded to include producers in the other non-Classico zones, and they, too, may use the *putto* seal.

The quality of Chianti can vary greatly from one label to another, especially since some wines are bottled within a year and fade quickly, while others are aged in wood for two or three years and improve in bottle for another five. Whereas each vintage of the famous red wines of Bordeaux and Burgundy, for example, is kept in barrel approximately the same length of time before being bottled, the wines of Chianti are aged depending on their character and quality. It is not unusual for a firm to be bottling the wines of a recent light vintage while the bigger wines of a previous vintage are still maturing in large casks. This leads to another distinction to be made among the wines of Chianti, based on the age of the wines. A Chianti that is at least two years old may be labeled *Vecchio*, which means old, and one that is three years old can be sold as a *Riserva*. The required aging need not take place entirely in cask, but may be a combination of cask and bottle. A Chianti Classico Riserva produced by a member of the *consorzio* will display a special black-rooster emblem in which the red circle is in turn surrounded by a gold circle bearing the words Chianti Classico Riserva. Most producers bottle *Riservas* only in the best years, and wines so labeled generally represent the finest Chianti available.

About eighty miles west of Venice, and just east of Lake Garda, is the historic city of Verona, whose local wines are almost as well known as is Chianti: Soave, Valpolicella, and Bardolino. The village of Soave produces a pale, dry white wine with a great deal of charm if it is consumed young. Until recently, it was common here to bottle white wines two or three years after the vintage, which gives them more character but less delicacy. Valpolicella and Bardolino are among the most enjoyable red wines of Italy—fresh, light-bodied wines with a characteristic dry aftertaste. Valpolicella is the sturdier of the two, Bardolino somewhat paler in color and lighter in body. The picturesque town of Bardolino is located along the eastern shore of Lake Garda, and many of its hillside vineyards are exposed to the extra sunshine reflected off the surface of the lake. Valpolicella is a valley north of Verona whose hillsides are covered with vines. The adjoining zone of Valpantena produces red wines very similar to those of Valpolicella, which can be marketed as Valpolicella-Valpantena.

An unusual red wine, Recioto della Valpolicella, is made in limited quantities from selected bunches of grapes that are spread out on trays and left to dry until they have withered. The resulting wine has more alcohol and more flavor than a Valpolicella, and may be matured in giant casks for five years or more. A wine labeled Recioto della Valpolicella is likely to be slightly sweet and usually has some sparkle as well. If such a wine has been fermented out dry, it is labeled Amarone. Recioto della Valpolicella Amarone is a particularly sturdy, full-flavored, and long-lived wine, very different in style from a Valpolicella.

The major shippers of Veronese wines include Bolla, Bertani, Lamberti, Masi, and Folonari.

At the southwestern end of Lake Garda, in the Lombardy region, are vineyards producing some agreeable red wines and rosés. The wines, entitled to the DOC Riviera del Garda, are made primarily from the Gropello grape. The rosés are labeled Chiaretto or, occasionally, Chiarello. The nearby village of Lugana is known for its pleasant white wines.

The best selling of all Italian wines in this country is

Lambrusco. Virtually unheard of only a decade ago, in recent years it has accounted for as much as 60 percent of all the Italian wines shipped here. Lambrusco is a slightly sweet red wine with just enough sparkle so that the wine sometimes foams up when it's poured and leaves a prickly sensation on the tongue when it's drunk. The wine is moderately priced and, served chilled, has become quite popular with people who find most red wines too dry.

Lambrusco is made from the grape of that name near Modena, in the Emilia-Romagna region. It is the traditional wine of Bologna—considered the gastronomic capital of Italy as Lyons is of France—and Lambrusco's freshness, acidity, and slight sparkle make it a good accompaniment to the rich cooking of that city. There are four DOC Lambrusco wines, the best known of which, Lambrusco di Sorbara, gets its name from the village of Sorbara, just north of Modena. Lambrusco entitled to a DOC accounts for only a small part of the total production, however, and virtually all of the wines imported to this country come from outside the DOC zones. It is also likely that some of these wines do not even come from Emilia-Romagna, but are produced from Lambrusco grapes grown in other regions of Italy. What is more certain is that the wines shipped here are generally grapier and sweeter than the dry, sturdy wines that created the reputation of the wine in Bologna. The style and sweetness of Lambrusco varies from one shipper to another: Riunite, the best-selling brand here, is less sweet than most.

Chianti, Soave, Valpolicella, Bardolino, and Lambrusco may be the wines that are the best known in this country, but it is the Piedmont region, in northwest Italy, that is generally acknowledged to produce the greatest variety of fine red wines. Turin, the capital of this region, is the center of the vermouth trade. Asti, thirty miles away, is world-famous for its sweet, aromatic sparkling wines: Asti Spumante and vermouth are discussed elsewhere. It is the table wines that concern us here, and the best of these are made from the Nebbiolo grape. *Nebbia* means mist, and the name of the grape apparently derives from the mist that usually covers the hillside vineyards of Piedmont in October, when the Nebbiolo grapes are harvested.

The most famous Nebbiolo wine is Barolo, produced around the town of that name southwest of Alba. Like most wines made from the Nebbiolo, Barolo is full-bodied, sturdy, long-lived, and needs several years to develop its qualities. According to the DOC law, Barolo must have a minimum alcoholic strength of 13 percent when bottled (compared, for example, to a minimum requirement of 11.5 percent for the *grands crus* of Burgundy and 12.5 percent for Châteauneuf-du-Pape), and the wine must be aged for at least three years, two of them in cask. A wine labeled *Riserva* must be at least four years old, one labeled *Riserva Speciale*, five years. Barolo and several other red wines of the Piedmont are often compared to the Burgundies and Rhône wines of France, but the comparison can be misleading. Barolo is a big wine, but it also has a distinctive undertaste, sometimes described as tarry, that sets it apart from French wines. In addition, the time Barolo spends in wood contributes bouquet at the expense of fruit, and results in a more evolved and mature taste than is found in, say, a Burgundy of equal age. There are about 500,000 cases produced annually of Barolo, which is less than a fifth as much wine as is made in the Chianti Classico district.

The village of Barbaresco, a dozen miles northeast of Barolo, gives its name to another famous wine made entirely from the Nebbiolo. The wine is somewhat lighter than Barolo and matures in less time. Only two years of age are required by law, of which one in wood, and only three years for a *Riserva*. The third famous Nebbiolo wine of the Piedmont comes from vineyards around Gattinara, which is situated in the Novara Hills, about seventy-five miles north of Barolo. Up to 10 percent of Bonarda grapes are permitted in Gattinara, and the wine must age for at least four years, two of them in wood. Gattinara is the smallest of the three appellations, producing only thirty or forty thousand cases of wine, compared to 200,-000 or so for Barbaresco. Only wines from hillside vineyards can be labeled Gattinara, and some producers market wines from adjoining vineyards as Spanna, which is the local name for the Nebbiolo. Spanna is not a DOC wine, and the quality is variable; some examples, such as those of Vallana, are on a par with the wines of Gattinara.

Five other villages around Gattinara produce DOC wines—Ghemme, Boca, Fara, Sizzano, and Lessona. Although all these wines are made primarily from the Nebbiolo, each appellation has different minimum requirements, and as much as 50 or 60 percent of other varieties can be used as well. These wines must undergo two or three years of aging in cask, and their flavor is, unsurprisingly, similar to that of Gattinara. Ghemme is the best known, but the wines are not often seen here, as all five appellations together rarely produce more than forty thousand cases.

Two other Nebbiolo wines that get their names from the villages near which they are made are Carema and Donnaz. Both come from grapes grown at fairly high altitudes, Donnaz from the Val d'Aosta, in the northwest corner of Italy, Carema from the border between Val d'Aosta and Piedmont. These attractive wines, produced in limited quantities, tend to be lighter and fruitier than other Nebbiolo wines.

The Nebbiolo grape is widely planted throughout Piedmont, as are such red-wine varieties as Barbera, Grignolino, Freisa, and Dolcetto. All these names appear on labels, most often Barbera, but the varietal wines that are entitled to DOC status are also defined by their region of production, such as Barbera d'Alba, Freisa di Chieri, Grignolino d'Asti, Nebbiolo d'Alba, and so on. Different varieties are planted in each region—Barbera d'Asti, Dolcetto d'Asti, Freisa d'Asti, Grignolino d'Asti—and the same variety may be planted in more than one region—Barbera d'Alba, Barbera d'Asti, Barbera del Monferrato. Confusingly, these red wines can be dry or semi-sweet, still or sparkling. The examples shipped here are usually dry, but their individual characteristics naturally vary depending on the grape variety and the zone of origin. In general, Grignolino is the lightest, Freisa has the most fruit, Barbera is more assertive, and Dolcetto, despite its name (*dolce* means sweet), is dry and full-flavored. Some dry white wine is also made in the Piedmont, from the Cortese grape. The DOC is Cortese di Gavi or just Gavi. Some of the best-known Piedmont firms are Antoniolo, Bersano, Borgogno, Brugo, Calissano, Contratto, Duca d'Asti (Granduca), Fontanafredda, Giri, Kiola, Pio Cesare, Prunotto, and Travaglini.

The Valtellina vineyards, situated northeast of Milan, are in the Lombardy region, but as they are planted primarily with a variety of the Nebbiolo called Chiavennasca, the wines bear some similarities to those of Piedmont. The steeply terraced vineyards extend along the north bank of the Adda River, which flows from east to west at this point on its course to Lake Como. Although some white wines are made here, the DOC Valtellina applies only to red wines, and these are made at least 70 percent from the Chiavennasca. Wines entitled to the higher appellation Valtellina Superiore account for about half of the region's wines, and these must be made at least 95 percent from the Chiavennasca. Although the wines are identified as Valtellina Superiore, their labels usually feature the name of one of the inner zones—Valgella, Sassella, Grumello, and Inferno, of which the first two have the biggest production. Fracia, a place-name not included in the DOC laws, seems to be used by only one firm, which also uses the name Castel Chiuro as a proprietary brand for both a red and a white wine. In addition, an unusual dry wine, similar to an Amarone from Valpolicella, is made from slightly dried grapes and labeled Sfursat or Sforzato; it is higher in alcohol than other Valtellina wines and is likely to have more body as well. Nino Negri, Rainoldi, and Polatti are three producers whose wines are shipped here.

After Soave, the most popular Italian white wine shipped here is Verdicchio. It is a dry white wine named after the grape variety from which it is primarily made. Just as Chianti is associated with the straw-covered *fiasco,* so Verdicchio owes some of its success to the distinctive, amphora-shaped bottle in which it is marketed. The wine is produced inland from Ancona, a city on the Adriatic coast in central Italy. The complete name of the DOC district is Verdicchio dei Castelli di Jesi, and most wines are so labeled. Those from the delimited inner district are entitled to the additional Classico designation as well. Farther south is another, smaller DOC district, Verdicchio di Matelica, but this name is rarely seen here. Fazi-Battaglia is the best-known brand of Verdicchio.

About halfway between Florence and Rome, in the region of Umbria, the walled town of Orvieto is perched on a hilltop. The town is dominated by its famous cathedral, begun in the late thirteenth century, and tourists are attracted to its mixture of Etruscan, medieval, and Renaissance art. The white wine of Orvieto has a long history, but its popularity was gradually eclipsed by such wines as Soave and Verdicchio. In the past few years, however, a number of Tuscan firms have taken a greater interest in this wine, and it is now much more widely available here. Orvieto is made at least 50 percent from the Trebbiano grape and is marketed either as *secco*, dry, or *abboccato*, semi-sweet. It is the *abboccato* version that established the fame of this wine, which was traditionally bottled in a distinctive, squat straw-covered flask called a *pulcianella*. Today, in response to the consumer demand for dry white wines, it is Orvieto *secco* that is most often seen, and standard bottles have pretty much replaced the more expensive *pulcianella*.

A white wine with the colorful name Est! Est!! Est!!! di Montefiascone comes from vineyards situated about fifty miles north of Rome. The name derives from a story—whose details vary from one version to another—about a German bishop who was journeying to Rome and instructed his servant to travel ahead and chalk *Est!* (it is) on the side of those inns whose wines were worth a stop. The servant was so taken with the wines of Montefiascone that he wrote *Est! Est!! Est!!!* on the wall of a local inn. The bishop stopped and apparently concurred, as the legend states that he settled in Montefiascone and spent the rest of his days enjoying its wine. The story is better than the wine, which is not often seen here.

Visitors to Rome will find themselves drinking the attractive white wines of the Castelli Romani, a group of once-fortified hill towns about twenty miles south of the city. Although this district produces red wines as well, it is the whites that are much better known and that are entitled to DOC status. The wines are made from the Malvasia and Trebbiano grapes, and although they can all be vinified either dry or semi-sweet, the ones shipped here are almost always dry. Among the various appellations, the wines of Marino, Colli Albani, and Colli Lanuvini can be found here, but it is the light-bodied dry white wine of Frascati that is the best known of all.

The northernmost region of Italy is Trentino-Alto Adige, whose appealing light-bodied red and delicate white wines are perhaps closer in style to those of Austria, to which this part of Italy once belonged, than to most Italian wines. The Trentino district extends south from the city of Trento to the northern end of Lake Garda, and its best-known appellation is Teroldego Rotaliano, a red wine made from the Teroldego grape. The broader appellation Trentino is usually combined with a specific varietal name, such as Merlot del Trentino or Trentino Cabernet. Other varieties cultivated include Pinot Nero, Riesling, Pinot Bianco, and Traminer.

Bolzano, about thirty miles north of Trento, is the principal city of the Alto Adige, which gets its name from the Adige River. German is widely spoken in this region, and its wines, marketed in tall, sloping bottles, are increasingly labeled with German names. The two best-known red wines of the Alto Adige, both made from the Schiava grape, are Caldaro or Lago di Caldaro (whose German names are Kalterer or Kalterersee), and the somewhat fuller Santa Maddalena (or St. Magdalener). Terlano (or Terlaner), the best-known white wine, is made at least 50 percent from the Pinot Bianco (or Weissburgunder). White wines made primarily from another variety are labeled as such—Terlano Sylvaner, Terlano Traminer, and so on. Similarly, the other major appellation of the region, Alto Adige (Südtirol in German), is combined with that of the grape variety from which the wine is made—Alto Adige Merlot (or Südtiroler Merlot), Alto Adige Pinot Bianco (or Südtiroler Weissburgunder), Alto Adige Pinot Grigio (or Südtiroler Ruländer), and so on. Schiava is the most widely planted variety, and Lagrein is another local variety used to make light reds and rosés, the latter labeled Lagrein Rosato (or Lagrein Kretzer).

The wines of northeastern Italy are becoming more widely available here, and many of these are labeled with such familiar varietal names as Merlot, Cabernet, Pinot Nero (Pinot Noir), Riesling, Sylvaner, Traminer, and Sauvignon. Tocai, which produces a dry white wine that bears no relation to the Tokay of Hungary, is the most widely cultivated white variety, but Pinot Grigio (the Pinot Gris of France) is the varietal white wine most often seen here. Merlot and Cabernet are the most frequently seen red wines. In addition to these French and German varietals, such Italian varieties as the red Refosco and the white Malvasia, Verduzzo and Picolit are also occasionally encountered. These varietal names are usually combined with that of a specific appellation entitled to DOC status, and in such cases the wine must be made from a minimum of 90 percent of the variety named. Among the DOC names that you are likely to see on varietal wines from the Friuli-Venezia Giulia region, in northeastern Italy, is Colli Orientale di Friuli (Colli and Collio mean hills), Grave del Friuli, and Collio Goriziano, sometimes shortened to Collio. In the Veneto region, the Colli Berici district, between Verona and Padua, and the wines known as Vini del Piave, or simply Piave, are the best known. Prosecco, a white-wine grape grown in the province of Treviso, north of Venice, makes still and sparkling wines labeled Prosecco di Conegliano. The red and white wines sold as Venegazzú are produced nearby.

Chianti is the best-known wine of Tuscany, but there are a number of other interesting wines produced there as well. The village of Montalcino, twenty miles south of Siena, gives its name to what is probably the most expensive red wine of Italy, Brunello di Montalcino. Made from a selection of the Sangiovese grape called Brunello, the wine must be aged in cask for a minimum of four years. It was first made in the late nineteenth century by Ferruccio Biondi Santi, whose firm is still the best known of the sixty-odd producers of this wine. Within the district entitled to this DOC, about two thousand acres are planted, and less than 200,000 cases or so of Brunello di Montalcino are bottled annually.

From Montepulciano, situated east of Montalcino, comes a red wine called Vino Nobile di Montepulciano. Made primarily from the Sangiovese grape, and similar in style to Chianti, it should not be confused with wines made from the Montepulciano grape in Abbruzzo. The *nobile* does not derive from the character of the wine, but from the fact that it was first produced by members of the local nobility in the fourteenth century.

Vernaccia di San Gimignano is a white wine made from the grape of that name near San Gimagnano, a picturesque medieval town between Florence and Siena, just west of the Chianti district. Vin Santo, or Vino Santo, is an unusual Tuscan white wine made from specially dried grapes. The wine, which has an alcohol content of 16 percent or so, is aged for several years in barrels that are not completely filled, and the resulting oxidation gives this wine a distinctive taste. Most examples are sweet, some are dry. Similar white wines labeled Vin Santo are also produced in other parts of Italy.

A variety of wines are produced in southern Italy near Naples, and some of them occasionally find their way here. The islands of Ischia and Capri both give their names to wines, mostly white, which are readily found in local restaurants. The resort town of Ravello, south of Naples, is also known for red, white, and rosé wines. Lacryma Christi, or Tears of Christ, is a fanciful name for white wines (some red is also made) whose origins were never strictly defined. Recently, the DOC Vesuvio was established for wines produced near that volcano, and the best of these wines can now be labeled Lacryma Christi del Vesuvio. Aglianico del Vulture is a red wine produced from the Aglianico grape on the slopes of Mount Vulture, east of Naples; Taurasi is another red wine made from the Aglianico grape. Fiano di Avellino and Greco di Tufo are white wines made in this region, whose best-known producer is Michele Mastroberardino.

There are, in addition, a number of individual wines that are occasionally seen here, and they are listed for reference. Torgiano is a small district in Umbria, south of Perugia, whose attractive red wines are made primarily from the Sangiovese, and the whites from the Trebbiano. Lungarotti, the best-known firm, uses the proprietary name Rubesco for its red wine, Torre di Giano for the white.

Frecciarossa, which means "red arrow," is actually the proprietary brand of a producer who makes red, white, and rosé wines. The firm is in Lombardy, between Milan and Pavia. The Oltrepó Pavese district is also situated here—the name refers to that part of the Pavia region that is beyond the Po River. In Romagna, in a district southeast of Bologna, three DOC wines are made—the red Sangiovese di Romagna, the dry white Trebbiano di Romagna, and Albana di Romagna, a white wine that can be either dry or semi-sweet. Cinqueterre is the appellation of a rather well-known white wine produced along the Ligurian coast, south of Genoa. The red Montepulciano grape and the white Trebbiano are widely planted in the Abruzzi region, southeast of Rome, and they produce two DOC wines labeled Montepulciano d'Abruzzo and Trebbiano d'Abruzzo. The former should not be confused with the famous Vin Nobile di Montepulciano produced near Siena. Rosso Conero and Rosso Piceno both come from central Italy, near the Adriatic coast, not far from the Verdicchio district.

The island of Sicily produces more than 10 percent of Italy's wines, but much of it is used for the production of vermouth, or to add body and alcohol to wines made elsewhere. The best-known wine of Sicily is Marsala, a fortified wine described further on. Red, white, and rosé wines produced in a number of communes near the volcano Mount Etna are entitled to the DOC Etna. Regaleali is an estate near Palermo, Corvo is a proprietary wine produced in Casteldaccia, Segesta is the brand name of a red and white Sicilian wine. The red and white wines of Sardinia are also shipped here; Sella & Mosca is the best-known firm.

It's obvious that Italy produces a great many different wines, yet many consumers have not gone much beyond the half-dozen most popular ones. The adventurous wine drinker who seeks out less-familiar names is bound to come across interesting wines and good values that will repay the effort made to find them.

OTHER EUROPEAN WINES

SPAIN

A tremendous amount of wine is made in Spain, which ranks third in production among western European countries, after Italy and France. Most of the wine shipped here from Spain, however, consists of sweet, fruit-flavored *sangría*. What's more, Sherry, which accounts for less than 3 percent of the wine made in Spain, also outsells traditional Spanish table wines here. Nevertheless, as any visitor to Spain knows, a wide range of table wines are produced throughout that country including many sound red wines, and these are becoming more widely available here.

The best wines of Spain, and the ones most often seen here, come from the Rioja district in northern Spain, not far from the French border. The vineyards extend for about eighty miles along the Ebro River, from Haro to Logroño and on to Alfaro. The district gets its name from a little river, the Río Oja, that flows toward the Ebro near Haro. Wines have been made in this region for several centuries, and in fact, the first attempt to guarantee the authenticity of these wines dates back to 1560. Rioja is one of the most carefully controlled wine districts in Spain, and since 1925 labels of authentic Rioja are all imprinted with a seal that resembles a small postage stamp.

Although the wines of Rioja have a long history, the character of the wines produced was altered less than a hundred years ago, when phylloxera struck the vineyards of Bordeaux. A number of winemaking families moved across the Pyrenees to the nearby Rioja district and brought with them their vinification techniques. Now history has turned the tables, and as the Bordeaux growers have adopted more modern winemaking methods, those of Rioja remain in many ways as they were in the nineteenth century. Basically, the fermenting must is kept in contact with the grape skins for an extended period, so that the red wines are particularly rich in color and tannin, and the better wines are kept in barrel a comparatively long time: five or six years is not uncommon. As a result, red Riojas are often more mature when they are bottled than similarly priced red wines from other countries. Unfortunately, many white Riojas still suffer from excessive aging in wood, but some producers are now adopting the modern custom of bottling white wines within a year of the vintage to retain their fresh and lively taste.

Rioja is a comparatively large viticultural area, producing about ten million cases of wine. The vineyards are planted with a number of grape varieties, including Garnacha, Tempranillo, and Graciano, and are parceled out among thousands of farmers, most of whom also tend other crops. Consequently, the endless rows of vines typical of most wine regions are replaced here by plots of vines interspersed among wheatfields and olive groves. In recent years cooperative cellars have become increasingly important and now account for over half of the annual production of Rioja.

Although a few of the major Rioja shippers own vineyards, just about all of them buy wine from farmers and cooperative cellars and blend them in their own cellars to produce a consistent house style. Most shippers also blend together wines from the three inner districts within Rioja—Rioja Alta, Rioja Baja, and Rioja Alavesa—so the relative merits and characteristics of the wines from each district are not of much concern to the consumer.

Rioja is a blended wine, and there are no famous individual vineyards in Rioja, as in France and Germany, so most shippers in this region traditionally market their wines with several different brand names. This can be confusing to the consumer at first, because the names seen on Rioja labels, such as Viña Real, Viña Pomal, Monte Real, Banda Azul, and Brilliante are proprietary names belonging to individual shippers. Thus a firm's dry white wine will have one name, its mellow white wine another; a young red wine and an older red wine will each be marketed with a different name.

A traditional practice in Rioja is for each shipper to market some wines in Bordeaux bottles, others in Burgundy bottles. As a general rule, red wines in Bordeaux bottles are somewhat lighter and more delicate, those in Burgundy bottles fuller and rounder, with perhaps a degree more alcohol. These distinctions are arbitrary at best, since the wines in both bottles have been made the same way from the same grapes grown in the same soil.

Vintages in Rioja do not have the same significance as in many other countries. Rioja is often a blend of several years, and a date on the label—sometimes preceded by the word *Cosecha,* or vintage—might only be meant to indicate the wine's relative age among the grades marketed by that shipper.

More important than a vintage date is the word *Reserva,* which indicates that the shipper has specially selected this wine, as it matured in his *bodega,* for further aging in cask and bottle. Some firms market their *Reservas* with an individual proprietary name, others use the same name for a younger wine and a *Reserva.* For example, Viña Real and Viña Pomal are available both in a recent vintage and as a *Reserva,* with the *Reserva* selling for about twice as much. *Reservas* from the best shippers in Rioja represent the best wines that are made in this district, and they can be very good wines indeed.

To assure continuity of quality, only those firms that have a minimum annual production equivalent to about one million bottles are permitted to export their wines, and there are less than forty firms that qualify. Some well-known Rioja firms (and their popular brands) include AGE (Siglo), Bodegas Bilbaínas (Viña Pomal, Brillante, Cepa de Oro), Compañía Vinícola del Norte de España, or CUNE (Viña Real, Imperial), Domecq Domain, López de Heredia (Viña Tondonia, Viña Bosconia), Marqués de Cáceres, Marqués de Murrieta, Marqués de Riscal, Bodegas Muerza (Rioja Vega), Federico Paternina (Banda Azul, Viña Vial), and Bodegas Santiago (Gran Condal).

The district of La Mancha in central Spain is the most important one from the standpoint of quantity. Red and white wines are made, of which the somewhat pale red is more easily found here. Within this district—the home of Don Quixote—the town of Valdepeñas produces the best-known wines of all.

Along the Mediterranean shore, north and south of Barcelona, are a number of districts producing interesting wines generally grouped together as Catalonian wines. The village of Alella produces a dry red wine and both sweet and dry white wines. Tarragona, south of Barcelona, was once famous for its fortified red wine, known as Tarragona Port. Nowadays, production consists mostly of inexpensive red, white, and rosé table wines. The most readily available wines of Catalonia come from the region of Penedés, situated about halfway between Barcelona and Tarragona. The best-known firm is that of Torres, in Vilafranca del Penedés, whose well-made branded wines include Sangre de Toro and Coronas, both full-flavored red wines, and Viña Sol, a dry white wine.

PORTUGAL

The most-famous wine of Portugal is Port, but it actually accounts for only 5 percent of the country's wine production and most of it is exported. Table wine, on the other hand, is very much a part of the Portuguese way of life: almost as much wine is produced in this small country as in the United States, and annual consumption is 125 bottles per person.

The most popular wines of Portugal shipped here are the many pleasant rosés that are to be found in just about every store and restaurant. Often shipped in distinctive bottles and crocks, these agreeable wines have undoubtedly converted many people to the pleasures of wine drinking. The best-known brands are Mateus and Lancers.

Apart from rosé, however, Portugal produces a variety of inexpensive red and white wines that are becoming more widely distributed in this country. The best of these wines are made under the supervision of the Portuguese government, which has established wine laws similar in style and intent to the *Appellation Contrôlée* laws of France. At present, the six appellations for which controls have been established (apart from Port) are Vinho Verde, Dão, Colares, Bucelas, Carcavelos, and Moscatel de Setúbal. Bottles of each of these wines are entitled to bear a distinctive neck label as a guarantee of authenticity.

Vinho Verde, very popular in Portugal, is now becoming better known in this country. Its name literally means green wine, but only in the sense of new wine: it can be red or white. Vinho Verde is produced in the northwest of Portugal, in the Minho province, north of the Douro River. These light-bodied wines are comparatively low in alcohol, and when consumed locally they are noted for their refreshing acidity. Red Vinho Verde—one of the few red wines that is normally served chilled—has a rather harsh taste and is rarely exported. If Vinho Verde is bottled early, within a few months of the vintage, malolactic fermentation takes place in the bottle, giving these wines a slightly sparkling quality that adds to their charm. This natural *pétillance* is usually absent from Vinho Verde that is exported, and some of the white Vinho Verde that is available here is mellow rather than crisply acid.

The Dão wines come from an extensive region in the central part of Portugal. The red wines—more easily found here than the mild, agreeable whites—are generous, full-flavored wines, often well aged and quite dependable.

About twenty miles from Lisbon, along the Atlantic coast, are the vineyards of Colares, which produce a very good long-lived red wine (and a little bit of undistinguished white wine). Although Colares is rarely seen here, the vineyards themselves are quite unusual and deserve mention. For one thing, the vines grow in sand dunes near the ocean, and planting new vines requires digging special reinforced trenches ten or twenty feet deep in the sand. For another thing, the Ramisco vines of Colares have never been attacked by phylloxera, so that this wine is one of the very few wines in Europe still being made from vines that have not been grafted onto native American rootstocks.

Carcavelos and Moscatel de Setúbal are both fortified sweet white wines produced in very limited quantities and rarely exported. Bucelas, rarely seen here, is a light, dry white wine from a village of that name about fifteen miles north of Lisbon.

The vineyards along the Douro River are best known for Port, but they also produce table wines that are among the best to be found in Portugal. Because of the importance of Port in this district, official appellation laws have not yet been established for table wines from the Douro, and shippers therefore market their red and white wines with proprietary brand names. The village of Pinhel, just south of the Douro, gives its name to a very agreeable red wine produced there.

Colheita, or vintage, *Reserva*, and *Garrafeira* are words sometimes found on Portuguese wine labels. One or another is used by a shipper when he wants to indicate that he has especially selected the wine for additional aging because of its superior quality.

SWITZERLAND

The little nation of Switzerland, with a population smaller than that of New York City, imports nearly as much wine as does the United States. Switzerland also produces a certain amount of wine, most of it white, and much of it agreeable enough: dry, crisp, refreshing, and uncomplicated.

Some wine is made in the Italian part of the country, notably Merlot del Ticino, but almost all of Switzerland's wines come from the French-speaking region known as La Suisse Romande. The cantons, or districts, that are best known for their wines are those of Neuchâtel, Vaud, and Valais. The most widely planted white wine grape is the Chasselas, known in the Valais as the Fendant and in the Vaud as the Dorin.

Neuchâtel, the most familiar of Swiss wines, comes from vineyards along the northern shore of the Lake of Neuchâtel. This pleasant white wine sometimes has a *pétillant*, or sprightly, quality, the result of malolactic fermentation, which produces a small amount of carbon-dioxide gas often retained in the wine. Cortaillod, a village along the shore of Lake Neuchâtel, gives its name to an attractive red wine made from the Pinot Noir grape. A rosé, Oeil de Perdrix, is also produced in this district.

The canton of Vaud, along the shore of the Lake of Geneva, is divided into two main wine districts: La Côte is the district west of the city of Lausanne, Lavaux is the district to the east. The wine villages of Dézaley and Saint-Saphorin, whose names appear on Swiss wine labels, are in Lavaux. Beyond Lavaux is the Chablais district, which encompasses the villages of Aigle and Yvorne. All of these wines are exported to this country, and they may be labeled with the name of the producing village, such as Saint-Saphorin or Yvorne, or with the village and district, as Dézaley de Lavaux or Aigle de Chablais.

The vineyards of the Valais lie along the Rhône River, on either side of the city of Sion. The wines of this district are labeled with the name of the grape from which they are made, sometimes in conjunction with the name of the district or its principal city—Fendant, Johannisberg (actually the Sylvaner), Fendant de Sion, Johannisberg du Valais, and so forth. Dôle is a light red wine made in the Valais from a combination of Pinot Noir and Gamay grapes.

AUSTRIA

Vienna may be famous for its coffeee and pastry, but wine is very much a part of the Austrian way of life: the per capita consumption of wine in that country is over fifty bottles a year. Almost all of the wine made in Austria is white, and the Austrian's casual approach to wine is nowhere more evident that in the *Heurigen*, or wine taverns, that are found throughout each wine region. Everyone who has *Heurige*, or new wine, to sell hangs a bough or wreath outside his establishment to alert passersby, and these refreshing wines are consumed on the premises—by the glass or from open carafes—in a tradition that dates back almost two hundred years. Some *Heurigen* are open all year round, others sell wines for only a few weeks in the spring and summer. The new wine may actually be more than a year old, since a wine can be sold as *Heurige* until November of the year following the vintage.

The most widely planted grape in Austria is Grüner Veltliner, whose mild, agreeable wines account for about a third of the total production. Other white wine grapes include Müller-Thurgau, Welschriesling, Rheinriesling (which is the true Riesling of Germany), Traminer, Neuburger, and Weissburgunder (Pinot Blanc). The principal red wine grapes are Portugieser, Blaufränkisch, Saint Laurent, and Zweigeltrebe (a cross of Blaufränkisch with Saint Laurent).

As in Germany, late-picked and overripe grapes are used to make wines labeled Kabinett, Spätlese, Auslese, Beerenauslese, and Trockenbeerenauslese. These words, which were freely used in the past, have now been clearly defined by new Austrian wine laws and have virtually the same meaning as in Germany.

A Viennese who wants to drink local wines does not have far to travel, because wines are made at the edge of Vienna itself, at Nussberg and Grinzing. A dozen miles south of Vienna is the village of Gumpoldskirchen, which produces one of the best known Austrian white wines. Gumpoldskirchner (the suffix *er* is added to the village or district name when it appears on a label) is usually made from three varieties—Rotgipfler, Zierfandler (also called Spätrot), and Neuburger.

About forty miles west of Vienna, along the Danube, is a region that produces some of Austria's most appealing white wines, primarily from Grüner Veltliner. Dürnstein and Loïben are the best-known wine villages of the Wachau district, and the villages of Krems and Langenlois each gives its name to adjoining districts.

Another important wine region is Burgenland, southeast of Vienna. The region is dominated by the Neusiedlersee, a long shallow lake that tempers the climate of the vineyards that surround it. The picturesque village of Rust is the most famous in Burgenland, and a number of nearby villages are now entitled to use its name for their wines. Apetlon, Mörbisch, Oggau, and Donnerskirchen are other well-known wine villages. Climatic conditions in Burgenland are particularly conducive to the appearance of *Edelfäule*, or noble rot, and in good vintages a surprisingly high proportion of the crop consists of Beerenauslese and Trockenbeerenauslese wines. Most of these botrytised wines are made from Weissburgunder, Müller-Thurgau, and Neuburger grapes, rather than the Riesling, as in Germany. *Ausbruch*, a word traditionally found on the labels of some sweet wines from Burgenland, has now been legally defined, and may be used only for wines whose quality is between a Beerenauslese and a Trockenbeerenauslese.

Austrian wines may be labeled with the name of a grape variety, with that of the district or village of origin, or with a combination of both, such as Kremser Grüner Veltliner, Langenloiser Rheinriesling, Dürnsteiner Müller-Thurgau, Apetloner Weissburgunder, and Oggauer Blaufränkisch. In addition, a number of Austrian wines are labeled with proprietary brand names. For example, the firm of Lenz Moser markets Schluck (which means sip), Blue Danube, and Alte Knabe; and Kremser Schmidt is a popular wine produced by the cooperative cellar at Krems.

HUNGARY

Although Hungary is not one of Europe's biggest wine-producing countries, it has always maintained a special position among wine lovers as the home of the famous sweet wines of Tokay. At one time these luscious dessert wines were considered an essential part of any complete cellar, and the finest examples were served at royal banquets and state occasions. Tokay was assumed to possess special invigorating qualities that led doctors to prescribe it to dying patients, and bridegrooms would consume a glass to ensure male heirs. No longer as popular as in the past, Tokay is nevertheless an interesting and unusual wine, enhanced by the legends that surround it.

The village of Tokay (spelled Tokaj locally) is situated in the northeast corner of the country, at the foothills of the Carpathian Mountains. A number of neighboring villages are permitted to market their wine as Tokay, and these hillside vineyards are planted, for the most part, with the Furmint grape. The volcanic soil of this district imparts a distinctive *terroir* to Tokay, a tang or undertaste that distinguishes it from the sweet dessert wines of Sauternes and the Auslese and Beerenauslese wines of Germany.

Tokay is made in a very special way. After the normal harvest, grapes are left on the vines to develop the same noble rot that affects the grapes in Sauternes and along the Rhine and Moselle. These shriveled grapes, with their much higher concentration of sugar, are known as *aszu*. The *aszu* grapes are specially picked and put into containers or butts, known as *puttonyos*. A certain number of *puttonyos* are then added to the normally ripe grapes, and the lot fermented together. The more containers of *aszu* berries that are added to a vat, the sweeter and richer the resulting wine will be, and consequently bottles of Tokaji Aszu (as the wines are labeled) indicate the number of *puttonyos* that were added: five *puttonyos* is the highest grade available in this country. Very limited quantities of Tokay were once made entirely from the free-run juice of *aszu* berries, and this essence, Tokaji Eszencia, has achieved legendary fame. Wines labeled Tokaji Eszencia are still produced in good vintages, but rarely exported.

Apart from Tokaji Aszu, there are also other wines made in the Tokay vineyards. Tokaji Furmint is the normal wine of the district, and its label may carry the word *edes,* meaning sweet. Tokaji Szamorodni is made from grapes harvested without special attention to the *aszu* berries among the vines (*szamorodni* means as it is grown). The wine may consequently be dry or sweet, depending on the proportion of shriveled berries that turn up in the vats, and this will be shown on its label. Bottles of Tokaji Aszu and Tokaji Szamorodni contain only a pint, two-thirds of a normal wine bottle.

Famous as it is, Tokay accounts for less then 5 percent of Hungary's wines, which are produced in a number of districts situated throughout the country. For the most part, Hungarian wines are labeled with a combination of the village of origin plus the grape variety used. A notable exception is the most famous red wine of Hungary, Egri Bikavér. The wine comes from vineyards around the village of Eger (just as German wine villages take on the possessive *er* when used on wine labels, so Hungarian towns add *i*), but Bikavér means Bull's Blood. This full-bodied dry red wine is made primarily from the Kadarka grape. There are other variations as well on the village-plus-variety labeling rule among the limited number of wines imported here: Vörös simply means red wine, as in Szekszárdi Vörös; from Villány comes Villányi Burgundi; and Leányka is a white-wine variety whose name may appear alone on a label, without that of a village of origin.

A number of white wines are produced along the shore of Lake Balaton, which is the largest lake in central Europe. Vines are grown along the slopes of Mount Badacsony, on the north shore of the lake, and two of the better-known wines are Badacsonyi Szürkebarát and Badacsonyi Kéknyelü. The latter, the drier of the two, is named after a grape variety, but Szürkebarát is a fanciful name meaning Gray Friar: the wine is made from the Pinot Gris. From the village of Debrö comes a sweetish wine with a peachlike bouquet, Debröi Hárslevelü.

GREECE

The vine may have appeared in Greece as early as 1500 B.C., and wine was certainly a common beverage in Homer's time, twenty-seven hundred years ago. Ancient Greek literature abounds in reference to wine, and it's quite possible that these early Greek wines were of exceptional quality. Greece continues to produce a variety of wines today, and if they are not remarkable, many of them are nevertheless attractive.

To many people, Greek wine means Retsina, and in fact

most Greek table wines are in this category. Retsina is a generic name applied to any wine that has been flavored, during fermentation, with a small but unmistakable amount of pine resin. Retsina has an unusual and pungent flavor that is described by those who do not like it as the taste of turpentine. Those who enjoy Retsina find it to be an excellent complement to the oily dishes that abound in Greek cuisine. Retsina is usually a white wine, but is also made as a red wine and a rosé, and is then labeled Kokinelli.

Apart from Retsina, there are a number of enjoyable red, white, and rosé table wines characterized by a distinctive and robust flavor that goes very well with rich foods. The problem for the consumer when buying Greek wines is that some names found on their labels are generic, many are the proprietary brand names of individual firms, and a few refer to a place or to a grape variety. For example, Roditis or Roditys is a name used by many firms for a dry rosé. Castel Danielis is a branded red wine from one firm, Achaia-Clauss, which also markets red and white wines labeled Demestica; and another firm, Cambas, uses the brand name Hymettus for red and white wines and Pendeli for a red. Naoussa and Nemea are place-names. In a store, read a Greek wine label carefully. If you're in a Greek restaurant, tell the waiter whether or not you want Retsina, and if not, tell him just how dry you want your wine to be. For example, the most famous red wine of Greece is Mavrodaphne, but it's a sweet dessert wine similar in style to Port, and not the best choice to accompany a meal.

YUGOSLAVIA

A number of moderately priced Yugoslavian wines can be found here, from vineyards situated throughout that country. The best-known wines come from the northern province of Slovenia, part of which once belonged to Austria. It is, therefore, not surprising that extensive plantings now exist of Riesling, Traminer, and Sylvaner, as well as Cabernet and some Merlot for the reds. The villages of Lutomer and Maribor are often seen on Yugoslavian wine labels, coupled with the grape from which the wine is made: Lutomer Riesling, Sylvaner de Maribor, and so forth. A few years ago, some of the biggest wineries combined to market their wines in this country under the brand names Adriatica, Navip, and Slovin. These wines are labeled both with the name of the grape and with the village or district of origin. Among the names to be found are Cabernet from Istria, Rizling from Fruska-Gora, Sipon from Maribor, and Prokupac from Yovac. Sipon (pronounced *shee-pon)* and Prokupac (pronounced *pro-koopats)* are native Yugoslavian grape varieties.

ROMANIA

Romania produces a variety of red and white wines from such native grape varieties as Grasă and Fetească, as well as Furmint, Kadarka, and increasingly, such traditional varieties as Cabernet Sauvignon and Pinot Noir. The sweet white from Cotnari, often compared to the Tokay of Hungary, is Romania's most famous wine. Tîrnave and Murfatlar are other traditional white-wine districts. Some of these wines have occasionally been shipped here in very limited quantities. Moderately priced Romanian wines labeled Cabernet Sauvignon, Pinot Noir, and Tarnave Castle are now being marketed here under the Premiat label.

RUSSIA

The vineyards of Russia have been considerably expanded in recent years as part of a government-sponsored program to increase the production both of table grapes and of wines. More than three million acres of vines are planted, and Russia is now the third largest wine-producing country in the world, after Italy and France. Many different sweet and dry table wines are made, as well as fortified wines and a considerable amount of sparkling wines.

THE WINES OF THE
UNITED STATES

CALIFORNIA

For the American consumer, California is the most interesting, varied, and exciting wine region in the world today.
For several decades California has supplied almost three-
quarters of all the wine consumed in this country, and the
quality of its moderately priced everyday jug wines has
long been acknowledged. It is only in the past ten years or
so that the excellence and diversity of its best wines have
attracted the attention and admiration of wine drinkers
here and abroad, and that California has been widely
recognized as one of the world's fine wine regions.

One indication of the pace at which changes have occurred is that as recently as the early 1960s, half of the
state's wine production consisted of inexpensive fortified
wines such as Port, Sherry, and Muscatel. Dessert wines
(as all fortified wines are referred to in this country,
whether they are sweet or dry) have gradually declined in
importance, but it was not until 1973 that table wines—
red, white, and rosé—actually accounted for more than
half of California's total production. The increased production of table wines, and especially of fine table wines,
is a reflection of growing consumer interest. Just as the
great wine châteaux of the Médoc prospered only when,
in the nineteenth century, an affluent middle class was
prepared to pay a higher price for wines of better quality,
so the increased plantings of the best grape varieties in
California became possible only when enough American
consumers began to discriminate among wines and were

willing to pay a premium for the best of them. In 1969 there were only 110,000 acres of wine grapes in California; ten years later an additional 220,000 acres had been planted, most of them in the early 1970s. The acreage of Cabernet Sauvignon, Chardonnay, Johannisberg Riesling, and Pinot Noir increased from less than nine thousand acres to almost sixty thousand. There is now twice as much Cabernet Sauvignon in California as in the Médoc district of Bordeaux, three times as much Chardonnay as in Burgundy's Côte d'Or.

Just as the interest in fine wines led to more vineyard acreage, so it encouraged the creation of many small new wineries. In the past, the commercial distribution pattern for wine in this country was such that large wineries and even medium-sized ones were expected to offer a complete line of wines, including a variety of table wines, dessert wines such as Port and Sherry, and sparkling wines as well. While a number of wineries successfully continue to produce a range of twenty to fifty different wines, the American consumer's current willingness to pay a premium price for fine wines has enabled both new wineries and some established ones to focus their attention on relatively few wines. There are now a great many new wineries whose total production is between fifteen and twenty-five thousand cases, no more than is produced by many châteaux in the Médoc and a number of estates along the Rhine and Moselle.

The quality of California wines has developed so quickly that several of the wines that are considered among the finest ever produced in the state, and on a par with the best in the world, have come from wineries that did not even exist as recently as 1970. Every year a number of new wineries introduce their first wines, and some of them are remarkable enough to establish what is virtually an overnight reputation. Whereas almost all of the world's great vineyards are already well-known, California's best wines are still being discovered. Because most of California's vineyards are planted with vines that, although bearing, are not yet mature, and because so many of the wines are being made by relatively young winemakers who are still developing their styles, it is certain that as good as California wines are today, the state has yet to produce its finest wines.

Most wine drinkers no longer make the mistake of grouping all California wines together, and have learned to distinguish among, say, an inexpensive jug of Mountain Burgundy, a distinctive Zinfandel, and a remarkable Cabernet Sauvignon produced in limited quantities by a small Napa Valley winery. Many consumers also realize that California table wines cannot be compared as a group to the European wines that are available here. Although the wines that are imported are by no means limited to the cream of the crop, they certainly include the finest examples from the best vineyards of Europe. A tremendous amount of cheap and ordinary wine is made in France, Germany, Italy, Spain, and other wine-producing nations that we rarely see here. What we do see all the time are our own moderately priced, dependable table wines of which California produces tens of millions of gallons annually. The unflattering connotations of the word "domestic" have probably contributed a great deal to the condescending attitude that many Americans have had about their own wines. Considering that many of the great European wine regions were established five hundred or a thousand years ago, it's remarkable what a long way we've come in such a comparatively short time.

It was only two hundred years ago that the first vines were planted in southern California by Spanish missionaries. These Franciscans established additional missions throughout the state, and they planted vineyards as far up the coast as Sonoma, north of San Francisco. By the 1830s, when these clerical holdings were secularized, European immigrants and farmers from the East had begun to set up commercial vineyards in California.

In the 1850s a Hungarian, Agoston Haraszthy, made a significant contribution to the wine industry by publishing the results of his experiments in grape growing and winemaking. He later brought over about 100,000 vine cuttings from Europe, which greatly increased the number of grape varieties available to California winemakers.

The gradual development of the California wine industry owes a great debt to the many Europeans who established wineries in the second half of the nineteenth century and the early years of this one. They include Italians (Giuseppe and Pietro Simi, John Foppiano, and Samuele Sebastiani), Frenchmen (Paul Masson, Pierre

Mirassou, Georges de Latour at Beaulieu Vineyard, and Etienne Thée and Charles Lefranc at Almadén), Germans (Carl Wente and the Beringer brothers), Czechs (the Korbel brothers), a Finn (Gustave Niebaum at Inglenook), an Irishman (James Concannon), a Prussian (Charles Krug), and a Hungarian (Agoston Haraszthy at Buena Vista). Then, less than a hundred years after it began, this industry was crippled by Prohibition. Many wineries went out of business and only a few were able to survive by producing sacramental wines or by growing grapes for home winemaking, which was still legal. The better wine varieties were uprooted and replaced by high-yield, thick-skinned grapes that could be shipped east without damage. As recently as 1971 two-thirds of the California crush—as the harvest is usually referred to—was made up of table and raisin grapes, primarily Thompson Seedless. Wine grapes accounted for more than half the total crush for the first time in 1974.

After the repeal of Prohibition, commercial winemaking started again almost from scratch, as there was a shortage of vinification equipment, of tanks and barrels to store the wine, of land planted in anything but high-yield varieties, of skilled personnel, and of a public accustomed to drinking table wines. It's not unfair to say that winemaking in California is less than fifty years old.

California table wines are often divided into two broad categories based on the way they are marketed: *generic wines,* labeled for the most part with the names of famous European wine regions; and *varietal wines,* labeled with the name of the specific grape variety from which each wine is primarily made. The most familiar generic names for red wines are Burgundy, Claret, and Chianti, and for white wines, Chablis, Sauterne (usually spelled without the final *s* in California), and Rhine Wine. These names are among the best known to wine drinkers and have, therefore, been used almost from the beginning of California winemaking to suggest, in a general way, the kind of wine contained in the bottle. Actually, generic wines have more in common with each other than with the European wines whose names are being used. Most California wineries sell generic wines, and their popularity is such that they account for most of the table wine sold in this country. While generic names are here to stay, there is also a trend away from the use of European place-names, and some wineries now label their less expensive wines simply as Red Table Wine, Mountain White Wine, Premium Red, and so on.

Generic wines—by which is meant all nonvarietal wines, however they are labeled—are among the least-expensive table wines available in this country, and many of them provide excellent value. Most of them are sold in jugs, and now that metric sizes have been adopted, the familiar half-gallons and gallons have been replaced by the 50.7-ounce magnum and the 101.4-ounce jeroboam. If there is a problem with generic wines, however, it is not that they don't taste like the European originals, but that there are no standards to help the consumer find his or her way among different brands. Perhaps the most important variable among generic wines is that some are dry and many are not. While a certain amount of sweetness in both white and red wines appeals to a large segment of the public, those who prefer completely dry table wines cannot simply assume that a Chablis will be drier than a Sauterne or a Rhine wine. For one thing, some wineries market identical wines under different generic labels. For another, many wineries maintain a minimum amount of sweetness in all their wines, others in none of them. The sweetness, which usually comes from grape concentrate added just before bottling, is often 1 percent and not infrequently 2 percent, which is far from dry.

As a rule of thumb, California Chianti and Barberone are generally less dry than wines marketed as Burgundy and Claret, and wines with Italian names, such as Fior di California, Fortissimo, Paisano, Vino da Tavola, Rustico, and Cappella are usually semi-sweet. Conversely, generic wines produced by small wineries are likely to be dry.

As pleasant as generic wines can be, it is among varietal wines that the finest California wines are to be found. Consumers were not always as familiar with the name of individual grapes as they are today, and as recently as the 1950s many wineries found it easier to sell a wine made primarily from Cabernet Sauvignon as Claret than with its varietal name. Today the situation is completely reversed. As more consumers have discovered that the best varietal wines represent the best that California has to offer, varietal labeling has caught on to such an extent that there are now more than two dozen varietal names in general use (they are described further on). The number of wineries marketing the most popular varietals increases every year: Cabernet Sauvignon is offered by nearly two hundred wineries, Zinfandel and Chardonnay by more than 150, and over a hundred firms market Pinot Noir, Johannisberg Riesling, and Chenin Blanc.

A varietal wine must be made at least 51 percent from the grape named on its label, and in 1983 the minimum requirement will be raised to 75 percent. In practice, the finest wines are made entirely, or almost entirely, from the named grape. Less-expensive varietal wines, however, are often stretched by blending in neutral wines. Since it is the specific character of each grape variety that distinguishes these wines and gives them their personality, the extent to which a Cabernet Sauvignon or Chardonnay is diluted can have an important effect on its taste.

If one factor that affects a wine's quality is its varietal content—that is, the percentage of the named variety actually in the wine—another factor that is just as important is where the grapes were grown. Although some consumers may still think of California as a single wine area, the state includes regions as cool as Bordeaux, Burgundy, Champagne, and the Rhine, and as warm as the Rhône Valley, central Italy, southern Spain, and North Africa. Certain parts of the state are best suited to high-yield grape varieties that can be blended to produce fortified dessert wines, others to ordinary table wines, and certain limited areas to the production of red and white wines with the finesse and individual distinction of the best European wines. Just as European winemakers have established, through trial and error, that specific varieties produce the finest wines only in delimited regions, so California growers are gradually determining the best sites for each of the major wine grapes. The principal technique in use is that of heat summation, based on the average daily temperature during the six-month growing season from April to October. The coolest areas are designated as Region I, the warmest as Region V, whatever their actual location, and these designations are widely used to determine which grape varieties will flourish best in a particular district.

The traditional fine wine area in California has been the

North Coast counties that fan out from San Francisco—
Napa, Sonoma (which includes the Alexander Valley),
Mendocino, the Livermore Valley in Alameda, and Santa
Clara. In the last ten or fifteen years, winemakers have
discovered that fine wines can also be made in such
regions as Monterey, San Luis Obispo, Santa Barbara, and
Amador, among others. As new vineyards and new
wineries have been created, there has been an increasing
use of appellations of origin on California labels. The
place of origin—Napa, Sonoma, Monterey, Livermore,
and so on—can appear on a label if at least 75 percent of
the wine comes from grapes grown in that region. If the
wine shows a vintage date, then 95 percent of the grapes
must come from the named region. A winery may also use
a dual appellation, such as Santa Clara-Monterey or Napa
and Alexander Valleys, but only if that dual appellation
was in use before 1978; otherwise, such a wine may now
carry only a California appellation.

There may also be specific inner districts within each
county that possess a distinctive microclimate: a particular
combination of temperature, elevation, cooling breezes,
drainage of the soil, and so on. Some, such as Sonoma's
Alexander Valley and Alameda's Livermore Valley, are
officially recognized as appellations of origin. Others, such
as the Dry Creek Valley in Sonoma, the Carneros district
in Napa, and the Santa Ynez Valley in Santa Barbara, are
not yet officially recognized, but their names are used on
labels.

Consumers have become increasingly familiar with the
names of individual districts of origin in the coastal counties, but what is perhaps the most basic distinction to be
made among California wines is that between the wines
produced in the coastal counties and those produced in the
San Joaquin Valley. The San Joaquin Valley, also known
as the Central Valley, stretches for more than two hundred
miles from Lodi (pronounced *low*-die) down to Bakersfield, and it is in this warm interior valley that most of
California's wine grapes are grown, as well as almost all of
its table and raisin grapes. Most of the new vineyards
planted since 1969 are in the San Joaquin Valley: two-
thirds of the Petite Sirah and Zinfandel planted was in this
valley, and almost all of such varieties as Barbera, Ruby
Cabernet, Chenin Blanc, and French Colombard. Despite

the tremendous increase in coastal vineyards, more than 80 percent of California wine made from wine grapes (that is, excluding that made from table and raisin grapes) comes from the San Joaquin Valley.

The interior valley has always been a source of generic wines, but as more consumers have associated varietal wines with quality there has been a tendency to label comparatively undistinguished wines with varietal names. Every wine, after all, is made from one or more grape varieties, but in the past, producers of inexpensive generic wines saw no advantage in labeling such wines with the name of the grape from which each was primarily made. The extensive new acreage in the San Joaquin Valley made it possible for varietal wines to be produced in large quantities from such grapes as Barbera, Ruby Cabernet, Zinfandel, Chenin Blanc, and French Colombard. Generally speaking, wines made from grapes grown in the warm interior valley tend to have less varietal character, individuality, and liveliness than those from cooler regions. Winemakers recognize this by paying two or three times as much for a ton of Zinfandel or Chenin Blanc from the coastal counties as from the Central Valley. Consequently, while some varietal wines from the San Joaquin Valley are well made and moderately priced, a number of others are no more distinctive than the generic Burgundy and Chablis they are meant to replace. Because California wines are not identified by a specific appellation of origin, as in Europe, the principal quality distinction, especially in the past twenty years, has been between generic and varietal wines. This distinction, however, was based on varietal wines produced in the cool coastal regions. Some of the new varietal wines have blurred this distinction, and suggest that varietal names are not in themselves a mark of superior quality.

In addition to table wines, dessert wines, sparkling wines, and vermouth, there is a category known as special natural wines, which are flavored, usually sweet, sometimes lightly carbonated, and which includes wines made from apples or pears as well as from grapes. Some, such as Thunderbird, contain 20 percent of alcohol. Others, which are known as pop wines or refreshment wines, contain about 10 percent alcohol. Bali Hai, Boone's Farm, T J Swann, and Annie Green Springs are among the best known in this category. In the early 1970s, special natural wines accounted for as much as one out of every six bottles of wine consumed in this country, but the fad for these fruit-flavored wines seems to have peaked.

It has often been claimed that there are no bad vintages in California, along with the corollary statement that there are no variations from one California vintage to another. The first claim has some validity. In most of Europe's fine wine districts grapes don't ripen fully every year, whereas in California it is unusual for grapes to be unripe at the time of the harvest. Nevertheless, there are years when a very cool growing season in parts of California has resulted in grapes that never fully ripened; there have been years when rains during the vintage caused a certain amount of rot to form on the grapes; and years when extensive drought conditions affected the quality of the wines. As the range of vintage-dated varietal wines has increased, consumers have become much more aware of vintage variations in California, as well as of varietal and regional differences. After all, when grapes as different as Cabernet Sauvignon, Pinot Noir, and Johannisberg Riesling grow side by side, it's inevitable that a particular growing season will favor one variety over another. And just as there are differences to be found in a given vintage between wines produced in the Médoc and in Saint-Emilion, or between Rieslings from the Moselle and the Rheingau, so there are bound to be differences between Cabernet Sauvignon from Napa and Mendocino, or between Chardonnays produced in Sonoma and Monterey, which are nearly two hundred miles apart. Ironically, just as Bordeaux vintages represent, for many consumers, all of France, so the relative success of Napa Valley Cabernet Sauvignon is often, and erroneously, used as a vintage guide to all California wines.

Although there are important distinctions to be made between one California vintage and another when discussing the finest varietal wines, the fact remains that an individual winemaker's skill and intent probably plays a more important role in California than in most of the world's wine regions. Some of the finest California wines have been made by individual wineries in years whose growing conditions were not considered ideal.

If a California wine bears a vintage date, it must be

made 95 percent from grapes harvested that year. Most California wines are not vintage-dated, including almost all generics and many popular varietals as well. The problem with nonvintage wines is that the consumer has no way of knowing how old the wine is, or rather, how long the wine has been in bottle. This is particularly important for delicate white wines, rosés, and light red wines, especially inexpensive ones that are meant to be consumed soon after bottling. Even when a label does not indicate a wine's vintage, it is sometimes possible to guess when it was bottled anyway. Glass manufacturers keep tabs on their production by means of a code blown into the bottom of the bottle, and this sometimes includes two digits indicating the year the bottle was made. Because wineries do not keep large inventories of glass on hand, you can assume that the wine was bottled in that year, which enables you to determine, in a general way, whether or not the wine is too old.

The basic information conveyed by a California wine label can be more or less explicit depending on the wine. As described above, certain minimum requirements must be met concerning grape variety, region of origin, and vintage. In addition, some wineries label certain of their wines as Reserve, Vintage Selection, Special Reserve, and so on to indicate superior quality. Many wineries also add additional information on their labels, or on a special back label, about such matters as the exact varietal content of their wines, the sugar content of the grapes when they were picked (expressed in degrees Brix), and if the wine is not dry, just how much residual sugar is present. Some wineries even indicate fermentation temperatures and the amount of time each wine was aged in barrel. A few wineries make separate lots of wine from individual vineyard plots and these are indicated by labeling the wine with a vineyard designation or with the name of the grower whose grapes were used.

One other indication of a wine's origin is conveyed by the phrase *Produced and Bottled by* . . . which means that at least 75 percent of that wine was fermented by the named winery. *Made and Bottled by* . . . means that as little as 10 percent may have been fermented by the named winery and the rest bought in bulk. Some wineries get around the implications of *Made and Bottled by* . . .

by using such terms as *Perfected and Bottled by* . . . or *Cellared and Bottled by*. . . . Actually, a winery's reputation is the most reliable guide to quality of its wines, and in the descriptions of individual wineries further on, the words "produced" and "made" are used interchangeably without reference to their legal implications.

One of the factors that has contributed to the continuing improvement of California wines is new winemaking technology. Perhaps the most significant development of the past twenty years has been the widespread adoption of temperature-controlled stainless-steel fermentation tanks. This has enabled both large and small wineries to ferment white wines slowly at low temperatures, which retains the wine's fruit and delicacy while diminishing the possibility of browning and oxidation. In addition, the personality of each grape variety is retained in the wine, rather than being dissipated by fast, warm fermentation, as often occurred in the past. The importance of temperature-controlled fermentation is understood throughout the world, of course, but California wineries have the capital to install expensive stainless-steel fermentors, whereas in many other countries, especially those with uncertain governments, winery owners have been reluctant to make the necessary investment. This is perhaps the principal reason that California white wines, including inexpensive generic wines, are so well made. The fermentors also enable winemakers to safely use higher temperatures to bring out the flavors of certain red wines.

Another technological advance has been the widespread use of ulta-fine membrane filters to clarify wines before they are bottled. This process, called microfiltration, removes all yeast and many of the bacteria which might otherwise remain in the wine at the time of bottling. The result is cleaner wines, without the baked taste sometimes caused by pasteurization or the acrid taste of oversulfured wines. In fact, few California wineries still pasteurize their wines today.

Along with technological advances, there have been other developments as well. One of the most dramatic in recent years has been the recognition of *Botrytis cinerea* in California vineyards. This beneficial mold, called *pourriture noble* in Sauternes and *Edelfäule* in Germany (both mean noble rot), shrivels ripe grapes, intensifies their flavor, and increases the sugar content of the juice. It was long believed that climatic conditions in California would not permit *Botrytis cinerea* to develop, but in 1969 Wente Bros. harvested naturally botrytised Johannisberg Riesling grapes in their Arroyo Seco vineyards in Monterey County. The earliest examples of such wines were labeled Spätlese and Auslese to suggest their similarity to German wines. The use of German words is no longer permitted, and such wines are usually labeled Late Harvest or Selected Late Harvest. The label must also indicate the sugar content of the grapes at the time of harvest and the wine's residual sugar after fermentation, so that the consumer can determine just how sweet each Late Harvest wine is. A number of California examples, notably those from Freemark Abbey, Joseph Phelps Vineyards, and Chateau St. Jean, have an intensity and richness equal to Beerenauslese and Trockenbeerenauslese wines from the Rhine. Most California Late Harvest wines have been made from Johannisberg Riesling, as in Germany, although a few have been made from Sémillon and Sauvignon Blanc, as in Sauternes, and from Chenin Blanc, as in the Loire Valley.

One of the most significant aspects of California's approach to wines, and of the informed consumer's reaction to those wines, is based on the awareness that a California winemaker has much more flexibility in making his wines than does his European counterpart. A number of options are available to winemakers everywhere: fermenting selected wines in small oak barrels rather than large tanks to add to their complexity; leaving the grape skins in contact with the fermenting must for an extended period in order to extract more color, tannin, and flavor; making a given white wine more or less sweet; and so on. A European winemaker, however, is to a large extent bound within established norms: the limits of the vineyard or of the appellation have been defined for quite some time; the grapes he may use are regulated by law; and the winemaking techniques are traditional. In contrast, a California winemaker can choose the site on which to establish his vineyard or the region from which to buy his grapes. He can select the specific grape varieties with which to produce wines, and can add a new variety or drop an old one from one vintage to the next. A winemaker from Bordeaux cannot suddenly produce Burgundies or Rhine wines, but a California winemaker specializing in Cabernet Sauvignon can begin to make Chardonnay or Johannisberg Riesling just by finding a source for those grapes. Winemaking styles also vary widely: some top California winemakers strive for wines that are elegant, distinct, and well-balanced; others deliberately produce wines that are powerful, tannic, and almost impenetrable without several years of bottle age.

Perhaps the most controversial of the many factors that contribute to the style of California's best varietal wines is the length of time each wine is aged in wood and the kind of wood used. Some traditional wineries continue to market rounded, mature red wines that have been aged for long periods in giant redwood vats; others have adopted the use of small oak barrels, as in Bordeaux and Burgundy, to add complexity, nuances of flavor, and longevity to certain red wines and such whites as Chardonnay. Many winemakers are constantly experimenting to find the kind of oak that best suits each varietal wine: some choose American oak, others use Yugoslavian, and many prefer to age their wines in French oak, making a further distinction between oak from Limousin, Nevers, and Tronçais. A number of winemakers, however, believe that wood obscures a wine's fruit and varietal character and prefer not to age their white wines in wood at all.

Whether or not fine varietal wines are improved by blending in another variety—adding some Merlot to Cabernet Sauvignon is the most familiar example—is another variable that plays an important role in determining a wine's style and flavor. Wines are usually fined, or clarified, before being bottled to remove impurities, but fining may also strip a wine of some of its character. Many wineries favor heavy fining to produce brilliant wines; others do not fine at all, in order to retain more depth and richness of flavor in certain red wines.

The choices available to California winemakers represent a challenge and an opportunity, but they also pose a problem for the consumer. As winemakers are finding their way with individual varieties and with the overall style of the wines they produce, the wines themselves do not always maintain a continuity of style. From one year to the next, a dry Johannisberg Riesling may become semi-sweet; a rich, intense Zinfandel may become lighter and fruitier; and so on. Among the established European wines, the primary difference between one year and the next is based on the character of the vintage; in California, the style of a particular varietal wine may change arbitrarily. This provides the interested consumer with an ongoing sense of discovery, but it sometimes makes it difficult to define the style of a winery and of its individual wines, or to choose wines on the basis of past experience.

The Principal Grape Varieties

Most European wines are labeled with the name of the district, village, or vineyard from which each one comes, as defined by its appellation of origin. In California, a wine's origin has played a less important role than the grape variety from which it is primarily or entirely made. Even among fine varietal wines, the name of the grape is often as much as the consumer is told about the wine in the bottle. Consequently, whereas someone tasting European wine will often discuss its appellation character, a person describing a California varietal wine is likely to comment on its varietal character. Just as a wine drinker can learn to recognize and evaluate the particular characteristics of a Médoc, Beaujolais, Sancerre, Meursault, Barolo, Chianti, or Rioja, so he or she looks for certain varietal characteristics in a Cabernet Sauvignon, Chardonnay, Johannisberg Riesling, or Zinfandel.

Anyone who takes an interest in California wines soon learns to distinguish among the different varietal names with which so many of these wines are labeled today. Most of the acreage devoted to classic grape varieties was planted in the early 1970s and a few figures indicate just how extensive these new plantings were. The acreage of Cabernet Sauvignon, for example, increased from 4,000 in 1969 to 26,000 ten years later, Chardonnay from 1,800 to 13,000, Pinot Noir from 2,000 to 10,000, Johannisberg Riesling from 1,000 to 8,000, Sauvignon Blanc from 600 to 5,000, Sémillon from 750 to nearly 3,000, Gewürztraminer from 400 to 2,800, and perhaps the most dramatic increase of all, Merlot jumped from about 100 acres to 4,000. As impressive as these increases are, these eight classic varieties account for less than 10 percent of the total production of wine grapes, less than 5 percent of all the grapes crushed in California.

There are no production limits per acre in California as there are in the top European districts, but the yield of the best varieties planted in the best sites is not large. Two or three tons per acre is not unusual (a ton of grapes will give about sixty cases of wine), four or five tons is considered quite good. In the San Joaquin Valley, where such varieties as French Colombard, Chenin Blanc, Ruby Cabernet, Barbera, and Petite Sirah are widely planted, yields of ten tons per acre or higher are normal.

What follows are descriptions of the grape varieties most likely to be seen on California wine labels.

Red Wines

Cabernet Sauvignon, the classic red grape of Bordeaux, is responsible for the finest red wines of California. The wines, noted for their tannic, austere qualities when young, have a complexity that comes from the variety and, in some cases, from the small oak barrels in which the wine is often matured. A certain amount of Merlot is used in the Médoc region of Bordeaux to soften the harshness of young Cabernet Sauvignon, and this practice has been adopted in California as well. As more *Merlot* was planted in California, it was inevitable that it would be bottled on its own as a varietal. (After all, the wines of Saint-Emilion and Pomerol are made primarily from Merlot.) A number of wineries now market a Merlot, and some even blend in Cabernet Sauvignon to add backbone to the rich, but somewhat softer wines made from this grape. A very small amount of *Cabernet Franc* is planted in California, and is sometimes blended with Cabernet Sauvignon to add bouquet.

Ruby Cabernet, a cross of Cabernet Sauvignon with Carignane, has been widely planted in the Central Valley, where it gives an abundant yield of agreeable wines.

Pinot Noir, from France's Burgundy region, is generally acknowledged to be the least successful of the classic grape varieties in California. California Pinot Noir is often light and indistinct, but even attractive, full-bodied examples usually lack the complexity of flavor and elegance of fine red Burgundies. Selected clones, or variants, of Pinot Noir have been planted in districts more suited to this variety, and winemakers have also been experimenting with different vinification techniques, often with encouraging results. *Red Pinot* is not a Pinot at all, and the name is almost never seen anymore. *Pinot Saint George* is another name for the Red Pinot.

Gamay Beaujolais is now known to be a clone of Pinot Noir, and wines made from this variety may legally be sold under either name. Since the name Gamay Beaujolais is popular with consumers, most wineries continue to sell lighter-bodied examples with that name, and market fuller ones as Pinot Noir. Nevertheless, wines labeled Gamay Beaujolais tends to be sturdier and less fruity than French Beaujolais. It is the variety called *Gamay*, or *Napa Gamay*, that is the one cultivated in the Beaujolais region, and it makes fruity and appealing wines in California. Both Napa Gamay and Gamay Beaujolais are usually bottled early and meant to be drunk while they are still young. Several wineries even produce a Gamay Beaujolais Nouveau, in the style of France's Beaujolais Nouveau, which is bottled and sold within weeks of the harvest.

Zinfandel, although of European origin, is often considered an indigenous American variety, since it has no exact counterparts anywhere else. The origin of Zinfandel, historically described as a Hungarian variety, was for years something of a mystery, but it has now been traced to the Primitivo of southern Italy. Plantings of Zinfandel have more than doubled in the past ten years, and it is now the most widely cultivated wine grape in California. When grown in the Central Valley, it usually produces undistinguished wine suitable for blending into generics. In cooler areas, its distinctive spicy or berrylike aroma and taste are evident, and it makes a very individual and appealing wine. Some winemakers make a light, fruity Zinfandel to be consumed young. Others prefer a Zinfandel that is big, tannic, and intense, and that needs some bottle age to develop. There are, in addition, some Late Harvest Zinfandels made from especially ripe grapes that produce wines with 15 or 16 percent of alcohol. Some are completely dry; others are vinified to retain some natural sugar.

Petite Sirah produces intensely-colored, full-flavored,

and tannic wines that were used for many years in generic blends. This variety is widely planted in the coastal counties and in the Central Valley, and many wineries now market the wine as a varietal. It is generally agreed that California Petite Sirah is not the Syrah of France's Rhône region, but the lesser Duriff. True *Syrah*, used to make such wines as Hermitage and Côte Rotie, has also been planted in California.

Barbera is widely grown in northern Italy and in California's Central Valley, where it produces an agreeable wine without any distinctive character. A limited amount of Barbera is made in the coastal counties as well, and is characterized by good flavor and lively acidity.

Charbono, another north Italian variety, is similar to Barbera, although softer and fuller-bodied. For many years Inglenook was the only one to market the wine as a varietal, but limited amounts of Charbono are now produced by other wineries as well.

Grignolino, also from northern Italy, is occasionally seen as a varietal wine. It is characterized by a light, orange-red color and slightly tart taste.

Carignane, widely planted in southern France (where it is spelled Carignan), is a high-yield variety that produces more total tons each year than any other wine grape in California. It is used almost entirely as a blending wine, but a few wineries market it as a varietal.

Carnelian, a new cross of Cabernet Sauvignon, Carignane, and Grenache, was developed as a high-yield variety for use in the Central Valley, and is occasionally bottled as a varietal wine. *Carmine* and *Centurion* are other Cabernet-based crosses.

In response to an increased demand for white wines, a number of wineries market white wines made from black grapes, often referred to as *Blanc de Noirs*. The color in red wine is extracted from the skins during fermentation, so if black grapes are pressed immediately after picking and the juice fermented away from the skins (as in the Champagne district of France), the result is white wine. Pinot Noir is the variety most often used, and the wines are usually marketed as Pinot Noir Blanc or Blanc de Pinot Noir. Zinfandel, Gamay, and Cabernet Sauvignon have also been used to make white wines. In practice, these wines are usually salmon-pink in color, or even light red, so the Blanc on the label is not really accurate. The wines are marketed as if they were white wines, however, and are meant to be served chilled on occasions when white wines are called for.

White Wines

Chardonnay, the classic grape of Burgundy, is considered the most successful white-wine variety in California. (Although it has been established that Chardonnay is not a member of the Pinot family, some wineries continue to use the traditional name Pinot Chardonnay on their labels.) At their best, Chardonnays are rich, full-flavored, complex, and elegant, and they are the longest-lived of dry white wines. Many winemakers now age Chardonnay in small oak barrels, so that the bouquet of these wines often combines oak with the natural fruit of the grape. Unlike Cabernet Sauvignon, Chardonnay is not a wine that benefits from blending, and some inexpensive examples that have been stretched with, say, French Colombard or Chenin Blanc lack varietal character and complexity. *Pinot Blanc* is not widely cultivated in California, but there is probably more acreage in California today than in Burgundy. The wines are similar to Chardonnay, but perhaps a bit lighter and less distinct.

The Riesling grape that is grown along Germany's Rhine and Moselle rivers is called *Johannisberg Riesling* or *White Riesling* in California. It produces fragrant and charming wines that usually have more body and alcohol than Rieslings from Germany, and that are, therefore, closer in style to full-flavored Rhine wines than to the delicate and piquant wines of the Moselle. A few wineries make a dry Johannisberg Riesling, as in Alsace, but most retain a certain amount of sugar to produce a semi-dry wine. In addition to the wide range of medium-dry Johannisberg Rieslings produced in California, winemakers there have also been remarkably successful at making Late Harvest wines similar to the Auslese, Beerenauslese, and even Trockenbeerenauslese wines of Germany.

Sylvaner can be sold in California as Riesling, and most of them are, although some wineries label this wine Riesling-Sylvaner or Franken Riesling. The wine does not have the fragrance and elegance of a true Riesling, but good examples have perhaps more distinction in California than in Germany. Some California Rieslings are just off-dry, others are semi-sweet.

Grey Riesling, which is not a Riesling at all, is capable of producing wines that are dry, crisp, and relatively flavorful, although most examples are semi-dry and undistinguished.

Emerald Riesling, a cross of Riesling with Muscadelle, produces pale-colored, light-bodied, rather neutral wines, which are often blended with Muscat to add aroma and flavor.

Chenin Blanc, used to make such Loire Valley wines as Vouvray, Anjou Blanc, and Saumur, produces fruity, appealing wines in California. A few Chenin Blanc wines are completely dry, but most range from semi-dry to semi-sweet, the exact degree of sweetness varying from one winery to another. (For that matter, Vouvray, too, is made as a dry, semi-dry, and sweet wine.) A very few wineries occasionally market a dry Chenin Blanc as White Pinot, which is misleading, since this grape bears no relation to the Pinot Blanc. The name probably derives from the Chenin Blanc's local name along the Loire—Pineau de la Loire.

Sauvignon Blanc is the grape used, usually in combination with Sémillon, to make Bordeaux Blanc and Graves, which can be dry or semi-dry. It is also used by itself along the Loire to make such assertive dry wines as Pouilly-Fumé and Sancerre. Sauvignon Blanc had never been a popular varietal wine until Robert Mondavi introduced a dry, flavorful Sauvignon Blanc labeled Fumé Blanc. Many wineries now market dry versions of this varietal as Fumé Blanc or Blanc Fumé; others continue to use the name Sauvignon Blanc for a wine that may be dry or semi-dry.

Sémillon is the grape that gives Sauternes its special character when attacked by noble rot, but few California winemakers have attempted to make a botrytised wine from this grape. This distinctive wine is marketed by relatively few wineries, and the label usually indicates whether the wine is dry or semi-sweet.

Wines labeled *Gewürztraminer* have a spicy aroma and a pronounced taste that makes them one of the most distinctive white wines in the world. *Gewürz* means spicy, and even muted versions of this wine still retain its characteristic penetrating bouquet and intense flavor. In France's Alsace region, Gewürztraminer is almost always dry; in California, most examples range from semi-dry to semi-sweet.

French Colombard, an anonymous component of many generic blends, is the most widely planted white-wine grape in California. Increasingly bottled as a varietal, it can be made into a pleasant off-dry wine with a touch of acidity, especially in the cooler coastal regions. Inexpensive semi-sweet versions are often bland.

Moscato di Canelli, an intensely flavored grape widely cultivated in northern Italy to make Asti Spumante, is planted to a limited extent in California, where it produces a distinctive and aromatic wine. Most examples are sweet, a few are semi-dry. (The Muscat of Alexandria, widely planted in the San Joaquin Valley, is a raisin grape historically used to make cheap Muscatel.)

Green Hungarian is such an appealing name that a few firms market this varietal, although the wine itself is fairly neutral.

Folle Blanche, known in France's Muscadet region as Gros Plant, makes a light-bodied, dry wine marketed only by Louis M. Martini.

Flora, a cross of Sémillon and Gewürztraminer, has not been widely planted and is rarely seen as a varietal.

Rosés

Most California rosés are blended from different varieties and sold as Vin Rosé or with a proprietary brand name. Of the varietal rosés, Grenache Rosé, popularized by Almadén, is the best known. Grenache is grown in southern France, and is one of the varieties used to make Tavel, France's best-known dry rosé; California Grenache Rosé is usually medium dry. Rosés are also made from Zinfandel, Gamay, Pinot Noir, Petite Sirah, and Cabernet Sauvignon. The best of them, which retain the varietal characteristics of the grape from which each is made, are among the most attractive rosés available.

The California Wine Regions

The changes that are continually taking place in California today mean that any description of its wine regions and wineries must necessarily be tentative. New winemaking districts are being created where vines were not previously cultivated, and microclimates particularly suited to one or another variety are being discovered within established vineyard regions. Wineries are in an even greater state of flux. The personality of a winery may change almost overnight because of new ownership or a new winemaker, and other factors play a role as well. A winery that has traditionally produced generic wines may introduce a line of varietal wines; one known for certain varietal wines may decide to market others in even greater quantities; a winery may produce its wines from purchased grapes until its own vineyards are fully bearing, at which time the style of its wines may change. Nor is a winery's history easy to establish: some winemakers made their first wines under someone else's roof while their own wineries were being constructed; others began by making such limited amounts of wine that it was not until the second or third crush, or vintage, that they were able to bottle enough wine to market commercially. The following brief descriptions of more than a hundred wineries is meant to be no more than an introduction to the diversity that characterizes the California wine scene today.

Napa

Of all the California wine regions, Napa is probably the most famous to consumers and the one with the finest reputation. The reasons for this are not hard to discover: not only does the Napa Valley contain some of California's best-known wineries, but the number of fine wines produced there since Repeal is greater than anywhere else. There are vintage-dated varietal wines, especially Cabernet Sauvignon, from such wineries as Beaulieu Vineyard, Inglenook, Charles Krug, and Louis M. Martini going back to the 1930s and 1940s, while Sonoma and Monterey, for example, began to produce such wines only in the 1960s. Today, outstanding wines are made in other regions as well, and many winemakers would agree that certain varieties grow even more successfully in other counties than in Napa. Nevertheless, Napa retains its reputation, which has been further enhanced by a number of excellent new wineries created in the 1970s.

The Napa Valley wineries are particularly accessible to visitors. The city of Napa is fifty miles north of San Francisco, and the distance from Napa to Calistoga by way of Yountville, Oakville, Rutherford, and St. Helena is about twenty-five miles. The Silverado Trail, at the base of the mountains east of the valley floor, parallels the main highway through Napa, and to the west the Mayacamas Mountains separate Napa and Sonoma counties.

There are about 25,000 acres of vineyards in Napa, of which more than 5,000 acres are Cabernet Sauvignon. Pinot Noir and Chardonnay account for about 2,500 acres each, and another 8,000 acres are planted in Zinfandel, Johannisberg Riesling, Chenin Blanc, Napa Gamay, Petite Sirah, Sauvignon Blanc, and Merlot. These ten varieties make up three-quarters of the vineyards in Napa. There are no officially defined inner appellations within Napa, but winemakers and grape growers have ideas of their own about the relative merits of specific districts for individual varieties. The cool Carneros district, for example, situated southwest of the city of Napa, is considered the best place for Pinot Noir and Chardonnay. The region around Calistoga, to the north, is actually warmer than the southern part of the Napa Valley, and a further distinction is made between grapes grown on the valley floor and those from hillside vineyards to the east and west. Wine labels rarely indicate the exact origin of the grapes, but these distinctions suggest some of the variables that grape growers take into account when planting their vineyards and that winemakers recognize when buying their grapes.

This description of Napa wineries begins with the largest ones, all of which are located along an eight-mile stretch from Oakville to just past St. Helena. Beaulieu Vineyard, founded by Georges de Latour in 1900, is best known for its Cabernet Sauvignon. The winery, usually referred to as BV, now produces three Cabernets: one is made entirely from that variety; another, labeled Beau Tour, is blended with 20 percent of Merlot; the third, produced in limited quantities, is the famous Georges de Latour Private Reserve. The Private Reserve, traditionally one of the finest Cabernets made in California, comes from a specific group of vineyards near Rutherford, and is the biggest and longest-lived of BV's Cabernets. BV also makes several other varietal wines, including Gamay Beaujolais, Johannisberg Riesling, a dry Sauvignon Blanc, and a sweet Sauvignon Blanc labeled Chateau Beaulieu. André Tchelistcheff, a Russian-born enologist, joined BV in 1938, and was responsible for the style and quality of its wines for thirty-five years. He pioneered the use of small oak barrels as an adjunct to large redwood tanks to age wines, and was one of the first to recognize the potential of the Carneros district as Napa's best site for Pinot Noir and Chardonnay. After his retirement from BV in 1970, Tchelistcheff became a consultant to BV until 1973, and thereafter to a number of other wineries throughout the state.

Inglenook, founded by Gustave Niebaum in 1879, is less than a mile from Beaulieu Vineyard. In 1964 the winery was sold to United Vintners, which was in turn acquired by Heublein, Inc., in 1968. (Heublein also bought Beaulieu Vineyard in 1969.) In recent years Inglenook has marketed three lines of wines: estate-bottled varietals, which now represent only a small part of the firm's sales; Inglenook Vintage wines, such as Chablis, Burgundy, and Rhine; and the Inglenook Navalle line of generic and varietal wines, which are made in the San Joaquin Valley and bottled there and at the Italian Swiss Colony winery in Sonoma. While the popular Navalle line provides the consumer with moderately priced wines, it is the estate-bottled wines that maintain the Inglenook tradition. They include a wide range of varietal wines including Charbono, an unusual red wine, a dry Chenin Blanc labeled White Pinot, and special cask bottlings in limited quantities of Cabernet Sauvignon, Pinot Noir, and, until recently, Red Pinot (which is actually the Pinot Saint George).

Louis M. Martini wines were first made in Napa in 1934. The firm owns more than a thousand acres of vineyards, but because they are located both in Napa and Sonoma, the wines bear a California appellation. Martini has achieved a particular reputation for such red wines as Cabernet Sauvignon, Zinfandel, Barbera, and Pinot Noir, and the winery is among the few whose white wines, such as Johannisberg Riesling, Chenin Blanc, and Gewürz Traminer, are dry. Wines given extra aging are eventually marketed as Private Reserve, and individual lots of wines are sometimes bottled separately and labeled Special Selection.

The Charles Krug winery, just north of St. Helena, was founded in 1860 and eventually purchased by the Mondavi family in 1943. Krug, which was the first winery to successfully market Chenin Blanc as a varietal wine, produces a full range of generic and varietal wines, as well as a separate line of less-expensive wines under the name CK Mondavi.

Not far from Krug is the picturesque nineteenth-century Rhine House, which serves as a tasting room for Beringer/Los Hermanos. The Beringer Brothers winery was revitalized in 1970, when it was purchased by Nestlé of Switzerland. Myron Nightingale was brought in as winemaker, a new winery was built, and the company now offers a full range of wines, including two proprietary wines, the red Barenblut and the white Traubengold. Beringer has achieved particular success with a line of generic and varietal jug wines marketed with the Los Hermanos label.

The Christian Brothers, a teaching order founded in France in the seventeenth century, first planted vineyards in California in 1882 and moved to the Napa Valley in 1930. They own about fourteen hundred acres in Napa and most of their table wines bear a Napa appellation. In addition, they own a thousand acres in the San Joaquin Valley, where they make dessert wines and brandy. In addition to the usual range of generic and varietal wines, the Christian Brothers also market a dry Sauvignon Blanc as Napa Fumé Blanc, a Napa Gamay as Gamay Noir, a medium-sweet Chenin Blanc as Pineau de la Loire, and a sweet Muscat wine as Chateau La Salle. They were also the first major winery to make a varietal wine labeled Pinot Saint George. With very few exceptions, the Christian Brothers produced only nonvintage wines until 1979, when the winery first introduced a range of vintage-dated varietal wines. The Christian Brothers, in association with Fromm & Sichel, a company that has been marketing its wines since the 1930s, created the Wine Museum of San Francisco, which was opened to the public in 1974.

The newest of the large Napa wineries is that of Robert Mondavi, which was built near Oakville in 1966. When Mondavi left Charles Krug, his intention was to produce only vintage-dated varietal wines, which was a much more unusual concept at the time than it is today. From the beginning, Mondavi experimented with various aspects of winemaking, including fermentation temperatures and the effects of different kinds of oak on the flavor and complexity of each varietal wine. The winery, which now owns more than a thousand acres in Napa, continues to produce a wide range of varietal wines. The most popular are Cabernet Sauvignon and Fumé Blanc, which is the name Mondavi originated for a dry Sauvignon Blanc. Specially selected lots of Cabernet Sauvignon and Chardonnay are bottled and sold as Reserve wines. Mondavi also operates a winery in Acampo, near Lodi, where the popular Red and White Table Wines are made. In 1977 Mondavi acquired the name and inventory of Oakville Vineyards in Napa.

In addition to these seven wineries, there are more than thirty Napa wineries whose names are known to interested consumers. Many of them were founded in the 1970s, most of them produce less than twenty-five thousand cases a year, and several do not sell much wine outside of California. They are described in a loose geographical order, starting on the Silverado Trail near the city of Napa, continuing north toward Calistoga, and then doubling back along the main highway and the western side of the Napa Valley.

Clos Du Val is unusual in that it was originally set up to make only two wines—Cabernet Sauvignon, which accounts for four-fifths of its production, and Zinfandel. The first wines, made in 1972 under the direction of Bernard Portet, a Frenchman who grew up in Bordeaux, established the winery's reputation for elegant and stylish red wines. In 1978, Portet began to make a small amount of Chardonnay as well. The Stag's Leap Wine Cellar, located a mile from Clos Du Val along the Silverado Trail, was established by Warren and Barbara Winiarski. More than half of its production is devoted to Cabernet Sauvignon, which established the winery's fame. Stag's Leap also makes Gamay Beaujolais, Johannisberg Riesling, Merlot, and limited quantities of Chardonnay. The Stag's Leap

Vineyard, located nearby, is an unrelated new winery known primarily for its Petite Syrah (as it is labeled) and Chenin Blanc.

Donn Chappellet established the Chappellet Vineyard on Pritchard Hill, east of the Napa Valley. The first wines were produced in 1969 in a dramatic new winery built in the shape of a three-sided pyramid. Chappellet, best known for its intense and long-lived Cabernet Sauvignon, also produces Merlot, Gamay, Chardonnay, Johannisberg Riesling, and a dry Chenin Blanc. The Pritchard Hill label, once used for certain wines, has been discontinued.

Villa Mt. Eden, near the Silverado Trail, produces limited quantities of several varietal wines from its own vineyards. Caymus Vineyards is a winery established by a grape grower who decided to keep some of his grapes to make his own wines. Caymus also uses the name Liberty School. Not far away is the winery built by Pillsbury and named Souverain of Rutherford. In 1976 the winery was sold to a partnership, some of whom are also partners in Freemark Abbey, and they renamed the winery Rutherford Hill.

The Heitz Cellars were established in 1961 by Joe Heitz, considered one of California's finest winemakers. He has achieved particular success with Cabernet Sauvignon and Chardonnay, and is also known for Pinot Noir and occasional lots of Grignolino. Heitz's most famous wine is Martha's Vineyard Cabernet Sauvignon, which comes from a twelve-acre plot near Oakville owned by Tom and Martha May. This single vineyard wine was first produced in 1966, and the total quantity varies from one thousand to four thousand cases.

The Joseph Phelps winery was built in 1974 and quickly established a reputation for its white wines. Its German-trained winemaker, Walter Schug, has made distinctive Gewürztraminers and a full range of Johannisberg Rieslings, including Late Harvest wines of Auslese quality and Selected Late Harvest wines of Beerenauslese and Trockenbeerenauslese quality. Phelps produces about equal quantities of red and white varietal wines, primarily Cabernet Sauvignon and Johannisberg Riesling, and was the first to market a wine from the true Syrah of the Rhône Valley. In addition, every year a limited amount of claret-like red wine is specially blended from such varieties as

Cabernet Sauvignon, Merlot, and Cabernet Franc, and labeled Insignia, without a specific varietal appellation.

In 1972, Tom Burgess bought the original Souverain estate located in the hills east of the valley, and renamed it Burgess Cellars. Most of the winery's production is Cabernet Sauvignon, Chardonnay, and Zinfandel from grapes grown in both Napa and Sonoma counties. Cuvaison, located farther north near the Silverado Trail, has recently been specializing in three varietals—Chardonnay, Zinfandel, and Cabernet Sauvignon.

One of the most striking wineries in California is that of Sterling Vineyards, modeled on the spare white churches found on some Greek islands. Visitors take an aerial tramway from the base of a hill to the winery above. The first wines Sterling marketed were from the 1969 vintage, and their production consists primarily of Cabernet Sauvignon (including special lots labeled Private Reserve), Merlot, Sauvignon Blanc, and Chardonnay. The winery was one of the first to market Merlot as a varietal, and they have built a following for this distinctive wine. In 1977 Sterling Vineyards was acquired by the Coca-Cola Company of Atlanta. Down the road from Sterling is the small, new Stonegate Winery which produces Cabernet Sauvignon and Chardonnay from its own hillside vineyards.

North of Calistoga is Chateau Montelena, whose vineyards are situated both in Napa and in Sonoma's Alexander Valley. Chateau Montelena's first wines were made in 1972 and it first achieved fame with its Chardonnay. The winery specializes in Chardonnay, Cabernet Sauvignon, Zinfandel, and Johannisberg Riesling. Some of its wines are marketed under a second label, Silverado Cellars.

Diamond Creek Vineyards, near Calistoga, specializes in Cabernet Sauvignon. The wines are labeled with the names of different parcels within the small vineyard—Volcanic Hill, Gravelly Meadow, and Red Rock Terrace. Stony Hill Vineyard is a famous small winery in the hills south of Calistoga. It was founded by the late Frederick McCrea and his wife, Eleanor, in the early 1950s and planted primarily with Chardonnay, although Gewürztraminer, White Riesling, and a sweet Sémillon de Soleil are also made there. These wines became known to connoisseurs even though production was so small that the wines were almost all sold at the winery. Schramsberg and Hanns Kornell, whose sparkling wines are described elsewhere, are both located in this part of Napa. The Conn Creek Winery was established here in time for the 1976 vintage.

The Freemark Abbey name, originally created in the 1930s, was revived by a partnership in 1967. The winery specializes in a limited number of varietals—Cabernet Sauvignon, Chardonnay, Petite Sirah, and Johannisberg Riesling. Freemark Abbey produces a single vineyard wine labeled Cabernet Bosché, which comes from a fifteen-acre vineyard in Rutherford owned by John Bosché. In 1973 the winery made a very sweet Johannisberg Riesling from botrytised grapes that was labeled Edelwein. In 1976 it produced an even richer wine labeled Edelwein Gold. The Round Hills Vineyards winery, close by, was founded in 1977; St. Clement Vineyard, situated along the highway, produced its first wines in 1976.

Spring Mountain Vineyards was established in 1968 by Michael Robbins and has established an excellent reputation for its Cabernet Sauvignon and Chardonnay. Spring Mountain also produces a Sauvignon Blanc and has bottled Cabernet Franc as a varietal wine. Nearby, Chateau Chevalier specializes in Cabernet Sauvignon and Chardonnay. The winery also uses the name Mountainside as a second label. The Robert Keenan winery began producing Cabernet Sauvignon and Chardonnay in 1977. Yverdon, named after a village in Switzerland, is another winery located on Spring Mountain.

South of St. Helena, the Sutter Home Winery has become known for its intensely flavored Zinfandel, made from Amador County grapes, and for a Muscat wine labeled Moscato Amabile. Franciscan Vineyards, located near Rutherford, produces a wide range of varietal and generic wines. The owners of Franciscan also produce a limited amount of specially selected Cabernet Sauvignon at Silver Oak Cellars. Raymond Vineyard, close by, is a small new winery whose first wines were marketed in 1977. Not far from Rutherford is the new Grgich Hills Cellars, founded in 1977 by Yugoslavian winemaker Mike Grgich and Austin Hills. Grgich, the first winemaker at Chateau Montelena, is specializing in Johannisberg

Riesling and Zinfandel. Farther down the road, Jack and
Dolores Cakebread established Cakebread Cellars.

High up in the Mayacamas Mountains, on the slopes of
Mt. Veeder, is Mayacamas Vineyards, which was purchased by Bob and Nonie Travers in 1968. The winery is
known for its intensely flavored Cabernet Sauvignon and
Chardonnay, both produced in very limited quantities. In
addition, a Late Harvest Zinfandel is made in certain
years from especially ripe grapes. The wine, fermented until it is dry, contains 16 or 17 percent of alcohol and is
considered a collector's item. Down the road are the Veed-
ercrest Vineyard and the small Mount Veeder Winery of
Michael and Arlene Bernstein.

The sparkling wines of Domaine Chandon, owned by
Moët-Hennessy, are described elsewhere. The winery, lo-
cated near Yountville, also makes two still wines—
Chardonnay and Pinot Noir Blanc—under the Fred's
Friends label. These wines are available at the elegant
Domaine Chandon restaurant, which has become very
popular with visitors to Napa.

Not far from the city of Napa, John and Janet Trefethen manage more than six hundred acres planted in a
number of varieties. Most of Trefethen's grapes are sold to
other wineries but the winery produces Chardonnay, White
Riesling, and Cabernet Sauvignon, and also markets a red
and white proprietary wine labeled Eshcol. Carneros Creek
Winery, near the road from Napa to Sonoma, is the only
winery actually situated in the Carneros district. It produces Pinot Noir from its own vineyards and Zinfandel
from Amador County grapes, among other wines.

Sonoma

Sonoma is a region in transition, and it does not yet
project as clear an image to consumers as does Napa. One
reason is that the county encompasses several vineyard districts, each with its own microclimate and its own appellation of origin. Another is that the producers include
traditional wineries that have only recently begun to
change their marketing policies and winemaking techniques, large new wineries that have experienced growing
pains, and many small new wineries that are just starting
to market their wines. Napa's fame, for example, is attrib-

utable to a number of long-established wineries whose reputations added prestige to that of the county. There are relatively few existing wineries in Sonoma whose identities go back more than fifteen years: most of them did not sell much wine under their own labels until the 1960s, and much of what they did sell was in jugs with generic names. For example, as recently as 1970, Sebastiani still sold more wine in bulk to other wineries than it did under its own name. Foppiano, founded in 1896, marketed its first Cabernet Sauvignon in 1972, its first Chardonnay in 1979.

The shift toward the production of fine wines can be seen in Sonoma, as in other California counties, by new plantings of better grape varieties. In 1969 there were 11,-000 acres planted in Sonoma, two-thirds of them made up of Zinfandel, Carignane, Petite Sirah, and French Colombard. Ten years later there were more than 26,000 acres, half of which are Cabernet Sauvignon, Merlot, Pinot Noir, Chardonnay, Johannisberg Riesling, and Gewürztraminer. Sonoma had long been a proven, if neglected, area for fine wines, but it wasn't until the early 1970s, when vineyard land in Napa became very expensive, that a number of new winemakers turned to Sonoma.

The extensive new vineyards created throughout Sonoma County present a special problem for the casual wine drinker because the geographical origin of Sonoma's wines cannot be grasped as easily as those of Napa. The well-known wineries that created the Napa Valley's reputation, and many of the newer ones as well, are concentrated along a fifteen-mile stretch from Oakville to Calistoga, and easily grouped on a map. In Sonoma County, however, there are two main wine regions, one in and around Sonoma itself, and the other near Healdsburg and Geyserville, almost fifty miles away. What's more, many Sonoma wineries do not feature the county appellation on their labels. Some, who get grapes or wine from other counties, use California, North Coast, or Northern California, but even those who could use the Sonoma appellation often prefer a more specific inner appellation such as Alexander Valley, Dry Creek Valley, Russian River Valley, or Sonoma Valley.

It was near the town of Sonoma, at the southern end of Sonoma County, that the first vineyards north of San

Francisco were established. Sonoma is only forty miles from San Francisco and just fifteen miles due west of the city of Napa, which is on the other side of the Mayacamas Mountains. Of the wineries in this part of the county, known as Sonoma Valley, or the Valley of the Moon, Buena Vista has the longest history. Founded by Agoston Haraszthy in 1857, it was revived in the 1940s by Frank Bartholomew, who sold it in 1968. The new owners, who considerably expanded its vineyards and built a new winery, produce a full range of wines, including those for which Buena Vista has become known—Gewürztraminer, Green Hungarian, Zinfandel, and a Cabernet Sauvignon rosé called Rosebrook.

The biggest winery in Sonoma (excepting Italian Swiss Colony) and one of the biggest family-owned wineries in California is Sebastiani. Originally a supplier of bulk wines to other wineries, it has achieved tremendous success under its own name with a full range of generic and varietal wines. The firm is known for its traditional winemaking techniques and for such varietals as Barbera and Green Hungarian, but it is responsible for a number of innovations as well. A few weeks after the 1972 vintage Sebastiani introduced a Gamay Beaujolais Nouveau in the style of France's Beaujolais Nouveau, and more recently the firm was one of the first to make a Pinot Noir Blanc, which they label Eye of the Swan.

Hanzell was created in the 1950s by James Zellerbach, who was determined to make Pinot Noir and Chardonnay wines equal to the best of Burgundy. He is generally credited with having introduced European oak barrels to California (in this case, Limousin oak from France), a practice that has been widely adopted throughout the state to give many red and white wines additional complexity. The winery, which has changed hands more than once, continues to produce these two wines in limited quantities. Hacienda Wine Cellars, founded by Frank Bartholomew soon after he sold Buena Vista, produced its first wines in 1973 and quickly developed a reputation for the few wines it makes. The Gundlach-Bundschu Winery and its Rhinefarm vineyard, originally created in the mid-nineteenth century, was revived in the 1970s and produces limited quantities of fine varietal wines. ZD Wines is a small winery founded in 1969 by Gino Zepponi and Norman de Leuze.

About a dozen miles north of Sonoma, near the town of Kenwood, is the Chateau St. Jean winery, whose first wines were produced in 1974. Winemaker Richard Arrowood makes red and white varietal wines in comparatively limited quantities, and has made a particular reputation with Chardonnay and Johannisberg Riesling. In some vintages, Chardonnay from as many as seven different vineyards, or ranches, were vinified, aged, and bottled separately. Arrowood has also made a number of Late Harvest botrytised Johannisberg Rieslings of Auslese, Beerenauslese, and even Trockenbeerenauslese quality, the last with more than 30 percent residual sugar.

The old Pagani Brothers winery, situated nearby, was sold in 1970 and renamed Kenwood Vineyards by its new owners, who now produce a range of generic and varietal wines. The small Grand Cru winery, situated between Sonoma and Kenwood, makes a limited number of wines, including Gewürztraminer, Chenin Blanc, and in most vintages, a botrytis-infected Gewürztraminer with more than 30 percent residual sugar.

Another group of wineries are situated in the area bounded by Healdsburg—forty miles north of Sonoma— and Geyserville. The impressive and original Sonoma Vineyards winery, built in Windsor in 1970 under the direction of winemaker Rodney Strong, produces a full range of varietal wines plus limited amounts of estate-bottled varietals labeled with the name of individual vineyards. The best known of them is Alexander's Crown, a sixty-one-acre plot of Cabernet Sauvignon; 1974 was the first vintage bottled. Sonoma Vineyards also continues to sell wines by mail order under the name Tiburon Vintners.

Simi, founded in 1876, was revitalized in the early 1970s and is now owned by Schieffelin & Company, a new York importing firm. Simi has achieved a reputation for such varietal wines as Cabernet Sauvignon, Zinfandel, Gewürztraminer, and an unusual Rosé of Cabernet Sauvignon. The appellation of origin for many of Simi's wines is Alexander Valley, which runs along the Russian River for several miles from Geyserville to a point just east of Healdsburg. Foppiano, established at the end of the nineteenth century, has gradually shifted from bulk wine production and jug wines sales to varietal wines, many of them labeled with a Russian River Valley appellation. The new Jordan Winery near Healdsburg is focusing on Cabernet Sauvignon and a limited amount of Chardonnay.

Souverain, a large, modern winery built in 1973 by the Pillsbury Company and now owned by an association of grape growers, is known for its wide range of well-made and often distinctive generic and varietal wines. Colombard Blanc, made from French Colombard, is one of its best-known wines. A restaurant at the winery has become a popular stopping place for visitors to northern Sonoma. Geyser Peak, another large winery, was considerably expanded in 1973 by the Jos. Schlitz Brewing Company. The Summit brand name is used for generic wines, and the best varietal wines, originally marketed under the name Voltaire, are now being labeled with the Geyser Peak name. Pedroncelli, a third winery located near Geyserville, has a history that goes back to 1927. They now produce a wide range of soundly made varietal wines including Gewürztraminer and a Zinfandel rosé, and two dependable generic wines labeled Sonoma Red and Sonoma White.

The Dry Creek Winery, founded by David Stare, produced its first varietal wines in 1972 and soon created a following for such wines as Cabernet Sauvignon, Zinfandel, Chenin Blanc, and Fumé Blanc. The vineyards are in the Dry Creek Valley, which is west of, and parallel to, the Healdsburg-Geyserville road, and the wines are labeled with that appellation. Trentadue, primarily a grape grower, produces a limited amount of varietal wine.

Farther north, the Italian Swiss Colony winery at Asti continues to receive a tremendous number of visitors every year, but the facility is used primarily to bottle the inexpensive line of Inglenook wines marketed as Inglenook Navalle. Italian Swiss Colony generic and varietal wines, which are now labeled simply Colony, are produced in Madera, in the San Joaquin Valley.

Korbel, located along the Russian River near Guerneville, is well known for its sparkling wines. Not far away, the Joseph Swan winery produces very limited amounts of several varietals, notably Zinfandel and Pinot Noir.

Other Sonoma wineries, most of them founded in the

mid-1970s and producing between three thousand and ten thousand cases, include Alexander Valley Vineyards, Davis Bynum, Clos du Bois, Field Stone, Hop Kiln, Johnson's Alexander Valley Wines, Lambert Bridge, Lytton Springs, Matanzas Creek, Mill Creek, and Preston.

Mendocino

Mendocino County is north of Sonoma, and its principal city, Ukiah, is 120 miles from San Francisco. Acreage has nearly doubled since 1969 and now amounts to ten thousand acres. For many years the only winery that was associated with Mendocino was Parducci, situated near Ukiah, which produces a full range of distinctive wines, including French Colombard, Chenin Blanc, and Petite Sirah. John Parducci has also explored the effects of different growing conditions within the county by bottling Cabernet Sauvignon from different vineyards separately, and has experimented with varietal characteristics by aging Cabernet Sauvignon in stainless steel rather than in wood. Parducci occasionally markets specially selected lots as Cellar Master's Selection.

Fetzer Vineyards, situated a few miles north of Ukiah, has established a following for its wines, especially such full-bodied reds as Cabernet Sauvignon, Zinfandel, and Petite Syrah. Husch Vineyards and Edmeades Vineyards, both founded in the 1970s, are situated near Philo in the Anderson Valley, about fifteen miles west of Ukiah. Each produces less than five thousand cases of such wines as Chardonnay, Gewürztraminer, and Cabernet Sauvignon.

The name Cresta Blanca, originally that of a winery created in 1882 in the Livermore Valley east of San Francisco, was bought by Guild in 1971. It is now used for a line of generic and varietal wines, some of which are produced at a cooperative cellar in Mendocino and bottled by Guild at Lodi.

Lake County, which adjoins Mendocino and northern Sonoma, now has about 2,500 acres of vineyards most of whose grapes are used by producers in other counties. The wines of Konocti Cellars are made from Lake County grapes, and the Lake County appellation appears on other labels as well.

Almost all of the vineyard acreage in Alameda County, east of San Francisco, is in the Livermore Valley, where Wente Bros. and Concannon are situated. As a result of urbanization, the vineyards in this county have been considerably reduced in recent years to about two thousand acres, most of it planted in white varieties. New legislation, however, by which agricultural land is taxed at a lower rate than that devoted to real-estate development, has enabled existing vineyards to continue and has even permitted new plantings.

Wente Bros., located near the city of Livermore, is best known for its distinctive white wines, including Chardonnay, Pinot Blanc, Grey Riesling, Sauvignon Blanc, Dry Semillon, and Le Blanc de Blancs, which is made primarily from Chenin Blanc. The firm also has extensive new vineyards in Monterey County, and as a result, some of their varietal wines still bear the Livermore appellation, some are labeled Monterey, and others have a California appellation. In 1969, Wente produced the first California Spätlese type of wine from botrytised Johannisberg Riesling grapes grown in their Arroyo Seco vineyard in Monterey.

Concannon, just down the road from Wente Bros., was established in the nineteenth century. Although it produces mostly white wines, including the unique Rkatsiteli, a Russian variety, the winery was one of the first to market Petite Sirah as a varietal wine. Concannon is also known for its Zinfandel Rosé and for specially aged lots of Cabernet Sauvignon and Petite Sirah labeled Limited Bottling.

Weibel is also in Alameda County, near Mission San Jose. The firm, which has planted additional vineyards in Mendocino, is known primarily for its sparkling wines, but produces a range of generic and varietal table wines as well. Llords & Elwood is a small winery that makes both table wines and dessert wines with such proprietary names as Dry Wit Sherry and Castle Magic Riesling. The J.W. Morris Port Works is located in Emeryville.

Santa Clara County now has only seventeen hundred acres or so of vineyards, and they are split up among several districts. Although the Santa Clara appellation is not often seen on labels, the region is known to many wine-minded tourists because the home wineries of two major firms—Almadén and Paul Masson—are located there. As real-estate developments have reduced the acreage in Santa Clara, these wineries have expanded into other counties—Almadén to San Benito and Monterey, Paul Masson to Monterey.

Almadén, which receives visitors at their winery in Los Gatos, traces its origins back to 1852, but it did not acquire its present name, which is Spanish for "the mine," until the late nineteenth century. Its present success really began in the 1940s, and in 1956 Almadén created a large new vineyard near Paicines in San Benito County. The firm later planted vineyards at La Cienega in San Benito and in Monterey as well, for a total of nearly seven thousand acres. Almadén introduced its popular Grenache Rosé in the 1940s, and markets a full line of generic and varietal table wines—the biggest sellers are Mountain Red Burgundy and Mountain White Chablis—as well as sparkling and dessert wines. The firm has also introduced vintage-dated varietal wines with such appellations of origin as San Benito, Monterey, and San Luis Obispo, as well as special lots of wine labeled with the name of one of the firm's founders, Charles Lefranc.

Paul Masson Vineyards also claims a founding date of 1852, but it was not until 1892 that Paul Masson, who came to America from Burgundy, gave the firm his name. Like Almadén, the firm owes its present success to new ownership in the 1940s. Most of the wines are bottled at the Paul Masson Champagne Cellars in Saratoga, visited by thousands of tourists every year, but almost all of Paul Masson's table wines are now produced at their Pinnacles winery in Monterey County, where most of their six thousand acres of vineyards are planted. Besides a full line of table, sparkling, and dessert wines, Paul Masson also markets such popular proprietary wines as Emerald Dry, Rubion, and Baroque. The firm has also introduced vintage-dated varietal wines from their Monterey vineyards labeled Pinnacles Selection.

The history of Mirassou, located near San Jose, also goes back to the mid-nineteenth century, but it was only in the 1960s that the firm actively began to promote its own name rather than selling its wine in bulk to other wineries.

Mirassou was one of the first to plant vineyards in Monterey, and both Santa Clara and Monterey appellations appear on their labels. Mirassou makes a full range of varietal wines as well as such proprietary wines as Monterey Riesling; Fleuri Blanc, a sweet wine with a Gewürztraminer base; and Petite Rosé, from Petite Sirah. Specially selected lots of certain varietals are marketed as Harvest Selection.

San Martin, another sizable Santa Clara winery, was created at the end of the nineteenth century and revitalized in the early 1970s. The winery produces a full range of wines from Santa Clara, Monterey, San Luis Obispo, Santa Barbara, and Amador grapes, and its labels indicate the percentage of each variety used in each wine and where they were grown. San Martin also pioneered the production of delicate, low-alcohol wines. Their Soft Johannisberg Riesling is a sweet wine that contains only 7 percent alcohol; others, such as Soft Chenin Blanc, Soft Gamay Beaujolais, and Soft Zinfandel are semi-sweet wines with about 10 percent alcohol.

Ridge, a small winery in the Santa Cruz Mountains, is known primarily for its intense and full-flavored red wines. The winery is generally credited with having changed the image of Zinfandel from a picnic wine to a big, long-lived wine that can compete with many Cabernet Sauvignons. Ridge makes individual lots of wine from grapes purchased in different parts of the state, and the origin of each wine is indicated on its label with such names as Montebello, which is the home vineyard, Fiddletown and Shenandoah from Amador, York Creek from Napa, Paso Robles from San Luis Obispo, and so on.

The Turgeon & Lohr Winery was established by Bernard Turgeon and Jerome Lohr, who planted nearly three hundred acres in Monterey County. The wines, labeled J. Lohr, are produced at their winery in San Jose. Martin Ray Vineyards, whose founder died in 1976, continues to produce a limited amount of Cabernet Sauvignon, Pinot Noir, and Chardonnay under the direction of Peter Martin Ray. Nearby, Mount Eden Vineyards produces wine from part of the vineyards originally established by Martin Ray.

A number of wineries, both new and old, are situated in the Hecker Pass district west of Gilroy, including Bertero,

Fortino, Hecker Pass, Kirigin Cellars, Thomas Kruse, and Live Oaks.

There are now only a hundred acres of vineyards in Santa Cruz, but a few small wineries have been created in this county. Perhaps the best known is that of David Bruce, who makes a limited amount of wine in a personal style that emphasizes body and barrel age. Felton-Empire Vineyards produces wine at what was the Hallcrest winery, and other new wineries include Smothers, established by entertainer Dick Smothers, Santa Cruz Mountain Vineyard, and Roudon-Smith Vineyards.

Monterey

As recently as 1969 there were less than two thousand acres of vines in Monterey; today, more than thirty-three thousand acres are planted. Mirassou and Paul Masson, unable to extend their holdings in Santa Clara, were the first companies to create vineyards in Monterey on a commercial scale. Wente and Almadén followed, and a number of ranching companies (as contrasted to wineries) have planted large vineyards as well. The vineyards are situated in the Salinas Valley between the Santa Lucia Mountains and the Gavilan Mountains. The vineyards are cooled by ocean breezes, and water for irrigation is supplied by wells drilled into an underground river. Since the vineyards were created in land that was never before planted with vines, it was assumed that the phylloxera louse would not be present in the soil. Most of the vines in Monterey are, therefore, planted on their own roots rather than being grafted onto phylloxera-resistant American rootstocks, as is the case elsewhere in California and throughout the world. Also, the rows of vines were deliberately set out to facilitate mechanical harvesting, whereby the grape bunches are shaken loose from the vines by machine rather than being picked by hand.

All of the principal varieties are planted in Monterey, and viticulturists are still determining which grapes are best suited to this region. Monterey winemakers feel that the region produces wines with a particularly intense and cleanly defined varietal character, but some consumers detect an odd vegetal flavor in some of the Monterey red wines. It may be that the region's long, cool growing season is more appropriate to such white varieties as Johannisberg Riesling and Gewürztraminer than to such red varieties as Cabernet Sauvignon. Pinot Noir is an exception among red varieties, however, and some of California's best Pinot Noirs have come from Monterey.

Almadén, Paul Masson, Mirassou, and Wente Bros. own vineyards in Monterey, and those firms are discussed elsewhere. The best-known winery in Monterey itself is The Monterey Vineyard, built in 1974 to the specifications of enologist Richard Peterson. The winery produces a full range of varietals, some of which are picked late in the season and labeled with such appropriate designations as Thanksgiving Harvest Johannisberg Riesling and December Harvest Zinfandel. The Monterey Vineyard uses the Austrian name Grüner Sylvaner for that variety, and has also marketed a botrytised Sauvignon Blanc labeled as such. In 1977 The Monterey Vineyard was purchased by the Coca-Cola Company of Atlanta.

Chalone Vineyard, on the Chalone Bench of the Gavilan Mountains, near Pinnacles National Monument, has achieved an excellent reputation for the wines it makes—in very limited quantities—from such varieties as Chardonnay, Pinot Blanc, Pinot Noir, and Chenin Blanc. Other Monterey wineries are the Monterey Peninsula Winery and Durney Vineyard, in the nearby Carmel Valley.

Other Wine Regions

San Benito County adjoins Monterey to the northeast. Almadén has planted more than four thousand acres there and uses San Benito as an appellation for some of its wines. Other firms have established vineyards in the San Ysidro district north of Hollister.

The acreage in San Luis Obispo, south of Monterey, has increased from less than five hundred acres in 1970 to more than four thousand, but there are few wineries there. Hoffman Mountain Ranch, near Paso Robles in the Santa Lucia Mountains, has already become known for its Pinot Noir and Chardonnay. Estrella Vineyards produced its first wines in 1978. Most growers in San Luis Obispo sell their grapes to wineries in other counties, who occasionally use the appellation on their labels.

Farther down the coast, in Santa Barbara County, vineyard acreage jumped from virtually none in the 1960s to about six thousand. The Firestone Vineyard has three hundred acres in the Santa Ynez Valley near Los Olivos, halfway between the cities of Santa Maria and Santa Barbara. Firestone made its first wines in 1975, and has won a following for Johannisberg Riesling, among other varietals. Other wineries in this region are the Santa Ynez Valley Winery, Sanford & Benedict, and Zaca Mesa.

Extensive vineyards were planted along the Sierra foothills in Amador County in the nineteenth century, but it is only in the past few years that Amador wines have become familiar to consumers. Most of the one thousand acres of vineyards are located in the Shenandoah Valley, about thirty miles southeast of Sacramento, and there is some acreage around Fiddletown as well. Amador has become best known for Zinfandel, and wineries in Napa, Sonoma, and Santa Clara buy grapes from that district and market them with the Amador appellation. Of the wineries in Amador County, the best known is Monteviña, which produced its first wines in 1973. Most of Monteviña's production is devoted to Zinfandel, but other wines are made as well, including Cabernet Sauvignon and Sauvignon Blanc. In addition, the winery makes Zinfandel Nuevo and Cabernet Sauvignon Nuevo in the style of France's Beaujolais Nouveau, and also produces limited quantities of unusual white wines from those two grape varieties.

The southernmost new wine region in California was established in the late 1960s by Ely Callaway in an area known as Rancho California. The Callaway winery, near Temecula, was built in 1974 and produces several varietal wines including intensely flavored Petite Sirah, Cabernet Sauvignon, and Zinfandel, and such white wines as Sauvignon Blanc, Johannisberg Riesling, and when weather conditions permit, a botrytised Chenin Blanc labeled Sweet Nancy in honor of Ely Callaway's wife.

San Joaquin Valley

The San Joaquin Valley, also known as the Central Valley, extends for more than two hundred miles from Stockton down to Bakersfield. More than 80 percent of California's wine grapes come from this region, and if the table and raisin grapes used for wine are included, the Central Valley (plus the vineyards around Lodi, twelve miles north of Stockton) accounts for more than 90 percent of the wine made in the state. There are a number of gigantic wineries situated in the valley; some produce wines that are shipped in bulk to other wineries throughout the state, some bottle their own wines and market them under a variety of brand names.

E & J Gallo, located in Modesto, is the biggest winery in the world, and accounts for one out of every four bottles of wine sold in this country. The winery, founded in 1933 by Ernest and Julio Gallo, markets a complete range of generic and varietal table wines, dessert wines, sparkling wines, and such special natural wines as Thunderbird, Spañada, and Boone's Farm. Gallo's most popular table wines are Hearty Burgundy and Chablis Blanc, and they also make such proprietary wines as Paisano and Rhinegarten, the Carlo Rossi Red Mountain wines, and André sparkling wines. Although Gallo wines are made primarily from Central Valley grapes, the firm also buys a significant share of the grapes grown in Napa, Sonoma, and Monterey.

United Vintners, owned by Heublein, Inc., is the second largest wine producer in the United States. Their brands, most of which are bottled at Madera, include Italian Swiss Colony, Inglenook, Petri, G & D, Fior di California, Jacaré, Lejon, and such special natural wines as Bali Hai, Annie Green Springs, and T J Swann.

Another large California wine company is Guild, a cooperative of a thousand grape growers. Most Guild wines are bottled at Lodi, and they market such brands as Winemasters' Guild, Cribari, Roma, Vino da Tavola, and Cresta Blanca. Some other Central Valley wineries are Franzia Brothers, East-Side (whose brands include Royal Host and Conti-Royale), JFJ Bronco, Giumarra, Gibson, California Growers Winery, California Wine Association (owned by the Perelli-Minetti family, and whose brands include Guasti, Ambassador, and Eleven Cellars), and the Bear Mountain Winery (which sells wines under the M. LaMont label).

In addition to these large companies, there are also a few wineries in the Central Valley producing distinctive wines in comparatively small quantities. Angelo Papagni, a grape grower with more than two thousand acres of vineyards, built a winery near Madera and began to make varietal wines in 1973, including one from Alicante Bouschet and a sweet Muscat wine called Moscato d'Angelo. Ficklin, also located near Madera, has been making limited amounts of Tinta Port since 1948, and in 1977 Andrew Quady built a winery in Madera to produce vintage-dated Port from Zinfandel grapes.

The number and variety of California wines available today may confuse and intimidate some consumers, but many others recognize the quality and value that so many of these wines offer. Just as some of California's best wineries did not exist a few years ago, so we can anticipate exceptional wines from wineries that have yet to be established.

NEW YORK AND OTHER STATES

Grape vines had to be specially introduced into California, but the earliest settlers in the eastern United States found a variety of native grapes already growing wild all along the Atlantic Coast. Encouraged by this profusion of vines, a number of colonists imported cuttings of European *Vitis vinifera* varieties during the seventeenth and eighteenth centuries, and tried to establish new vineyards on the East Coast. Invariably, these vines died, and we now know that this was a result of phylloxera, fungus, and very cold winter temperatures to which *vinifera* vines were not resistant. In the early nineteenth century, successful experiments were carried out with existing native varieties, notably Catawba, and native American wines began to be produced commercially in several states. These native grapes, made up for the most part of *Vitis labrusca*, impart a pungent aroma and distinctive flavor to the wines made from them, and their taste often seems strange to those who are used to European or California wines. This flavor is usually described as foxy, and its pronounced grapy character is most clearly demonstrated by the Concord grape—used for juice and jelly as well as for wine—which accounts for more than two-thirds of the vineyard acreage in New York State. The *labrusca* varieties that dominate the eastern vineyards are cultivated in only a few other places—such as Oregon, Washington, Canada, and Brazil—and the unique wines they produce should be approached with this in mind.

By far the biggest wine-producing area outside of California is in the Finger Lakes district of New York State, about three hundred miles northwest of New York City. The region gets its name from several elongated lakes that resemble an imprint made by the outspread fingers of a giant hand. Although the region is subject to great extremes of temperature, these lakes exert a moderating influence on the climate of the vineyards situated along their sloping shores. The first vines were planted in this district in 1829 in a clergyman's garden in Hammondsport, at the southern tip of Lake Keuka. A number of commercial wineries were established in the decades that followed, but production in the Finger Lakes is now dominated by four brands—Taylor, Great Western, Gold Seal, and Widmer's. New York State accounts for about 10 percent of the wines consumed in this country, but only half of that is made up of table wines, the rest is New York State Champagne, Sherry, and Port.

A wine labeled New York State may contain up to 25 percent of wines from outside the state. This permits New York wineries to diminish the intense *labrusca* taste of many of their wines by blending in neutral California wines. If more than 25 percent of wine produced outside the state is added, the wine must be labeled American, and there are wines so labeled bottled in New York State that contain 80 percent or more of California wine. Because *labrusca* grape varieties are typically low in sugar and high in acid, a wine's volume may legally be increased by as much as a third by the addition of sugar and water, which is called amelioration. The sugar increases the wine's eventual alcohol content, the water dilutes its acidity.

As in California, many New York State wines are marketed with generic place-names of European origin, such as Sauterne, Rhine Wine, Chablis, and Burgundy. Because *labrusca* grapes are used to make most of these wines, they bear no resemblance whatsoever to their French and German counterparts or to California wines, all of which are made from *vinifera* grapes. It's fair to say that a wine drinker who first experiences a New York State Chablis or New York State Burgundy is in for something of a surprise. Nevertheless, people who enjoy the distinct flavor of certain table grapes find these wines very pleasing indeed, and their wide distribution in this country attests to their popularity.

A number of New York State wines are made from specific native grapes and are so labeled. These varietals include Delaware, Moore's Diamond, Niagara, Dutchess, Missouri Riesling (no relation to the Riesling of Germany), Vergennes, Isabella, and Catawba. These wines all have a more-or-less-pronounced *labrusca* taste, and their more precise labeling makes it easier for the consumer to choose among them.

In recent years there has been a significant trend in the Finger Lakes vineyards toward French-American hybrids. These are crossings that combine the hardiness of the American vines and their resistance to disease and extremes of cold with the more delicate flavor of the *vinifera* grape. Hybrids are named after the individuals who developed them and carry the serial number of the original seedling, such as Baco 1, Seibel 5279, and Seyve-Villard 5276. Most of these hybrids were developed in France at the end of the nineteenth century, and over the years they have acquired names that are more attractive than the original combinations of name and number. The most popular hybrids (and the names by which they are commonly known) are, among the red varieties, Baco No. 1 (Baco Noir), Seibel 10878 (Chelois), Seibel 9549 (De Chaunac), Seibel 7053 (Chancellor), Seibel 13053 (Cascade), and Kuhlmann 188-2 (Maréchal Foch). The best-known white varieties include Seibel 5279 (Aurora), Seyve-Villard 5276 (Seyval Blanc), and Ravat 6 (Ravat Blanc). French-American hybrids account for about 15 percent of the wines produced in New York State—Aurora, De Chaunac, and Baco Noir are the most extensively planted. The wines, in which the *labrusca* flavor is considerably diminished or even entirely absent, are often blended with *labrusca* wines. Many are also bottled on their own as varietal wines.

The few hundred acres of *vinifera* grapes in New York State are the result of the pioneering work done by Dr. Konstantin Frank, who had successfully cultivated *vinifera* in his native Russia before emigrating to this country. Frank first began grafting European vines on native American rootstocks in the early 1950s for Charles Fournier of Gold Seal, and later went on to establish his own company—Vinifera Wine Cellars—to produce and market such *vinifera* varieties as Johannisberg Riesling, Chardonnay, Gewürztraminer, Pinot Noir, and Gamay. With the exception of Gold Seal, the major wineries have not planted much *vinifera*, but Dr. Frank's success, especially with his white wines, has encouraged many winemakers throughout the east to cultivate *vinifera*.

Each of the four major New York State wineries produces and markets a somewhat different range of wines. The Taylor Wine Co., located in Hammondsport, at the southern tip of Lake Keuka, is one of the largest wine firms in America. Most of Taylor's sales consist of dessert wines, but it has achieved great success with its sparkling wines and with such proprietary table wines as Lake Country Red and Lake Country White. The company was purchased by the Coca-Cola Company of Atlanta in 1977, and has since introduced the California Cellars line of wines that are blended and bottled in California at The Monterey Vineyard (which is also owned by Coca-Cola).

Great Western is the brand name of the Pleasant Valley Wine Company, also in Hammondsport, which was acquired by Taylor in 1961. Great Western is especially known for its sparkling wines and for its table wines, which consist of generic wines; of wines labeled with a combination of generic and varietal names, such as Aurora Sauterne, Delaware Moselle, Diamond Chablis, Dutchess Rhine Wine, and Baco Noir Burgundy; and of such varietal wines as Chelois, De Chaunac, and Seyval Blanc.

Gold Seal Vineyards, a few miles north of Hammondsport, has had particular success with one of its sparkling wines, Charles Fournier Blanc de Blancs Champagne, named after the man who was the firm's winemaker from 1934 until his retirement some years ago. Among Gold

Seal's many wines are two *viniferas*, Chardonnay and Johannisberg Riesling; two table wines that also bear the Charles Fournier signature, Chablis Nature and Burgundy Natural; and a full range of American—rather than New York State—generic wines. The company's best-selling wine is Pink Catawba, and it also produces a separate line of sparkling wines under the name Henri Marchant.

Widmer's Wine Cellars is located in Naples, at the southern tip of Lake Canandaigua. Widmer's is known for its barrel-aged Sherries, which are stored outdoors on the winery's roof, and for such *labrusca* varietal wines as Moore's Diamond and Delaware. Among its most successful wines are Lake Niagara, a sweet white wine, and Lake Roselle.

The Bully Hill winery, near Hammondsport, was established in 1970 by Walter S. Taylor, whose grandfather founded the Taylor Wine Company. The firm specializes in wines made from French-American hybrids: some are blended and marketed as Bully Hill Red and Bully Hill White, others are sold with such varietal names as Seyval Blanc and Chancellor Noir. Nearby, the small, new Heron Hill Vineyard produces wines from *vinifera* and hybrid varieties, as does the Glenora Wine Cellar, west of Seneca Lake.

The Hudson River Valley, the oldest wine-producing region in New York State, has witnessed a renewed interest in winemaking in recent years. Its best-known winery is Benmarl, located near Marlboro, seventy-five miles from New York City. The winery's small production consists of hybrids such as Seyval Blanc and Baco Noir as well as limited amounts of such *vinifera* varieties as Chardonnay and Johannisberg Riesling. Benmarl also produces a *nouveau* wine that arrives in New York City shops each fall a few weeks after the vintage. Other new wineries in the Hudson Valley region include the Great River Winery, Cascade Mountain Vineyards, and Clinton Vineyards.

One of the newest wineries in New York State is the Hargrave Vineyard in Cutchogue, on northern Long Island. Founded by Alex and Louisa Hargrave on the site of an old potato farm, the winery produces *vinifera* wines from its own vineyards. Its first wines were made in 1975, and the winery markets such varietals as Pinot Noir, Cabernet Sauvignon, Sauvignon Blanc, and Chardonnay.

The Canandaigua Wine Company has been very successful with such brands as Richard's Wild Irish Rose and Virginia Dare. The Monarch Wine Company in Brooklyn, New York, produces Manischewitz kosher wines primarily from Concord grapes, as does the Mogen David Wine Corporation based in Chicago.

A great many new wineries have been created throughout the country in the past few years, and wine is now made in more than thirty states. Of the more than seven hundred wineries in the United States, nearly three hundred are located outside of California. Many continue to make wine from *labrusca* grapes, others use hybrids and *vinifera* varieties. Most wineries around the country produce limited amounts of wine that they sell locally, but a few have come to the attention of a wider audience. One of the smallest firms is also one of the most important in the recent history of American wines: Philip Wagner's Boordy Vineyard, near Baltimore, Maryland. His pioneering work with French-American hybrids, which he first planted in the 1930s, is considered the major factor in the increased use of these varietals in other eastern vineyards. Boordy Vineyard produces small amounts of red, white, and rosé wines, most of which are consumed locally.

Ohio was one of the earliest sources of American wines, and once made more wine than California, but its production today is considerably less than that of New York State. Catawba and Concord are the most extensively planted varieties. Meier's Wine Cellars, the leading producer, continues to market a range of wines from native grapes, but is also cultivating hybrids and *vinifera* varieties as well. In the Ozark plateau region of Arkansas, Wiederkehr Wine Cellars makes wine from *labrusca,* hybrids, and from such *vinifera* varieties as Johannisberg Riesling and Chardonnay. Presque Isle Wine Cellars and Penn-Shore Vineyards in Pennsylvania's Erie County are also producing wines from hybrids and *vinifera* grapes. In northern Michigan, Chateau Grand Travers, near Traverse City, specializes in such *vinifera* varieties as Chardonnay and Johannisberg Riesling.

Several Washington and Oregon wineries are now making excellent wines from *vinifera* varieties. Most of Washington's vineyards are planted with Concord, but there are now nearly three thousand acres devoted to *vinifera* varieties. Ste. Michelle Vineyards, near Seattle, markets a wide range of such varietal wines as Johannisberg Riesling, Sémillon, Chenin Blanc, Sauvignon Blanc, Gewürztraminer, Cabernet Sauvignon, Merlot, and Grenache Rosé from vineyards in the Yakima Valley, 180 miles southeast of Seattle. Associated Vintners and the Preston Wine Cellar are two other Washington wineries. In Oregon, more than a thousand acres of *vinifera* vineyards are now planted in different parts of the state. The Hillcrest Vineyard is in the Umpqua Valley, and several wineries have been established in the Willamette Valley, not far from Portland, including Tualatin Vineyards, Eyrie Vineyards, Knudsen-Erath Vineyards, and Reuter's Hill Winery (formerly Charles Coury Vineyards).

THE WINES OF
SOUTH AMERICA

CHILE

Although Chile is not the biggest wine-producing country in South America, its wines, especially the reds, have traditionally been considered to be the best of that continent. Chile extends for about three thousand miles along the west coast of South America, in a thin strip rarely more than a hundred miles wide, between the Pacific Ocean and the Andes Mountains. The country has a wide variety of terrains and climates, and the best grape-growing area for table wines is in the central valley of Chile, north and south of Santiago. Wines were first brought to Chile by Spanish missionaries in the sixteenth century, but winemaking did not really get started on a commercial basis until the mid-nineteenth century. At that time French wine experts, many of them from Bordeaux, were brought over to Chile, as were a number of French grape varieties. To this day, there are extensive plantings of the classic Bordeaux vines, such as Cabernet Sauvignon, Merlot, Sauvignon Blanc, and Sémillon.

Most Chilean table wine is sold in barrels or in large jugs, and comparatively little is marketed in the familiar bottle sizes used in other countries. Exports, limited in the past, are being encouraged under government supervision. There has been an increase in the sales of Chilean wines here, and an improvement in the quality of the wines now available. Some wines are marketed with generic names, such as Burgundy and Rhine Wine, others with such varietal names as Cabernet Sauvignon, Pinot Noir, Riesling, and Sauvignon Blanc. There is actually very little Pinot Noir and Riesling planted in Chile: wines labeled Burgundy and Pinot Noir are made primarily from Cabernet Sauvignon, those labeled Rhine Wine and Riesling are usually made from Sémillon and Sauvignon Blanc. Two firms whose wines are distributed here are Concha y Toro and Viña Undurraga.

ARGENTINA

Argentina makes more wine than any other country in the Western Hemisphere, and is one of the five biggest producers in the world. Most of this consists of ordinary wine that is consumed within the country: the per capita consumption in Argentina amounts to well over a hundred bottles a year. In recent years, however, a number of Argentine producers have begun to export their wines to this country. Some are labeled with generic names; many with such varietal names as Malbec (by far the most widely planted of the better varieties), Cabernet Sauvignon, Chardonnay, and Chenin Blanc. Sylvaner is often marketed as Riesling, Chenin Blanc as Pinot Blanc. Argentine wines suffered in the past from old-fashioned winemaking methods and excessive aging in wood, which often resulted in faded reds and oxidized whites. In an effort to increase their exports, a number of wineries have adopted modern vinification techniques and are now producing more attractive wines. Andean Vineyards is a brand name created by an association of several leading wineries to market their wines in this country.

The wines produced in Brazil, made primarily from *Vitis labrusca* and French-American hybrid grape varieties, are rarely seen here. In recent years, a number of American and European wine companies have invested in Brazil, and new vineyards have been planted with *Vitis vinifera* grapes.

VARIOUS WINES

AUSTRALIA

There are interesting parallels to be drawn between wine production in Australia and the United States. Commercial winemaking began at about the same time in both countries, in the 1830s, and developed in several different regions rather than in a single area. Fortified wines were made in far greater quantities than table wines, and only in the recent past has each country reversed that trend. Twenty years ago, Sherry- and Port-type wines accounted for two-thirds of Australia's total wine production. Although the same quantity of fortified wines continues to be made, table-wine production has increased to such an extent that, along with sparkling wines, it now accounts for three-quarters of the wines made in Australia.

James Busby, a Scottish schoolteacher, is often referred to as the father of the Australian wine industry, and his role seems to have been quite similar to that of Agoston Haraszthy in California. Busby brought over a great many cuttings in 1831, distributed them to a number of growers in the Hunter River Valley, north of Sydney, and also contributed a treatise on viticulture to aid new winemakers. Vineyards were gradually established in different districts of Australia, in such places as the Barossa Valley (north of Adelaide, and nearly eight hundred miles from the Hunter River Valley), Coonawarra, the Murray River Valley, Clare and Watervale, Murrumbidgee, Mildura, Great Western, Tahbilk, and the Swan Valley near Perth, three thousand miles from Sydney.

Australia, halfway around the world and almost as big as the United States, has not yet developed much of an export market. Only 2 percent or so of its wines leave the country, and Canada and Great Britain are its biggest customers. As in California, the wines are made from a number of different grapes grown in a variety of soils. Many firms own vineyards in several districts, blend the wines together, and market them with proprietary brand names or with such generic names as Burgundy, Chablis, Moselle, Hock, and Claret. There is a trend toward using a combination of district and grape name on a label, but the exotic Australian place-names are still unfamiliar to consumers in other countries, as are some of the varietal names used. Shiraz is a red-wine grape, probably the Syrah of the northern Rhône, that is also sold as Hermitage. Cabernet is widely planted and sold as such, but a wine labeled Riesling is likely to be made from the Sémillon. The true Riesling of Germany is labeled Rhine Riesling. Nor is it unusual to see labels bearing the names of more than one variety, such as Cabernet Shiraz, Cabernet Malbec, or Pinot Hermitage. Although the way Australian wines are traditionally labeled may puzzle those who are not used to it, the wines themselves continue to gain admirers among those who have had the opportunity to taste them.

An interesting feature of the Australian wine scene is the importance given to the wine competitions held in various cities on a regular basis. Almost all of the wineries compete, and the prizes confer considerable prestige on those who win them. It has even been said that some Australian wineries employ two winemakers—one to make wines for the public, the other to make the wines that are entered in competition.

Some of the biggest Australian wine firms include Lindemans, Seppelt, Orlando, Penfolds, McWilliams, and Kaiser Stuhl, a cooperative in the Barossa Valley.

SOUTH AFRICA

Vines were first planted in South Africa by Dutch settlers in the middle of the seventeenth century, and its sizable production consists of table wines, brandy, and well-made fortified wines in the style of Sherry and Port. Most of its exports are shipped to Great Britain, its traditional customer, and to Canada.

Generic names, such as Chablis and Burgundy, are not widely used in South Africa, whose wines are most often labeled with proprietary names or with that of the grape variety. Steen, perhaps related to the Chenin Blanc, is the most widely planted white-wine grape. Pinotage, a cross of Pinot Noir and Hermitage (which is actually the Cinsault), is a popular red variety that is indigenous to South Africa, as Zinfandel is to California. Cabernet is also planted, especially in such highly regarded wine districts as Paarl and Stellenbosch, located about thirty miles east of Cape Town.

The Co-operative Wine Growers' Association, known as the K.W.V., controls wine production in South Africa, and accounts for most of the wines that are exported. The Stellenbosch Farmers' Winery markets most of the wines sold within the country.

ISRAEL

Although the wine production of Israel is relatively small by world standards (about one-third that of Switzerland, for example), Israeli wines are widely distributed in this country. Most of them are mellow red and white table wines and Sherry- and Port-type fortified wines, but many drier wines are now being marketed as well. Vines were growing in Palestine over three thousand years ago, but the modern wine industry of that country dates from the 1880s, when Baron Edmond de Rothschild sponsored the creation of new vineyards. Carignan, Grenache, and Alicante are the principal varieties cultivated, but in recent years there have been new plantings of Cabernet Sauvignon, Sauvignon Blanc, and Sémillon as well. A cooperative society formed in the early years of this century now accounts for about three-quarters of Israeli wine production, and for almost all of its exports to this country, under the brand name Carmel.

ALGERIA

Not long ago, Algeria was a relatively important producer of wines; today, its production is about a third of what it was in the 1950s. Algeria is a Muslim country, and Muslims are not permitted to consume alcoholic beverages, so Algeria is in the paradoxical situation of maintaining an industry whose product cannot be marketed within its own borders. Robust Algerian wines, almost all of them red, were traditionally shipped to France to add color, body, and alcohol to the lighter *vin ordinaire* produced in the Midi region. After Algeria obtained its independence from France in 1962, shipments to France decreased, and when the Common Market was established, French wine firms realized that it was economically more advantageous to import blending wines from Italy than from Algeria. Common Market regulations were modified in the late 1970s, and large quantities of Algerian wines are shipped to France in bottle and to other European countries in bulk. In recent years, however, the biggest customer for Algerian wines has been Russia.

At one time, a dozen Algerian wines were entitled to the French V.D.Q.S. appellation. More recently, Algeria set up its own appellation laws for seven of these wines: Medea, Dahra, Coteaux de Mascara, Coteaux du Zaccar, Coteaux de Tlemcen, Monts du Tessala, and Aïn Bessem-Bouïra. Their labels bear the phrase *Appellation d'Origine Garantie*, and some of them, such as Dahra and Medea, are being shipped here.

CHAMPAGNE AND SPARKLING WINES

Champagne, the most festive of wines, adds gaiety and distinction to any occasion at which it is served. Unfortunately, most of us drink Champagne only at crowded receptions, where we enjoy its convivial effect without the chance to really taste the wine as we would if it were served as a predinner aperitif or at the dinner table. It's a pity that Champagne is considered so special that it's reserved only for infrequent celebrations. Although good Champagne is never cheap (extra import duties are levied on sparkling wines), it is no more expensive than a good bottle of Bordeaux or Burgundy, and the appearance of a bottle of Champagne is usually greeted with pleasure and enthusiasm.

Because Champagne is marketed almost entirely by brand names, it is not a difficult wine to buy. It's a wine, nevertheless, that is made in a fairly exacting way, and visitor to any of the big Champagne houses in Reims, Ay, or Epernay invariably leaves with the impression that Champagne is not expensive considering the number of complex steps necessary to produce it.

There are any number of sparkling wines produced in France and throughout the world (these will be discussed separately), but true Champagne can be made only within the region of that name situated about ninety miles east of Paris. Although Champagne has been known as a wine for almost fifteen centuries, until the late seventeenth century the name was associated with still red wines. In the second

half of the seventeenth century, the Benedictine monk
Dom Pérignon, who was the cellar master at the Abbey of
Hautvillers, noted that the white wines of Champagne developed a sparkle in the spring following the vintage. In
effect, not all of the natural grape sugar had been transformed into alcohol at the time of the vintage, because
early winters tended to stop fermentation before it ran its
course. When warmer weather returned in the spring, the
remaining traces of sugar began to referment, and the
wines in barrel took on a natural effervescence. According
to tradition, Dom Pérignon devised a cork to replace the
ineffective pegs and rags that were then used to stopper
bottles, and this enabled him, for the first time, to bottle
the sparkling wines of Champagne in airtight containers.
Dom Pérignon is credited with having invented Champagne, but what he probably did was devise a better way
of retaining its natural sparkle so that the wine could be
marketed. He also seems to have realized that a better
sparkling wine was obtained if still wines from various
Champagne vineyards were blended together before the
second fermentation took place. He thus established the
concept of a *cuvée,* or blend, which has enabled the
Champagne shippers to maintain a consistent style year after year. It is this fact that makes Champagne unusual, for
unlike the best Bordeaux and Burgundies, which owe their
distinction to the soil and exposure of a particular
vineyard, Champagne is invariably a blended wine. More
specifically, it is a wine whose sum, as a blend, is more
distinctive than each of its parts: it is in blending that
Champagne achieves its personality. One indication of this
is the number of different Champagne firms in existence,
each producing a slightly different Champagne by blending
available wines in different proportions.

The Champagne vineyards are generally divided into
three sections: the Valley of the Marne, the Mountain of
Reims, and the Côte des Blancs. About two-thirds of the
Champagne region is planted in Pinot Noir and Pinot
Meunier grapes, the same varieties that are used to make
the great red Burgundies. The Chardonnay grape makes
up the rest of the plantings, and is of course predominant
in the Côte des Blancs. Although the shipping houses
market about two-thirds of the region's wines, they own
less than 10 percent of the vineyards, most of which are in

the hands of thousands of small proprietors. At vintage time, those farmers who are not members of cooperative cellars sell their grapes to the shippers—who cannot rely on their own acreage alone to maintain their stocks of wine—at a price per kilo that is negotiated each year just before the harvest. The established price of grapes is then multiplied by the official rating of the soil from which each particular load comes. There are a dozen villages whose vineyards are rated at 100 percent quality, including Ay, Cramant, and Avize. Others are rated on a sliding scale that goes down to 77 percent. About one-third of the wines produced in Champagne come from soil rated 90 percent or higher.

Because most of the grapes harvested are Pinot Noir and Pinot Meunier and because the color of red wines comes from pigments on the inside of the skin that dissolve in fermenting must, it is essential that the harvested grapes be pressed and separated from their skin as quickly as possible. For this reason the shipping houses maintain huge presses at strategic locations throughout the vineyards, so that the journey from vine to press is kept to a minimum. It is to these pressing houses that the growers take their grapes, which are then loaded in lots of four thousand kilos, or nearly nine thousand pounds. The presses are wide and flat, rather than high, so that the grapes can be spread out and the juice can run out of the presses quickly. Two or three fast pressings produce the equivalent of ten barrels, each holding about fifty gallons. This is known as the *vin de cuvée* or first pressing (although actually more than one pressing is needed to produce this much wine). Three more barrels of wine are produced, called *tailles*, and this too can be made into Champagne, although this wine is naturally worth much less. Sometimes a fourteenth barrel is squeezed out, known as the *rebêche*, but this cannot be made into Champagne. The thirteenth barrel, incidentally, may be worth only 50 percent as much as a *vin de cuvée*, and there are some shippers who seek out the *tailles* to make a cheap Champagne. If these shippers further specify that their *tailles* must come from vineyards rated at, say, 80 or 85 percent, there will be quite a difference between what they market and the wines of the leading Champagne houses.

The pressed juice is then transferred from the fields to

the cellars of the shippers or to the many cooperative cellars that exist in Champagne, and there the fermentation begins that will transform it into wine. When fermentation is complete, the temperature of the cellars is lowered, which enables the wine to rid itself of some of its tartrates, thus diminishing its natural acidity.

In January the tasting of the new wine begins, so that a *cuvée* may be made up for bottling. Each of the top shipping houses has, as always, obtained grapes from throughout Champagne to give itself flexibility in making up its usual blend. Tasting the new wines can take four or five weeks, and might take this form: first the wines of each pressing are tasted and compared to other lots from the same district. Then the wines of different districts within Champagne are compared, and their respective qualities noted. One village may produce wine known for its bouquet, another for its body, a third for its delicacy and finesse, and so on. Finally, wines on hand from previous vintages, called reserve wines, are tasted to determine in what proportion they should be used. Remember that a nonvintage Champagne (and this accounts for more than 80 percent of the total) is made up of wines of more than one harvest. Certain years may produce rather thin wines, others rich wines that lack elegance. The characteristics and flaws of each vintage can be adjusted by the use of reserve wines, which may account for 15 to 30 percent of a *cuvée*. This complicated and delicate blending process, in which a dozen to fifty different lots of wine may be combined, is the key to determining and maintaining a house style, upon which the reputation of each firm rests.

When a shipper considers that a particular vintage is especially successful, he will make a *cuvée* predominantly from grapes harvested that year, and the bottles will display the vintage year on their labels. Shippers do not always agree on the quality of the wines produced in any given vintage, and the years for vintage Champagne will vary from one shipper to another. Paradoxically, a vintage Champagne made entirely from the wines of a single harvest may not be typical of a shipper's traditional style, since the *cuvée* is not balanced by the use of reserve wines. In practice, however, it is likely that a certain amount of reserve wine is often used even in vintage Champagne, so that the wine displays both the personality of the vintage and the style of the shipper.

Once the *cuvée* has been made up, the wines are bottled. A little bit of sugar syrup—*liqueur de tirage*—is added to the wine, along with yeast, to provide the elements necessary for a second fermentation. The bottle is then firmly stoppered with a temporary cork—most firms now use a metal cap similar to that used for soft drinks—and is placed on its side. The sugar will now be transformed into alcohol and carbon-dioxide gas, and because the gas is imprisoned in the bottle, it must combine with the wine. This chemical combination is the reason why bubbles last so long in Champagne, compared to carbonated wines. The artificially induced second fermentation in the bottle, which is the essence of the Champagne process (*méthode champenoise*) takes a few months. Then the bottles, now filled with sparkling wine, are left to mature for a legal minimum of a year. A vintage Champagne must age in bottle for a minimum of three years.

It was 150 years after Dom Pérignon first conducted his experiments that the key step of bottle fermentation could be adequately controlled. A French chemist devised a way to measure any residual sugar left in the still wine after blending, as well as a method for calculating how much additional sugar had to be added to the wine to produce the desired amount of gas pressure in the bottle. Until then, Champagne making was a fairly hazardous undertaking, as the pressure resulting from a second fermentation could not be controlled, and the bottles of the day were not uniform. It was not unusual for half a cellar to be destroyed by a series of bottle explosions. Today such breakage has been reduced to less than 1 percent, but Champagne production is so immense that a big firm might still lose ten thousand bottles a year in this way.

The maturing bottles rest in piles that stretch out literally for miles below the ground. The extraordinary underground cellars of Champagne are carved out of the chalky subsoil of the region, and enable the Champagne producers to maintain their enormous stocks of bottles at a very constant temperature. There are about two hundred miles of underground cellars below the vineyards of Champagne, and some firms maintain little railroads to transport the bottles from one part of the cellar to another.

A by-product of the second fermentation is a cloudy deposit that makes the bottle essentially unsalable. A series of complicated steps now takes place whose sole purpose is to rid the bottle of this deposit without losing the imprisoned gas bubbles. The bottles are put into *pupitres*, A-shaped wooden boards with holes in which each bottle can be separately manipulated. A *rémueur*, the most highly paid worker in a Champagne house, now takes each bottle, which is at a slight downward slant, and gives it a little twist to dislodge the sediment, at the same time tipping the bottle over slightly to lower the corked end. This delicate process goes on every day for several weeks, and ends with each bottle standing upside down—*sur pointe*—with all of its sediment lying against the cork.

The *dégorgement*, or disgorging process, is most easily effected by dipping the necks of the bottles in a cold brine solution, which freezes the sediment to the temporary cork. In some firms a *dégorgeur* twists the cork with a pair of special pliers, and it flies out with the sediment and a bit of wine. The *dégorgeur* then places the bottle on a conveyor so that the final cork, the one we see, can be quickly inserted under tremendous pressure. Today, most firms use automatic equipment to disgorge their bottles.

Just before the final cork is inserted, some sugar syrup is added to the wine, along with as much Champagne as is needed to fill up the bottle again. This *liqueur d'expédition*, also referred to as the *dosage*, is what determines the relative dryness of a Champagne. The driest of all Champagne is Brut, which receives the least amount of dosage—no more than 1.5 percent. Extra Dry or Extra Sec, the next driest style, may contain 1.2 to 2 percent of sugar. Dry or Sec is somewhat sweeter and, in fact, not really dry, and Demi-Sec, with 3 to 6 percent of sugar, is the sweetest Champagne usually marketed.

A Champagne shipper will occasionally say that Americans like to see the word Brut on the label, but actually prefer the taste of Extra Dry, and that may be true. Fashions change, and a hundred years ago English wine merchants unsuccessfully beseeched their French suppliers to ship some dry Champagnes to counteract the prevailing taste for very sweet wines. It was only in the 1870s that dry

Champagnes established their present popularity, although certain markets—South America and Scandinavia, for example—still demand fairly sweet Champagnes. Because the relative sweetness of Champagne is determined only when the final cork is inserted, it is not difficult for any shipper to make up a Champagne that will conform to his customers' demands.

One aspect of Brut Champagne that deserves mention is that the less sweetening added, the better the wine has to be, as its quality cannot be masked. Also, a Brut does not taste at its best when served with a sweet dessert—the sugar in the food makes the wine taste slightly bitter by contrast—and it is the custom in Reims and Epernay to serve an Extra Dry with dessert.

It's worth noting here that the bottle-fermentation method described is used only for half-bottles, bottles, and magnums (which hold two bottles). Other sizes are produced by decanting bottles of Champagne into six-ounce splits and into larger sizes such as the jeroboam (four bottles) and methuselah (eight bottles). Obviously, splits have the greatest chance of going flat, and are in any case poor value, ounce for ounce, compared to a half-bottle or bottle.

The difference between a nonvintage and a vintage Champagne has been explained. A vintage Champagne from a major firm costs about three dollars a bottle more than its nonvintage, but I think most shippers would be happy to base their reputation—and your enjoyment—on their nonvintage.

In addition to marketing nonvintage Brut, vintage Brut, and Extra Dry Champagnes, a number of firms have also created a luxury Champagne that is two or three times the price of a nonvintage Brut. Moët & Chandon's Dom Pérignon is perhaps the most famous of these Champagnes, which are known as *cuvées speciales;* others include Taittinger Comtes de Champagne, Louis Roederer Cristal, and Laurent Perrier Grand Siècle. The *cuvées* for these Champagnes are prepared with particular care, the wines are usually aged longer, and most of them are marketed in distinctive, specially designed bottles.

Some Champagnes are marketed as Blanc de Blancs, which indicates that the wine has been made only from white Chardonnay grapes. A Blanc de Blancs tends to be lighter and more delicate, and there are many who prize its particular elegance. Note that this phrase has a very particular meaning in Champagne, where most of the wines are made from black grapes. But when the phrase is used on white-wine labels from other districts or other countries, it doesn't have any meaning, because white wines are made from white grapes as a matter of course.

Some shippers market a *crémant,* which is a wine that does not have the full sparkle of a Champagne, but rather a more delicate *pétillance. Crémant* should not be confused with Cramant, which is a village in the Côte des Blancs whose wines are occasionally marketed under its own name.

A quantity of nonsparkling wine is also produced in the Champagne district from the same vineyards and the same grapes as Champagne. Of course, all Champagne begins as a still wine, but these go to market as such. Until 1974, the still wines of the Champagne region were labeled *Vin Nature de la Champagne.* They were almost never exported and were difficult to find even in France. The wine was in short supply because for many years virtually all of the wines produced in Champagne were transformed into sparkling wines to meet the increasing worldwide demand. Also, shippers were reluctant to export a nonsparkling wine that had the word Champagne on its label, for fear it might confuse many consumers. In the past twenty years, however, new plantings have doubled the size of the Champagne vineyards, which now amount to sixty thousand acres, and production increased accordingly. In 1974, the name of the still wines of Champagne was changed to Coteaux Champenois, and what was then an excess of production was bottled as nonsparkling wine. For a few years both production and sales of Coteaux Champenois increased substantially, and examples from a number of different shippers were available both in France and in this country. Then, as a result of a very small crop in 1978, coupled with increased sales of Champagne, shippers were given permission to transform existing stocks of Coteaux Champenois from previous vintages into Champagne, and nonsparkling wines from this region have become less readily available once again.

Most Coteaux Champenois is white, but there is some still red wine produced in Champagne as well, the best known of which comes from the village of Bouzy. The white wine is light-bodied and comparatively high in acidity, which is typical of wines produced in northerly vineyards.

Here is an alphabetical list of Champagnes that can be found in the United States. There are, of course, other shippers doing business here, but these firms account for almost all Champagne sales in this country. Actually, the three firms of Piper-Heidsieck, Mumm, and Moët & Chandon ship two-thirds of all the bottles sold here.

Ayala	Laurent Perrier
Bollinger	Mercier
Canard-Duchêne	Moët & Chandon
Charbaut	Mumm
Veuve Clicquot-Ponsardin	Perrier-Jouët
De Venoge	Piper-Heidsieck
Deutz & Geldermann	Pol Roger
Heidsieck Monopole	Pommery & Greno
Charles Heidsieck	Louis Roederer
Krug	Ruinart
Lanson	Taittinger

Although the Champagne region of France produces, by general accord, sparkling wines with the greatest style, complexity, and finesse, a number of other sparkling wines are made in France and, of course, throughout the world. Many of them are produced by the bulk process of tank fermentation, also known as the Charmat process, after the Frenchman who first developed the technique about seventy years ago. The second fermentation of the base wine takes place in large sealed tanks rather than in individual bottles. The resulting sparkling wine is then drawn off under pressure and bottled. This method is obviously much quicker and cheaper than bottle fermentation: using the Charmat process, tanks of still wine can be transformed into bottles of sparkling wine in as little as two weeks.

A technique called the transfer process is often used—except in Champagne—to lower the costs of bottle-fermented sparkling wines. After the second fermentation has taken place and the wines have aged for some months, the sparkling wine is transferred under pressure into tanks, where the appropriate *dosage* is added. The wines are then filtered and rebottled. The transfer process is obviously cheaper than having to disgorge each bottle separately, and its use accounts for the fact that the labels of many sparkling wines—especially in the United States—carry the phrase "individually fermented in the bottle" while others are labeled "individually fermented in this bottle."

In France, all sparkling wines not produced in Champagne have always been called *mousseux*, no matter how they are made. There are *mousseux* made in the Loire, notably in Saumur, Vouvray, Touraine, and Anjou; in the village of Seyssel in the Haute-Savoie, and in Bordeaux. A great deal of *mousseux* is produced in Burgundy, both red and white, although the red is more popular here than it is in France. Because the word *mousseux* is used both for bottle-fermented sparkling wines and for less-distinguished ones, a new appellation was created in 1975 for certain bottle-fermented sparkling wines from *Appellation Contrôlée* regions. Crémant de Loire, Crémant de Bourgogne, and Crémant d'Alsace are names that can now be used for the best sparkling wines from these regions. Other French sparkling wines that are only occasionally seen here include Saint-Péray, a dry *mousseux* from the Rhône; the sweet Blanquette de Limoux, produced near Carcassonne; and the sweet, Muscat-flavored Clairette de Die.

The sparkling wines of Italy—dry and sweet, white and red—are labeled *spumante*. The most famous is Asti Spumante, produced in northern Italy around the village of Asti. Made from the distinctive and aromatic Muscat grape, Asti Spumante has a unique, intense bouquet reminiscent of ripe grapes and a sweet and pronounced taste that many people find delicious with fruit and dessert. Asti Spumante is relatively low in alcohol—under 9 percent—and contains as much as 8 or 9 percent of sugar. It is almost always made by the Charmat process, called *autoclave* in Italy. Sparkling wines are produced throughout Italy, and many appellations known here for their still wines can be found there in a sparkling version as well. Soave, Verdicchio, and Lacryma Christi are some examples of white sparkling wines, Nebbiolo and Freisa are made into red sparkling wines. In addition, many firms market branded sparkling wines and the dry ones are likely to be labeled Brut, Brut Riserva, Brut Nature, and so on. The words *Metodo Champenois* or *Fermentazione naturale in bottiglia* on a label indicate that the wine was bottle-fermented.

Sekt is the generic name for German sparkling wines, which are produced in tremendous quantities. Historically, the thin, acid German wines of poor years were used as the base for Sekt, but demand has become so great that quite a bit of wine imported from neighboring countries is now used as well. Today, more sparkling wine is made in Germany than in Champagne. Sekt is an agreeable wine characterized more by a fruity taste and a slight sweetness than by delicacy. Henkell Trocken is the best-known brand in this country.

A tremendous quantity of Spanish sparkling wine is produced in San Sadurní de Noya, near Barcelona. The best of these wines, which are quite attractive, are made by the Champagne method of individual bottle fermentation. The major firms are Codorníu and Freixenet.

About 85 percent of all sparkling wines sold in this country are made in California and New York State. The word "Champagne" can legally be used to describe American sparkling wines, preceded by an indication of its origin: California, New York State, American. A large proportion of American sparkling wines are made by the Charmat, or bulk process, and this fact must appear on the label. Whatever the method used—bulk process or bottle fermentation—the quality of the finished wine also depends on the quality of the base wine used. In California, it is often a neutral white wine that can be transformed into an agreeable, if undistinguished, sparkling wine, but many wineries are now upgrading the quality of their base wine to make a more interesting product. Two California wineries that specialize in sparkling wines are Korbel (which markets a Brut and a bone-dry Natural), and Hanns Kornell (which offers several styles, including the very dry Sehr Trocken). Some other major producers are Almadén, the Christian Brothers, Paul Masson, and Weibel.

Schramsberg is a small Napa Valley winery specializing in sparkling wines made primarily from Pinot Noir and Chardonnay grapes, and using the traditional methods of the Champagne region. Among its wines are Blanc de Blancs, Blanc de Noirs, and a semi-dry Crémant. The

French firm of Moët-Hennessy is now producing sparkling wines in California, partly from its own vineyards, at Domaine Chandon, a winery they built in the Napa Valley. They do not use the word Champagne to describe their wines, which are labeled Chandon Napa Valley Brut. Domaine Chandon also makes a wine from Pinot Noir grapes labeled Blanc de Noirs.

New York State Champagne is very popular throughout the country, and far outsells French Champagne. The native grapes, notably Delaware and Catawba, that give New York State wines a special grapy flavor have traditionally produced a very agreeable sparkling wine with a flavor of its own. Today, many of these distinctive sparkling wines display less of the taste of native grapes than in the past. The major producers of New York State Champagne are Taylor, Great Western, and Gold Seal.

The white and pink sparkling wines produced in America are usually called Champagne, the red wines are labeled Sparkling Burgundy. Cold Duck, a pink sparkling wine that was quite popular for a time, is supposedly a blend of Champagne and Sparkling Burgundy.

Champagne and sparkling wines are not inexpensive, and should be served with some care. There are few sounds that fill us with as much pleasant anticipation as the loud pop of a Champagne cork, but this is usually accompanied by a wasteful explosion of foam and wine. If you ever have occasion to open more than one bottle of Champagne at a time, it's worth noting the simplest and most effective means of doing it. The usual method is to grab the neck and start tugging at the cork. This means that the heat of your hand is applied to the narrowest part of the bottle, which is under greatest pressure, and the tugging serves only to increase that enormous pressure. Instead, put a napkin or handkerchief between your hand and the bottle (this is also a safety measure, if a bottle should ever crack), and then remove the foil and loosen the wiring. Make sure the bottle is not pointed toward you or anyone else, because once the wire is loosened, the cork may explode out. Hold the cork firmly in your other hand and twist the bottle away from the cork. The cork should come out easily, but if it doesn't, you'll have to carefully push the cork away from the bottle with your thumb. As the cork comes out, the bottle should be at a 45-degree angle, so that a larger surface of wine is exposed to the atmosphere, and there is consequently less chance of pressure building up at the neck and wine spilling out of the bottle. This procedure may be a bit too deliberate for celebrating a sports victory in a locker room, but you'll find it's easy enough in your home.

The so-called Champagne glasses often used at receptions—wide, shallow, sherbet-type—are in fact the worst of all. Their flat, wide bottom surface dissipates the bubbles very quickly, and they are clumsy and awkward to drink from. A tulip-shaped glass tapering to a point at the base, or the traditional flute in the shape of an elongated V, are both better glasses. If the bubbles rise from a single point, where the bowl is joined to the stem, they will last longer and present a more attractive appearance.

FORTIFIED
WINES

Fortified wines are those to which a certain amount of brandy has been added to bring the total alcoholic content up to 17 to 21 percent. Wine producers in this country refer to all such wines—whether they are dry or sweet—as dessert wines. Sherry and Port are the most famous examples of fortified wines, and Madeira, Marsala, and Málaga are also fairly well known. Vermouth is a fortified wine that has also been flavored with a variety of herbs and spices, and traditional aperitif wines are made in a similar way.

It is common to divide fortified wines into two classes—the dry wines, which are usually served before meals, and the sweet ones, which traditionally make their appearance after dinner. In practice, however, this division has too many exceptions. Many people enjoy a sweet Sherry before a meal, the French often drink a sweet Port before sitting down to dinner, and both sweet and dry Vermouth are often served along with cocktails.

SHERRY

Sherry is perhaps the most versatile of all wines: it can be bone-dry, mellow, or richly sweet; it can be served before or after a meal, or at almost any time of day. The name Sherry derives from the town of Jerez de la Frontera, in the southwest corner of Spain. Until the thirteenth century this part of Spain was under Moorish domination and Jerez was situated along the frontier *(frontera)* between the Moors and the Christians.

Jerez, which is the center of the Sherry trade, forms a triangle with the towns of Puerto de Santa María and Sanlúcar de Barrameda, and within this triangle are found the best grape-growing districts for the making of Sherry. The best soil, *albariza,* is made up of white chalk, and that district is planted entirely with the Palomino grape. A certain amount of Pedro Ximénez is also planted, and P.X., as it is called, is vinified in a special way to make very sweet wines used in the final blending of some Sherries.

Sherry, virtually unique among the world's wines, is made in a rather special way. The juice is fermented into a completely dry wine, with no residual sugar, and is then stored in butts, or barrels, in the *bodegas*—high-ceilinged warehouses—of the various firms. Whereas almost everywhere else barrels of new wine are filled to the top, so that air cannot get to the wine and spoil it, in Jerez the butts are not completely filled, and oxidation is actually encouraged. In the weeks following the vintage, each of the thousands of butts of new wine in a particular cellar develops somewhat differently. Even wines from the same vineyard, stored in adjoining butts, may not evolve into identical wines. In some, a white film of yeast cells, called *flor,* or flower, forms on the surface of the wine, and these are classified as Finos. Others develop very little *flor,* or none, and are classified as Olorosos. Finos and Olorosos are the two basic categories of Sherry, which is, in effect, a deliberately oxidized wine. The fuller-bodied and less-delicate Olorosos are fortified with brandy to 18 percent, and will be used primarily to make sweet Cream Sherries. Finos are fortified to only 15½ percent, so that the *flor,* which gives these wines their individuality, will not be destroyed. In time, Finos are classified once again: some remain Finos; others, slightly richer and fuller, become Amontillados.

Although it is true that two butts of Sherry from the same vineyard may turn out somewhat differently, their evolution is not quite as mysterious and unpredictable as it is sometimes made out to be. The shippers know, for example, that certain vineyards traditionally produce Finos, others Olorosos; that wines from severely pruned vines are likely to turn into Finos; and that younger vines will probably produce Olorosos. After all, if a particular shipper sells mostly Fino, he cannot just put new wine into barrels and hope for the best. His experience enables him to produce Finos, just as a shipper who specializes in Cream Sherry is able to make wines that will develop into Olorosos.

As Finos and Olorosos continue to age, the exact style of each butt of wine is determined, and it is earmarked to become part of a particular *solera* within the firm's *bodegas*. It is the *solera* system of blending and aging, unique to Sherry, that is at the heart of the production of this wine. A *solera* can be visualized as several tiers of barrels, all containing wines similar in style, with the oldest wines at the bottom. When some of the wine from each barrel in the bottom row is drawn off to be blended, bottled, and shipped, the loss is made up with wines from the second tier, which contains the next oldest wines. These, in turn, are replaced with wines from the third tier, and so on. At each level, the older wine already in the barrel is said to "educate" the younger wine that is added. Although the entire collection of barrels is usually referred to as a *solera*, technically speaking, it is the barrels containing the oldest wines that are the *solera;* each tier that feeds the *solera* is called a *criadera*, or nursery; and the youngest *criadera* is replenished from an *añada*, a wine only one or two years old. Because the amount of wine withdrawn from a *solera* is limited to, say, no more than a third of a barrel at one time, the *solera* system enables the shipping firms of Jerez to maintain a continuity of style for each of their Sherries, year after year. In practice, a *solera* system is more varied and complex than this simple visualization. A Fino *solera* may consist of four tiers, or scales; an Oloroso of seven or eight. Sometimes, the youngest *criadera* in an Oloroso *solera* may be replenished not by a young *añada*, but by the oldest wine in another *solera*, so that the wine that is bottled may have passed through twelve or fourteen scales. Since each scale in a *solera* may consist of two or three hundred barrels, they are not actually piled one on top of another, and may even be scattered throughout several cellars.

The amount of wine drawn off from a *solera* differs depending on the style of wine. One-third of a Fino *solera* may be drawn off four times a year, whereas in an Oloroso *solera* only a quarter may be withdrawn twice a year. Also, to make up a particular Sherry, a shipper will often combine wines from several *soleras,* so that the final blend consists of wines of slightly different styles. Since Sherry is produced by a system of fractional blending that includes a number of successive vintages, and wines from many vineyards, Sherry is never vintage-dated, nor is it identified by the name of an individual vineyard.

Although Sherries are classified as Finos and Olorosos, they are marketed in four main categories. A Manzanilla is a Fino that has been matured in the seacoast village of Sanlúcar de Barrameda, fifteen miles from Jerez. This bone-dry wine acquires a distinctive tang, sometimes attributed to the salt air, but more likely the result of higher humidity, which produces a richer *flor.* Curiously enough, if a Manzanilla is shipped back in barrel to Jerez, it gradually loses its special taste. A Fino is a dry Sherry, but many shippers do not emphasize this word on their labels, preferring instead to feature such proprietary brand names as La Ina or Tio Pepe. A good Fino, delicate and complex, is a difficult wine to make, and some cheap examples are not even dry. An Amontillado is usually described as nuttier than a Fino, and since they are often Finos with more barrel age, they tend to be fuller-bodied. The most obvious difference between the two, however, is that the Amontillados shipped here are distinctly sweeter than Finos. It is possible to find a dry Amontillado in Spain, where the best of them are very much admired, but the popular brands available here are all somewhat sweet, even those labeled as dry. As with Finos, the word Amontillado does not always appear on the labels of these wines. The fourth category of Sherry is Cream Sherry, which is almost always made from Olorosos. Although an Oloroso is completely dry as it ages in its *solera,* its bigger body and fuller flavor lends itself to transformation into a Cream Sherry by the addition of specially made sweet wines during the final stages of blending. Amoroso is still used occasionally on a label to indicate a golden Sherry that is between an Amontillado and a Cream Sherry in color and sweetness. Brown Sherry, rarely seen in this country, is even darker and sweeter than a Cream Sherry.

Dry sherries taste best chilled, and it's preferable to put a bottle of Fino in the refrigerator than to serve it with ice cubes, which dilute its delicate flavor. An open bottle of Sherry lasts longer than a table wine because of its higher alcoholic content. Nevertheless, most Sherry shippers agree that once opened, a good Fino will begin to lose its character within a week or two.

When buying Sherry, it is the name of the shipper that is important rather than that of a village or vineyard. Furthermore, many Sherry shippers have individualized certain of their wines by the use of proprietary brand names, some of which are better known than that of the firms that produce them. Some Sherry houses (and their leading brand names) are Croft (Original), Pedro Domecq (La Ina), Duff Gordon (Club Dry), Gonzales Byass (Tio Pepe), Harveys (Bristol Cream), Sandeman (Armada Cream), and Williams & Humbert (Dry Sack).

About one hundred miles northeast of Jerez is the Montilla-Moriles district, whose wines are labeled simply as Montilla. The name Amontillado is derived from Montilla, and these wines are similar in style to Sherry. They are made primarily from the Pedro Ximénez grape, which in this region is fermented out until the wines are dry. Montilla has a natural alcohol content of about 16 percent and, unlike Sherry, it is bottled and shipped without being fortified with brandy.

Wines labeled Sherry are also made in the United States, primarily in California and New York State; in fact, considerably more Sherry is made in this country than in Spain. However, most American Sherries are made by baking neutral white wines to age them artificially, which is a technique used in Madeira, not in Jerez. Consequently, the drier Sherries are often less successful than the Cream Sherries, whose baked taste can be more easily masked by sweetening. Some American wineries produce Sherries by aging the wine in small barrels instead of baking them, but the traditional *solera* system of blending is not in use here. In the past few years, many wineries have begun to use a submerged *flor* process: *flor* yeast is mixed with dry white base wines, left for ten days or so until the *flor* settles, and the wine is then drawn off the yeast and aged in barrels. Nevertheless, there is a difference between wines exposed to *flor* for a few days and those that react with *flor* for many years. Furthermore, many California *flor* wines are later blended with baked wines before bottling. Although Sherries produced in the United States generally lack the distinctive nutty quality and complexity of taste typical of Spanish Sherry, many of them are soundly made and the best of them are a good value.

PORT

Port is a sweet, red, fortified wine made along a delimited section of the Douro River in northern Portugal. (White Port has also been made for a hundred years, but most of it is used for blending.) Port takes its name from the town of Oporto, at the mouth of the Douro, although the offices and warehouses of the famous Port shippers are located across the river in Vila Nova de Gaia. Port has long been popular in Great Britain and was, in fact, specifically developed for the British market, but it has been slow to catch on in this country. Perhaps the image of cheap American Port has discouraged consumers from discovering how good authentic Port can be, or it may be that our drinking habits don't lend themselves to the appreciation of a sweet, red wine that is usually served after a meal.

In 1968, in an effort to distinguish true Port from imitations produced in this country, the Portuguese government took the unusual step of declaring that Port shipped from Portugal to the United States must be labeled Porto. Although wines bottled in Portugal now carry the phrase Vinho do Porto, many shippers continue to feature Port, rather than Porto, on their labels. In addition, the decree does not apply to wines shipped in bulk to England and bottled there for sale in this country. Despite the ruling, the wine continues to be called Port by both shippers and consumers alike.

The red wines of the Douro were known as unexceptional table wines until the early eighteenth century, when political considerations made it cheaper for the English to import wines from Portugal than from France. As more Portuguese wines were exported to England, some shippers began to add brandy to the wines to fortify them for the long voyage, and Port as we now know it gradually evolved. Today Port continues to be popular in England, but surprisingly enough, France now imports twice as much of this wine as does England. The French drink Port before the meal, as an aperitif.

Port is produced along the upper Douro River on steeply terraced vineyards planted with more than a dozen different grape varieties. Today, grapes are crushed by mechanical means, but as recently as twenty years ago all the grapes used for Port were crushed by foot in large cement troughs, and some firms still use this old-fashioned treading for selected lots of grapes. As the grapes are crushed, fermentation begins, converting the sugar in the juice into alcohol. At a certain point, brandy is mixed with the incompletely fermented wine. This sudden dose of alcohol stops the fermentation completely, and the resulting fortified wine contains 5 or 6 percent of unfermented grape sugar and about 19 percent of alcohol. White Port is also made in the same way and mostly used for blending with reds, although some is fermented out until it is dry and marketed as an aperitif wine. In the spring, following the vintage, the new wine is transported from *quintas,* or vineyard estates, along the Douro to shippers' cellars, called lodges, in Vila Nova de Gaia. There the wine is aged in wooden casks, called pipes. A pipe of Port, the traditional measure in that region, holds the equivalent of a little more than seven hundred bottles.

Young Port is a deep red-purple wine, quite fruity and grapy, which has not yet absorbed the brandy with which it was mixed. It is not a harsh or unpleasant wine—its sweetness masks its tannin and alcoholic content—but it is not fine or complex, and has yet to develop its character. Almost all Port is wood Port, that is, aged for several years in cask before being bottled. (The exception is Vintage Port, which will be discussed further on.) The two basic styles of wood Port are Ruby and Tawny. Ruby Port is darker in color, more fruity and vigorous in style. Tawny Port is lighter in color, as its name suggests, generally older, softer, more delicate, and often more complex. This distinction is blurred by the fact that the only requirement of wood Ports is that they be aged about three years before being shipped. It takes six or seven years for a young Port to develop into a Tawny, and fine Tawnies are aged considerably longer. Aging wines is expensive, of course, and consequently many Tawnies on the market are simply Rubies to which a certain amount of White Port has been added to lighten the color and soften the taste. It is by no means unusual for a shipper to market a Ruby and Tawny that are both three years old, the principal difference being that the Tawny contains as much as a third of white Port in the final blend. It is a mistake, therefore, to assume that an inexpensive Tawny is necessarily older than a Ruby, even though it is lighter in color. As a matter of fact, the Ruby may well be a more interesting and typical wine, since it retains the distinctive character and body of Port, compared to the somewhat diluted and bland taste of a Tawny that contains a lot of white Port. Ruby and Tawny Ports are ready to drink when they are bottled, and do not improve with bottle age.

Although wood Ports account for virtually all of the six or seven million cases of Port produced annually, the most famous and glamorous wine of the region is undoubtedly Vintage Port. It is a wine made entirely from the grapes of a single harvest and bottled after about two years in wood, so that it matures in bottle rather than in cask. A shipper "declares" a vintage only when he thinks the quality of the wine exceptional enough to warrant it, and this usually occurs only three or four times in a decade. The decision is not made until the second spring after the vintage, in case the second of two consecutive vintages turns out better than the first, and every shipper decides for himself whether or not to declare a vintage. For example, only fourteen shippers made a Vintage Port in 1958, twenty-seven in 1960, only four in 1962, twenty-five in 1963, twenty-one in 1966, only seven in 1967, thirty-nine in 1970, only four in 1972, and nearly forty in 1975. Even in a year when a shipper declares a vintage, only a very small part of his production, perhaps 5 percent, is set aside to be bottled as Vintage Port. The rest is needed to maintain the quality and style of his wood Ports. The total amount of Vintage Port produced in a given year rarely exceeds 200,000 cases, and even in an abundant vintage, only a few shippers bottle more than 12,000 cases each.

Vintage Port is unquestionably one of the finest wines made, and since it is bottled only in good vintages—unlike, for example, red Bordeaux—it is perhaps the most dependable of all fine wines. Wine ages in bottle much more slowly than in wood, however, and since the wines begin as exceptionally tannic and intense examples of

Port, most shippers suggest that a Vintage Port needs a minimum of ten or fifteen years to be drinkable. Since Vintage Port throws a heavy deposit as it ages, careful decanting is a necessity. Vintage Port was traditionally bottled in England, because that is where almost all of it is drunk. Since 1974 all Vintage Port must be bottled in Portugal; the 1975s, for example, are all Portuguese bottled. Despite the demands that Vintage Port makes on the patience of its admirers, there has been a resurgence of interest in this wine in the past few years, and a wide selection of recent vintages is now available in many shops in this country.

In addition to Vintage Port, there are two other styles of Port on whose labels the word "vintage" may appear. Late Bottled Vintage Ports, known as LBV, are, like Vintage Ports, produced from wines of a single vintage but are bottled only after four to six years in wood. (The year of bottling appears on the label.) Some shippers use the wines of a generally declared vintage year; most use intermediate years. They are meant to combine the character of a Vintage Port with additional barrel age and are, in a manner of speaking, specially selected aged Rubies. A shipper's LBV will be a richer and more intense wine than his Ruby, but more evolved than a Vintage Port of about the same age. They can be drunk when they are bottled, although some shippers say they will continue to improve in bottle for three or four years.

There are also a few bottles to be found labeled Port of the Vintage rather than Vintage Port. These wines have nothing whatever to do with Vintage Port, but are simply old Tawnies from a specific year, often refreshed with younger wines and bottled after many years in wood. (The date of bottling must now appear on the label.) These wines are almost always overpriced, and often misleadingly advertised as if they were Vintage Ports.

Crusted Port is a blend of two or more vintages bottled before the wine has matured. It throws a crust, or deposit, as it ages in bottle, hence its name. Crusted Port has pretty much been replaced by Late Bottled Vintage Port.

Some Port shippers whose wines are found in this country (and their best-known proprietary brands) are Cálem, Cockburn (Private Reserve), Croft (Distinction), Delaforce (His Eminence's Choice), Dow (Boardroom),

Fonseca (Bin 27), Graham, Harveys (Gold Cap, Directors' Bin), Hooper's, Niepoort, Robertson (Dry Humour), Sandeman (Partners'), Taylor Fladgate, and Warre (Warrior, Nimrod). Most of these firms also ship Vintage Ports, as do Offley Forrester, Rebello Valente, and Quinta do Noval, among others.

California Ports are produced by a great many wineries and vary widely in quality. The best of them are full, fruity, mellow wines that nevertheless lack the subtlety and complexity of the wines from the Douro. Four small wineries that have built a following for their distinctive California Ports are Ficklin, in Madera, which markets Tinta Port; Andrew Quady, also in Madera, whose firm produces vintage-dated Ports from Zinfandel grapes; the J.W. Morris Port Works in Emeryville, east of San Francisco, which markets Founder's Port as well as vintage-dated Ports; and Woodbury Winery in San Rafael, north of San Francisco, whose first vintage-dated Port was produced in 1977. Port made in New York State tends to retain more of the native *labrusca* flavor than does New York State Sherry.

MADEIRA

Madeira is a small Portuguese island off the coast of North Africa whose distinctive fortified wines range from fairly dry to very sweet. In colonial times, Madeira was probably the most popular wine in America, and was specially imported by connoisseurs in Boston, New York, and Charleston. Only a small quantity is imported today. The vineyards of Madeira were devastated by two plagues in the second half of the nineteenth century, first the fungus oïdium, then phylloxera, and its production has never regained its former size.

As is the case with Port, the fermentation of Madeira was traditionally stopped by the addition of brandy at a point determined by just how sweet the finished wine was meant to be. Although this technique is still occasionally used, most Madeira is now fermented out until it is dry, just like Sherry. In the past the fortified wines were then put in rooms called *estufas*, or ovens, and the wines slowly baked for several months. Today, large concrete vats heated by internal pipes are used to bake the wines. The wine must be baked for a minimum of ninety days at a temperature no higher than 122°F. This concentrated aging process is meant to approximate the beneficial effects of a long sea voyage, as it was discovered in the eighteenth century that the voyages to which all cargo was subjected seemed to improve the wines of Madeira.

Madeira has a special pungent taste that comes from the volcanic soil in which the vines are planted, as well as an agreeable cooked or burned taste that it acquires in the *estufas*. At the time of bottling each lot of wine is sweetened to produce the appropriate style of wine. Sercial is the driest of all Madeiras, Verdelho the next driest; Malmsey is the sweetest, and Bual, or Boal, is medium-sweet. Although these four names are those of specific grape varieties cultivated on the island, the wines are no longer made primarily from the grape with which each is labeled. The grape names are now used simply to indicate the relative style and sweetness of each wine. Some shippers also market their wines with proprietary brand names such as Island Dry, Saint John, Duke of Clarence, and Viva. Rainwater Madeira, typically pale in color, is a generic name for a medium-sweet wine. Madeira is among the longest-lived of all wines, and it is still possible to find fifty- or one-hundred-year-old single vintage Madeiras (as opposed to vintage-dated *solera* wines, which are actually blended from many vintages): good examples are by no means faded, and offer a remarkable tasting experience.

One of the principal shippers on the island is the Madeira Wine Association, which produces and markets such brands as Blandy's, Cossart Gordon, Leacock, and Rutherford & Miles. Other shippers include Barbeito, Borges, Henriques & Henriques, and Justino Henriques.

Marsala is a fortified wine made in Sicily. As is the case with Sherry, the wine is completely fermented until it is dry, then later fortified and sweetened. Even dry Marsala is not completely dry. Most firms market not only a sweet Marsala, but specially flavored Marsalas as well, using egg yolks, almonds, oranges, and so forth.

The city of Málaga, situated along the southern coast of Spain, gives its name to a sweet, fortified wine made primarily from Muscatel and Pedro Ximénez grapes. Málaga is rarely encountered here.

VERMOUTH AND APERITIFS

Vermouth, both sweet and dry, is most often used in mixed drinks, but it is also popular as an aperitif, and is usually served with ice and a twist of lemon peel. Vermouth has a wine base, and is fortified, sweetened, and flavored with various herbs, spices, and increasingly, flavor extracts, according to each firm's secret recipe. Traditionally, Italian Vermouth is red and sweet, while French Vermouth is pale and dry, but both types are made in each country, and a little more than half the Vermouth consumed here is made in this country. The French town of Chambéry, near the Swiss-Italian border, has given its name to a distinctive pale and dry Vermouth.

Anything that is drunk before a meal—Sherry, Vermouth, white wine, Champagne, or even a cocktail—could properly be described as an aperitif, but the term aperitif wine usually refers to certain proprietary brands, such as Dubonnet, St. Raphaël, Byrrh, and Lillet. They can be red or white and some are made primarily from *mistelle*, must whose fermentation has been arrested by the addition of alcohol, thus retaining a high proportion of grape sugar. Most aperitifs have a more pronounced and distinctive flavor than Vermouth because they are meant to be drunk by themselves, with ice and perhaps a splash of soda water. Quinine or an equivalent flavoring agent is a traditional ingredient that contributes a slightly bitter aftertaste that tempers the sweetness of the aperitif.

Pineau des Charentes is an unusual aperitif produced in the Cognac region of France. It is a blend of sweet, unfermented grape juice and young Cognac, and is bottled with about 17 percent of alcohol.

COGNAC AND
OTHER BRANDIES

Although this book is primarily concerned with wine, a meal at which good wines are served often ends with a glass of brandy, which is, almost always, distilled wine. The word is derived from *brandewijn*, a Dutch word for burned (distilled) wine. Wherever grapes are grown and made into wine, brandy of some kind is also made. The most famous and most highly regarded of all brandies is Cognac, which is distilled from wine produced in a specifically delimited area in southwest France, about seventy miles north of Bordeaux. All Cognac is brandy, but there is only one brandy that can be called Cognac.

It was in the early seventeenth century that the white wines produced in the valley of the Charente River were first distilled to make a *vin brûlé*, presumably to provide an alcoholic beverage that would be less bulky to ship than wine. The city of Cognac, which lies on the bank of the Charente, gave its name to this brandy in the eighteenth century, and only as recently as a hundred years ago did the various Cognac producers first begin to bottle and label their brandy in their own cellars, thus establishing the brand names by which almost all Cognac is marketed today.

We have seen how important soil is to the quality and characteristics of various wines, and this is equally true for the wines used to make Cognac. There are seven clearly defined districts whose wines are permitted to be distilled into Cognac. The two most important inner districts are called Grande Champagne and Petite Champagne, but these names bear no relation to the sparkling wines of Champagne. Champagne in French means open fields, a distinction made even clearer by the names of the five other districts, four of which refer to woodlands: Borderies, Fins Bois, Bons Bois, Bois Ordinaires, and Bois Communs. These legally delimited areas were established when it was discovered that the wines from each district, when distilled, produced Cognacs with marked differences in quality. The very best Cognacs come from Grande Champagne and Petite Champagne, which now account for about 30 percent of the total production of Cognac.

There are three grape varieties used to make Charente wines, but it is the Saint-Emilion (also known as the Ugni Blanc, and unrelated to the Bordeaux wine district) that has gradually replaced the Folle Blanche and the Colombard. The white wine of the Charente is thin and sour, usually under 10 percent in alcohol, and unattractive to drink. Oddly enough, the wine produced in Grande Champagne from its predominantly chalky soil tastes even worse than the rest, and yet it produces the finest Cognac. There are no quantity limits per acre to the wines produced in the Charente, but the growers vinify their wines carefully, because any off-taste or defect in the wine will show up even more strongly in the distilled brandy. Much of the annual wine crop is sold directly to big distilling houses that are owned by or under contract to the biggest Cognac shippers, but many thousands of small growers also distill their own Cognac, to be sold later to the shippers.

Once the wine has been made, distillation takes place in old-fashioned pot stills, which resemble giant copper kettles, and proceeds for several months on a twenty-four-hour schedule. The small grower-distillers move their beds near their pot stills and maintain a steady vigil over the distillation process. Cognac is unusual in that it is doubly distilled. The first distillation produces a liquid of about 60° proof (or 30 percent alcohol), called *brouillis*. This is redistilled to make the raw Cognac, known as the *bonne chauffe*, which comes out of the still at 140° proof. It takes about ten barrels of wine to make a barrel of Cognac. Distillation is deliberately slow, so that the characteristics of the wine are imparted to the brandy. The congeners, or flavoring elements, retained during distillation give Cognac its particular character, whereas a fast, high-proof distillation would result in a relatively flavorless alcohol.

The new Cognac, which is colorless, is then aged in oak barrels. These barrels were traditionally made of Limousin oak, but the forest of Limousin can no longer supply all the needs of the Cognac shippers. Today, about half the barrels in the cellars of Cognac are made of Tronçais oak, from a forest about two hundred miles away. It is the interaction between oak and brandy, as well as the continual oxidation that takes place through the porous wood, that gives Cognac its superb and distinctive flavor. The basic elements are present in embryonic form in the new Cognac, but it is barrel-aging (during which the brandy also picks up color and tannin from the oak) that refines a harsh distillate into an inimitable beverage. What's more, Cognac, like all brandies, ages only as long as it remains in wood, and undergoes no further development once it is bottled. It is not the vintage that matters, as with wine, but the number of years spent in wood.

Aging is expensive, however, not only because the millions of gallons of Cognac lying in the warehouses of the big shippers and in small cellars throughout the countryside represent an enormous capital outlay, but also because Cognac evaporates as it ages. It is claimed that as much Cognac evaporates into the atmosphere every day as is consumed in France, and this "angel's drink" adds to the final cost of an old Cognac. A barrel of Cognac kept in a cellar for twenty years without being topped up would shrink by almost half its volume. This explains not only why fine Cognac is expensive, but also why most Cognacs on the market are considerably younger than consumers imagine. The finest Cognacs will continue to improve in barrel for about forty years, after which there is a danger that they will dry out and take on a woody or stalky flavor. Very old Cognacs are therefore stored in glass demijohns, because brandy does not change once it is put into glass. Cognacs from lesser districts, on the other hand, will mature and mellow for only a few years, at which time they are already quite pleasant. They can naturally be improved by being combined with older Cognacs from other districts, and it is at this point that the blender's skill comes into play. Apart from Cognacs that may have been distilled especially for them, all the Cognac houses constantly buy young Cognacs from the thousands of grower-distillers in the region. Tremendous stocks of different Cognacs of various ages must be maintained by the shippers in order to make up their respective house styles on a continuous basis.

As Cognac ages, its alcoholic content diminishes slowly, but it is obviously not possible to age every Cognac until it arrives at a marketable strength—usually about 80° proof—and the shippers must therefore add distilled or deionized water to their final blends to achieve the desired proof.

Although Cognac takes on color from the oak as it matures, its pale-brown color will vary widely according to age and the kind of barrel used. It is, therefore, invariably augmented with harmless caramel coloring before being bottled, so that the color will be consistent year after year.

There are a number of markings—stars, initials, and phrases—that traditionally appear on Cognac labels, and some of these are more meaningful than others. Most of the Cognacs marketed here fall into two basic categories—those labeled Three Star or Five Star, and those labeled VSOP (Very Superior Old Pale). The stars on a bottle of Cognac are completely meaningless, except to place the brandy in the youngest age category. By French law a Cognac must be aged at least eighteen months, but our federal laws stipulate that all brandy must be at least two years old. Because stars have no legal meaning, and because so many other brandies have now adopted the star system that originated in Cognac, many shippers dropped this designation from their labels and introduced proprietary brand names such as Bras Armé, Sceptre, Régal, Célébration, and Gold-Leaf. More recently, shippers are replacing stars and proprietary brands with the initials VS (Very Special) or VSP (Very Special Pale), but neither of these designations has any added significance with respect to the age of the Cognac.

VSOP, however, does have a special meaning: any Cognac so labeled must be at least four years old. Clearly, the increasing use of the initials VS and VSP is an attempt not only to get away from the meaningless star system, but also to blur the distinction between younger Cognacs, which account for perhaps 80 percent of sales, and the

VSOPs. There is one other age designation: the word Napoléon can be used only on the label of a Cognac that is at least five years old. No Cognac can legally be described as older than five years today because the French government will no longer issue age certificates for Cognac beyond five years, on the reasonable assumption that it would be too difficult to monitor the two million or so barrels of Cognac currently aging in cellars throughout the region.

In addition to Three Star or VSP Cognacs and those labeled VSOP, some firms also market Cognacs that are even older. Many are labeled Napoléon, others are marketed with such proprietary names as Triomphe, Extra, Cordon Bleu, and XO. These generally cost about twice the price of a VSOP, and many of them are excellent. A comparison of Cognacs in this price category would indicate not only that they are noticeably older than the VSOPs, but that each shipper has developed an individual style that brandy connoisseurs can distinguish and appreciate.

A Cognac labeled Grande Champagne or Grande Fine Champagne has been distilled entirely from wines made from grapes grown in the Grande Champagne district, and this is the highest appellation possible. More familiar is Fine Champagne Cognac, which indicates that the brandy comes from both Grande and Petite Champagne, with at least 50 percent from Grande Champagne. Because of the importance attached to these appellations, some Cognacs are labeled Fine Cognac or Grande Fine Cognac, phrases as meaningless as they are misleading.

Finally, a word about Napoléon Cognacs that supposedly date from the days of the emperor. Even if you came across an authentic bottle dated, say, 1812, you would have no way of knowing how long the brandy had spent in wood. If the Cognac had been bottled in 1813, it would simply be a one-year-old Cognac, for once in bottle brandies no longer improve. As it happens, bottles of 1811 Napoléon Cognac regularly show up at London auctions. Experts believe that they were bottled at the turn of the century, and they have the heavy, somewhat caramelized taste that was preferred 80 years ago. No one really believes that they have anything to do with 1811 or with Napoléon.

Cognac is most often served in special brandy glasses, which are available in a variety of sizes. It is traditional to cup the bowl with your palm, so that the applied warmth releases the brandy's bouquet. For this reason very small and very big glasses are less comfortable than those with a bowl whose size is somewhere between that of a tangerine and an apple. Good Cognac is noted for its complex and refined bouquet, and in fact brandy glasses are also known as snifters. A professional Cognac taster actually relies more on his nose than on his palate when buying young Cognacs or making a final blend, and if you pause a moment to inhale Cognac before tasting it, you'll be surprised at how much this will tell you about its style and quality.

The best-known Cognac firms, listed alphabetically are

Bisquit	Hine
Camus	Martell
Courvoisier	Monnet
Delamain	Otard
Denis-Mounié	Polignac*
Gaston de Lagrange	Rémy Martin
Hennessy	Salignac

Cognac may be the most famous of all brandies, but there are quite a few others that serve admirably to round out a meal. After Cognac, the best known of all French brandies is Armagnac, which is somewhat richer and fuller in taste than Cognac. If it lacks the finesse and distinction of Cognac at its very best, Armagnac nevertheless offers good value: it ages more quickly than Cognac, and comparatively priced examples may therefore be softer and mellower.

Armagnac comes from southwest France, from a region near the Pyrenees that used to be called Gascony. The region is not widely traveled, and the inhabitants are determined individualists, with long memories for local history. When they speak of "the occupation" they usually mean the occupation of Gascony by the English in the fifteenth century. And how many people would display, as a proud exhibit in their local museum, a *bidon de fraudeur*, a flat metal container shaped to fit against a man's stom-

* This is the brand name used by UNICOOP, the largest cooperative cellar in Cognac.

ach, and used for smuggling Armagnac under one's clothes.

Until recently, many small farmers in this region had barrels of old Armagnac aging in their cellars or behind the barn. These farmers were able to produce brandy, despite their limited facilities, because it was the custom for portable stills to be carried throughout the region from November through the following April, transforming wine into Armagnac. These portable stills, which resembled small locomotives, are infrequently seen today, and half of the region's production comes from cooperative cellars.

As in Cognac, the white wine from the Armagnac region is thin and meager. It is also characterized by a special earthy taste, which finds its way into the brandy in a subdued form, and this is a basic characteristic of the taste of Armagnac. Distillation of Armagnac is one continual process (Cognac is twice-distilled) and traditionally the brandy trickled from the still at an average of 104° proof. Today, Armagnac can be distilled at 140° proof, as in Cognac, but nevertheless more of the original taste of the wine "comes over" during distillation, giving the brandy a more pronounced character. Armagnac is then aged in the local Gascon oak or, increasingly, in Limousin and Tronçais oak. As in Cognac, the VSOP designation can only be used for a brandy that has aged for at least four years.

Armagnac is usually marketed in the distinctive, flat-sided *basquaise* bottle. Relatively few brands are widely available here—the best known are Marquis de Caussade (the brand name used by an association of cooperatives), Marquis de Montesquiou, and Larressingle.

A brandy that provokes strong feelings pro and con is marc (pronounced *mar*), which is also produced in Italy as grappa. Marc itself, called pomace in America, is the residue of skins, pits, and stalks from which wine has been pressed out. Water is added to the marc, left to referment, and this mixture is then distilled to produce a very pungent and distinctive brandy. The best-known marc is Marc de Bourgogne, although the brandy is also produced in Champagne, the Rhône Valley, and Alsace, where an unusual Marc de Gewürztraminer is made. Marc, which has a strawlike bouquet and somewhat leathery taste, is occasionally made from pressings of an individual vineyard and so labeled, such as Marc de Chambertin. By comparison, the grappa of Italy is colorless and is not usually aged in wood. Consequently, it is likely to be more pungent and less mellow than the best French marc.

Brandies from France, labeled simply French Brandy, are widely available here, but they are the cheapest and least-interesting group of all. All French brandy is purchased by the shippers from the French government, which distills a certain amount of cheap wine each year. Despite this anonymity of origin, many French brandy labels bear such designations as Napoléon, VSOP, Ten Star, and Grande Réserve, none of which has any legal meaning at all. In fact, all of the leading brands available here are shipped in bulk and bottled in this country.

Spanish brandies, noted for their fullness rather than their finesse, are sweet compared to the brandies of France, and this mellowness must certainly contribute to their popularity here. Spanish brandies are distilled throughout that country from a number of different wines, and then blended in Jerez, which is best known, of course, for its Sherry. Fundador of Pedro Domecq is the best-known brand.

Asbach Uralt is the best-seller here among German imports; it is a dry, delicate and attractive brandy in the French style.

The United States produces 80 percent of all the brandy consumed in this country, and all of it comes from California. California brandies are very slightly sweetened, but they also have a distinctive, spicy, wood-fruit flavor that gives them a complexity of taste lacking in brandies that are merely sweet. California brandy is made primarily from raisin and table grapes, and the wines are distilled at 160° to 170° proof, producing a brandy that is relatively light, clean, fairly neutral, and does not require much aging. California brandies are inexpensive, and many of them are appealing, but they are often marketed as an alternative to whiskey and other traditional spirits in mixed drinks and highballs, rather than as a brandy to be drunk from a snifter. The Christian Brothers accounts for about one-third of all California brandy sales.

There are also a few well-known brandies that are made from fruits other than grapes. The most unusual, often the most expensive, and to some palates the finest of all brandies are those distilled from wild fruits in the mountains of Alsace and Switzerland and in the Black Forest of Germany. They are produced in very small quantities, and restaurateurs in France and Germany compete with a few importers for the finest examples. *Kirsch* (wild cherry), *framboise* (wild raspberry), *mirabelle* (yellow plum), *quetsch* (purple plum), and *poire* (pear) are the best known, and because they are colorless, they are known generically as *alcools blancs*, or white alcohols. Actually, all distillates are colorless when they come from the still, but we seem to be more comfortable in whiskies, rum, and most brandies are pale brown, although we accept gin and vodka in their natural state.

The *alcools blancs* are made in a special way. In the case of pears, cherries, and plums, clean, ripe fruit is crushed and allowed to ferment. The mash, called *marmalade*, is then distilled. Berries have too little sugar to ferment easily, so they are macerated in alcohol and that alcohol is then redistilled. Whatever process is used, the result is a colorless distillate that concentrates the essence of the fruit. A great deal of fruit is needed to produce a bottle of brandy—25 to 35 pounds of Williams pears for a bottle of *poire*, up to 40 pounds of raspberries for a bottle of *framboise*—which is one reason these brandies are so expensive.

Although the labels of most fruit brandies sold here state that the brandy "is a finished product when it leaves the still and does not require mellowing in oak to perfect its quality," the fact is that many fruit brandies are aged for two or three years, sometimes even longer. The aging usually takes place in glass demijohns, however, so that the brandies do not acquire any color. The containers are loosely stoppered, so that the brandy remains in contact with air, or they are uncorked and shaken up every few months. Either way, the bouquet develops finesse through oxidation without taking on color. It is the delicate and fragrant bouquet of these white alcohols, each reminiscent of the original fruit in its ripe and undistilled state, that makes the best of these brandies so remarkable and so different from grape brandies.

Fruit brandies are distilled at 100° proof and sold at about 90° proof: for all their haunting bouquet they are by no means bland. These *alcools blancs* bear no relation to various fruit-flavored brandies, such as blackberry brandy or apricot brandy, which are made in an entirely different way, appropriately colored, and quite sweet.

Another famous fruit brandy is Calvados, made from apple cider in the French *département* of Calvados, in Normandy. The best Calvados comes from the Pays d'Auge, where the fermented cider must be distilled in traditional pot stills similar to the ones used in Cognac. When properly aged, Calvados is a delicious brandy, with a distinctive applelike tang. A local custom is the *trou Normand*—a pause in the middle of a long dinner to swallow a shot of Calvados, which supposedly aids the digestion and makes room for the rich courses to follow. Applejack is the American equivalent of Calvados. Since it is a blend of cider brandy and grain neutral spirits, it is lighter than Calvados and has less of an apple taste.

When the moment is at hand for an after-dinner brandy, there is certainly no lack of choice. If you hesitate to buy a bottle of an unfamiliar brandy, one way to experiment is to try different brandies in restaurants. You're bound to discover something new that is very much to your taste.

THE ENJOYMENT
OF WINE

BUYING AND STORING WINES

Although every liquor store or wine outlet carries at least
a limited selection of wines from several countries and
from a number of American wineries, there are so many
different wines available and at such a wide range of
prices that it's well worth your while to shop around. In
almost every city there are several stores whose proprietors
are fully aware of the growing consumer interest in wines,
and who make an effort to have a large selection of well-
chosen wines from a variety of sources. Many such re-
tailers also publish price lists periodically, and if there is
any homework that a wine enthusiast can do, apart from
drinking wine regularly, it is to spend some free moments
looking through wine catalogs. This will enlarge your
awareness of what is currently available and at what
prices, and it also permits you to look up any unfamiliar
wine names, which you cannot do when you're standing in
a shop. If you live in a large city with several good wine
stores, get on their mailing lists. If the choice is limited in
your town, at least remember to pick up a catalog or two
when you travel, for reference purposes.

Once you've found a good wine source or two, try to
find a corner in your home that you can use to store wine.
This needn't be elaborate, and you might start with only
half a dozen bottles, but there are several reasons why it
pays to buy wines ahead of time. For one thing, you don't
have to run out at the last minute if guests are expected,
nor will you find yourself without any wine left halfway

through dinner. For another, you don't have to rely on the corner liquor store, which can be especially annoying if you've already discovered that the selection is limited and the prices high. Also, fine red wines that have thrown a deposit need at least a few days' rest if they've been shaken up. If you have a few such wines on hand, you'll be sure of getting the most they have to offer. Finally, don't underestimate the real pleasure of being able to choose a wine from your own collection—red, white, or rosé—that suits your dinner and your mood.

The wine cellar itself can be as simple as a whiskey carton turned on its side, and the guides to maintaining a store of wines are simple and logical. The first rule, of course, is to lay a wine bottle on its side, so that the cork is kept moist and expanded, preventing air from entering the bottle. Ideally, wines should be kept at a constant 55° to 60°F, away from daylight and vibrations. These conditions can obviously be met only by those who have access to a real cellar, or who are able to construct a self-contained temperature-controlled storage area. To keep wines in a home or apartment, you should remember that evenness of temperature is at least as important as the temperature itself, within limitations, because constant fluctuations of heat and cold will hasten a wine's evolution and eventual decline. Therefore, keep wines away from boiler rooms, steam pipes, or kitchen ovens. Don't store wines in a place where they will be subject to a lot of knocking about, such as the closet where the brooms and vacuum cleaner are kept. And keep wines away from direct exposure to sunlight, which seems to decompose them in a short time (whether in your house or in a retailer's window). If the temperature of your storage area stays much above 70°, you should limit yourself to no more than a six months' supply of wines. With these general rules in mind, you should be able to figure out a good place to store a few bottles.

Wine racks are available from most department stores and, in many states, from liquor stores. Many of these racks are designed to be stacked, and those are the ones you should look for, so that you can expand the capacity of your cellar. Never store fine red wines in racks in which the bottles lie at a downward angle, neck lowest. The cork will be kept moistened, but any sediment present in such wines will slide toward the cork and may adhere to it. You will thus drink cloudy wine from your first glass. It's also a good idea to store wine bottles with their labels facing up. This makes it easier to locate any bottle without having to twist it around and, in the case of red wines with sediment, you'll know that the deposit always lies along the side opposite the label.

As you determine the wines you like most, you will want to increase the size of your collection. There are sound reasons for buying wines to be consumed in the future. Certain wines, such as red Bordeaux, are usually least expensive when they first appear on the market, and then gradually increase in price. Other wines, such as Burgundies and the best of California, are often produced in such limited quantities that they disappear from retail shelves within a few months or a year. Those who invest in such wines have the satisfaction of knowing that their cellars include bottles that have become much more expensive or that are virtually unobtainable.

A certain amount is written about wine as a financial investment. It's true that if you buy the finest red wines in the best vintages they will almost certainly increase in value over the years. Nevertheless, it is illegal for a consumer to resell wine without the necessary licenses, which most people find complicated and impractical to obtain. It's therefore wiser to think of your wine purchases as an investment in future pleasure, rather than as a way of making a profit.

SERVING WINES

Serving wine—or more specifically, drinking wine—is certainly not very complicated and can be briefly summarized: chill white wines and rosés; serve red wines at cool room temperature; use large, stemmed glasses that are slightly tapered, and fill them only halfway. This covers the subject in a general way and gets you started as a wine drinker. There is so much conversation and snobbism about the proper way to drink wines, however, that it might be useful to describe the various steps in serving a wine. What follows is not meant to discourage anyone by its attention to detail, but rather to indicate, for reference, the most logical way to get a wine from the cellar into your glass. The degree of special effort to be made will depend on the wine and the occasion: a sandwich doesn't require special presentation, nor is an elaborately prepared dish best served on paper plates.

Older red wines, which may throw a slight and harmless deposit, should be stood upright on the dining-room table or sideboard an hour or two before the meal to permit any sediment to slide to the bottom. Red wines are supposed to be served at room temperature, which is to say, not at the cooler temperature of the ideal cellar. Because few of us have real cellars, the bottle has presumably been lying in a closet or in a rack along the wall, so the wine is already at room temperature. Remember that the concept of serving wines at room temperature originated before the days of central heating. Actually, red wines often taste dull and flat if served too warm, much above 70°, say, no matter what the temperature of the room is. In the summer, it's advisable to cool down a light red wine (Beaujolais, California Burgundy, Valpolicella) by putting it in the refrigerator for thirty minutes or so. This will give the wine an agreeable freshness and actually seems to improve its flavor. A complex red wine, however, should never be chilled: the wine will be numbed and may also taste bitter.

White wines and rosés are served chilled, because it is their refreshing quality that is their greatest virtue. Two hours in the refrigerator will do the job. If you need a chilled bottle of white wine at the last minute or a second bottle to serve with a dinner in progress, empty one or two ice trays into your biggest cooking pot, fill it with water, and put in the bottle. It should be cool in fifteen or twenty minutes. The trouble with most wine coolers or ice buckets is that they are too shallow and chill only half the bottle. Chilling a wine in ice water is both quicker and safer than putting the bottle in the freezer. The colder a wine is, the harder it is to taste, and some people use the trick of over-chilling a poor bottle of white wine to mask its defects. For the same reason, a fine bottle of white wine should not be chilled too much, or you will deaden the qualities for which you have paid.

A corkscrew is really the only piece of equipment that a wine drinker needs, and as it will last for years, it pays to look for a good one. In the first place, the screw part,

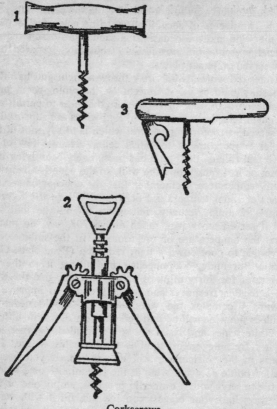

Corkscrews

A good corkscrew should have a bore at least two inches long with smooth edges, so that it can completely penetrate a long cork without crumbling it. The bore should also be in the form of a real coil, rather than having an awllike solid core: a corkscrew must be able to grip an old cork, not drill a hole in it. The simplest corkscrew. (1) may require some awkward tugging; a corkscrew with leverage (such as 2) is more convenient. This model is popular, easy to use, and usually effective, but note that it does not have a true coil, nor is the bore long enough to penetrate long corks. The folding corkscrew (3) is favored by waiters because it can be carried in a pocket, has a knife with which to cut the capsule, and has good leverage.

called the bore, should be at least two inches long. Because good wines are long-lived, they are bottled with long, strong corks, and a poor corkscrew will often break the cork of an expensive bottle of wine. Second, the bore should be in the form of a true coil, not a wiggly line. A coil will get a real grip even on an old cork, whereas a wiggly line will just bore a hole in it. Finally, get a corkscrew that gives you leverage. A simple T-shaped corkscrew, even with an excellent bore, requires too much tugging, and you will find yourself gripping the bottle between your feet or your knees, which can lead to messy accidents.

To open a bottle of wine, first remove the lead foil that covers the cork and part of the neck. Because lead foil may have an unpleasant taste, cut it off well below the lip of the bottle, so that the wine will not be in contact with the foil when it is poured. Wipe off the top of the cork and insert the corkscrew into the center of the cork. Remember to pull the cork gently, because if you give it a sharp tug, the vacuum that is momentarily created between the wine and the rising cork may cause some wine to splash out of the bottle.

If you break the cork, and this occasionally happens even with a bottle of sound wine, reinsert the corkscrew at an angle to get a grip on the remaining piece. If the cork crumbles, you can simply strain the wine into another container through clean cheesecloth or a tea strainer.

Incidentally, you should never wrap a wine bottle in a napkin: it's considered bad manners not to let your guests see what is being poured into their glasses. If you're worried that a few drops of wine may spill onto the tablecloth, you can tie a small napkin around the neck of the bottle.

Most wine drinkers believe that a red wine should be uncorked half an hour or an hour before it is to be served because this exposure to air, called breathing, will develop the wine's bouquet and soften the tannic harshness of a young wine. A number of enologists have tested this theory and feel that the surface of wine exposed to air in the neck of the bottle is too small to have any effect on the taste of the wine, even after several hours. It seems reasonable to assume that if exposure to air was beneficial to a red wine, a more effective way of letting a wine breathe would be either to pour it into a carafe or to pour it into large glasses fifteen or twenty minutes before starting to drink it. Many people assume that letting a wine breathe is synonymous with uncorking it, but there are obviously more efficient ways to achieve whatever improvements aeration may accomplish.

As to the concept of letting wines breathe, there are a number of professional wine people who believe that unnecessary exposure to air actually diminishes the quality of a wine. Older wines, which are often fragile, will fade in the decanter; younger wines will lose some of their intensity and definition without achieving any improvement in bouquet or flavor. Occasionally you may come across a wine, either red or white, that has an off-odor, and this may be dissipated by swirling the wine in your glass for a few minutes. Also, wines that have experienced several years of bottle age may require a few minutes in the glass for their bouquet and flavor to show themselves. Extended exposure to air, however, may well be an error. One exception to the view that wines should simply be opened and poured is in the case of older red wines that have thrown a deposit. Such wines should always be decanted (as described below) so that the sediment does not spoil one's enjoyment of the wine, but the decanting should take place just before the wine is to be served, which is usually not the same thing as decanting before the start of the meal.

The observation that wines are not improved by being allowed to breathe is a controversial one, but it's one that you can easily test for yourself. Next time you plan to serve two bottles of the same red wine, whether it be a young vigorous one or an older, mature one, simply decant one bottle an hour ahead of time, and then compare a glass of that wine with one from a bottle that has simply been opened and poured. After a few experiments of your own, you can decide whether or not you prefer the taste of wines that have been allowed to breathe.

It's customary in a restaurant for the host to taste the first glass of wine in case a bad bottle has been served and to prevent any bits of cork from reaching the glasses of his guests. This seems to me unnecessary in one's home, because you should taste the wine when you open it. There's no more logic to first tasting a wine when everyone is seated than for a cook to first taste a sauce after it's been served to guests. (Imagine the awkward scene if the bottle is defective.)

Decanting red wines may seem complicated or affected, but it's very simple and very useful. The sediment that red wines develop after ten years or so, although harmless, is also distracting when it appears in the last two or three glasses that are poured. Decanting a wine, which simply involves transferring it from its original bottle to another container, permits you to serve a wine that is completely brilliant and unclouded to the very end, and at the sacrifice of only an ounce or two of wine. First, you must stand the bottle up for an hour or two to allow all the sediment to fall to the bottom. Your decanter can be any clean container, whether it's a crystal wine decanter, an inexpensive carafe, or a glass pitcher. Hold the decanter firmly (remember, it will soon contain a full bottle of wine) and transfer the wine slowly in one motion—otherwise the sediment will wash back and forth. Traditionally, the shoulder of the wine bottle is held over a candle, so that you can see when sediment begins to come over into the decanter and can stop pouring at that moment. Because we now have electricity and because the heat of a candle is not going to do an old wine any good, you are better off using a flashlight standing on end, or pouring over any bright light.

If you are worried about decanting a ten-dollar bottle of wine, decant the next wine you drink, whatever it is, just to get the hang of it. Decanting is really the only way to get your money's worth out of older wines, when you can afford them. A decanter of wine on a dining table is also a most attractive and appropriate sight and enhances the enjoyment of wine. If you're concerned that a good wine will go unnoticed because it's unlabeled, you should know that it's customary to put the empty bottle alongside the decanter, so that your guests will know what they're drinking.

There is one other point about decanting, which may seem finicky, but remember, you've got an old bottle that cost you several dollars, and you want to get the most out of it. Because these bottles don't come our way very often, your decanter may be musty or have an off-odor from whatever was in it last. Therefore, you might first pour a few drops of wine into the decanter, rinse, and pour it

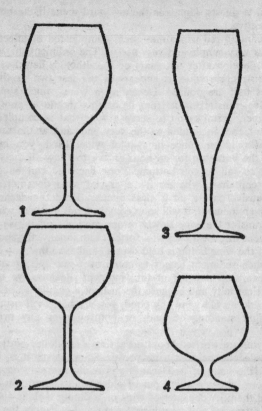

Wineglasses

The ten-ounce all-purpose wineglass (1) can be used for all table wines, as well as for Sherry and Port, if need be. It should be filled only about halfway, so that the wine can be swirled to release its bouquet. The first glass is in the traditional Bordeaux shape; the second all-purpose glass (2) is in the traditional Burgundy shape. The classic Champagne glass (3) displays bubbles more attractively and releases them more slowly than does the familiar wide-bottomed saucer-shaped glass. The traditional brandy glass (4) may vary in total capacity from about six to twelve ounces: a much smaller or much bigger glass is difficult to cup in one's hand, as is done to release the brandy's bouquet.

out. This will not only remove any odor that may be in the decanter, but will give the decanter the bouquet of the wine that's about to go into it.

Wineglasses have been discussed earlier, in the chapter on tasting, but to summarize: use a stemmed, clear glass with a bowl that is slightly tapered at the top to retain the wine's bouquet, and with a capacity of at least eight ounces. Small glasses seem stingy and don't permit a wine to be swirled to release its bouquet. Glasses with tall stems and colored bowls are sometimes recommended for German wines, but they only hide the delicate golden colors of a fine Moselle or Rhine wine. These glasses originated when winemaking techniques had not been perfected, and a bottled wine was apt to turn cloudy. Colored bowls hid this defect.

Almost every major wine region has its traditional glass, just as it has its traditional bottle, but it is completely unnecessary to have different glasses to serve and enjoy wine properly. When two or more wines are served at a meal, it does dress up the table to use differently shaped glasses, but even here an all-purpose wineglass is perfectly acceptable. If you do use glasses of two different sizes, the smaller one is traditionally used for white wines, the larger for reds. If you serve two reds, the better wine should be poured into the bigger glass.

As a general rule, expensive red wines will not keep a second day, and you had better plan to drink them when opened. Their flavor tends to become somewhat dulled and indistinct, at best, and may taste rather sharp and vinegary at worst. Almost all white wines can usually be kept in the refrigerator for several days and are only slightly the worse for wear. Inexpensive red and white wines, especially those from California, will keep much better, because they have been treated to remain more stable once they're exposed to air. It doesn't hurt to keep even red wines in the refrigerator, or at least in a cool place, just as you would with milk or any other perishable product.

The most helpful point to remember about leftover wine is to cork it up as soon as possible—it doesn't help a half-empty bottle of wine to be left open an extra hour or two.

When you put the cork back into a bottle for any reason, remember not to put the top, which is usually dirty, in contact with the wine. If the bottom of the cork has expanded, once pulled, and cannot be easily replaced, the simplest solution is to slice a quarter inch off the top and then reverse it.

If you do find yourself with leftover wine that has lost some of its flavor but that is still drinkable, there are several ways it can be used. You can use red wine to make *sangría*, a cold wine punch, by adding sugar or sugar syrup (which disguises the tartness of leftover or inexpensive wine), a couple of slices of lemon and orange, and ice cubes. When you pour out the *sangría*, add a splash of club soda to give it zest. You can use white wine to make a spritzer by adding club soda—it's a refreshing aperitif. And finally you can make your own wine vinegar. Although wine that's been left out for a while will be attacked by the vinegar bacteria and will soon taste sour, it will not actually turn to vinegar by itself. You must add a quantity of good vinegar to the leftover wine to start the process properly.

The amount of wine needed for a dinner will naturally vary depending on the occasion, the menu, and the extent to which each of your guests enjoys wines. Even assuming that we are talking about people who normally drink wine with their meals, the amount of wine you should serve seems to vary in an almost geometrical proportion to the number of people present. Two people having a light supper may be happy to share a half-bottle. Four people can easily drink two bottles, and six people at a big dinner might consume four bottles without any signs of overindulgence, especially if more than one kind of wine is served. The safest procedure is to have on hand—unopened—an extra bottle or two of whichever wine you're serving.

WINE AND FOOD

The question of which wine to serve with which food is one that seems to intimidate many people. Some will invariably choose rosé as a happy compromise. There are times, of course, when a rosé is the most appropriate choice: with a light luncheon, on a picnic, or in informal surroundings, its simple and refreshing qualities are perfectly in keeping with the mood of such occasions. What's more, there are an increasing number of unusual varietal rosés being produced in California from such grapes as Cabernet Sauvignon, Gamay, and Zinfandel, and some of these are quite appealing. There's certainly nothing wrong with choosing a rosé to accompany a meal, but it's not necessary to resign yourself to rosé as a compromise. There are so many red and white wines that are not only more interesting but that will also set off a carefully prepared dish more effectively that it's a pity not to be more adventurous when choosing wines. It's perhaps well to recall here, without prejudice, that a rosé is technically an incompletely made red wine and will rarely have the character or distinct personality of either a good red or white wine.

The established customs concerning the pairing of food and wine are simple and logical, but reaction to the very existence of these informal guidelines can be extreme. There are gastronomic societies whose members are so concerned that every wine must match perfectly the dish with which it is served that a special committee meets a few days before each gala dinner to taste its way critically through the entire menu and the accompanying wines. Then there are those who democratically maintain that any wine goes with any dish—if it pleases you. This attitude is perfectly acceptable if everyone shares your taste, but a little experimenting will soon convince most people that there are very sound reasons for the few general rules that most wine drinkers follow.

For one thing, there are some foods with which wine does not go very well. The acidity in a salad dressing alters the taste of any wine that is drunk at the same time, whether the dressing is made with vinegar or lemon juice. Chocolate tends to overwhelm wine, even the sweet white wines that sometimes accompany chocolate desserts. Spicy foods also overwhelm wine, and beer is the usual accompaniment for curries and highly flavored Chinese dishes. One last negative rule is that, generally speaking, red wines do not taste right with fish. The oiliness of most fish seems to give red wine a somewhat bitter and unpleasant taste, and the refreshing quality of a chilled white wine is much more enjoyable. It must be added, however, that a number of restaurateurs and gastronomes in France consider a light-bodied, chilled red wine such as Beaujolais to be an appropriate accompaniment to many fish dishes.

With these few admonitions out of the way, the most practical rule to follow in choosing wines is, the richer the dish, the richer the wine. For example, shellfish can be accompanied by a light, dry white wine, such as Muscadet or Soave. Fish served with a rich sauce calls for a wine with more body and more flavor, such as a white Burgundy or California Chardonnay. Simply grilled meats are enhanced by light, delicate red wines, whereas game or rich stews might better be accompanied by a positive and full-bodied red.

The common rule, white wine with white meat, red wine with red meat, is a good start, but there are any number of exceptions. For example, roast chicken is a perfect dish to set off a fine red Bordeaux or California Cabernet Sauvignon, and many people will prefer a Valpolicella or Chianti with *veal scaloppine*, especially if it's made with a cheese and tomato sauce. Conversely, in the summertime you may prefer a chilled glass of dry white wine with cold meats, even roast beef.

If wine is used in the preparation of a dish, it's traditional to use the same kind of wine as an accompaniment. Thus, *coq au vin* usually calls for a red wine, whereas the version made in Alsace, *coq au Riesling*, will naturally be accompanied by a white wine. This example suggests another useful guideline—pairing of regional dishes with regional wines. A rich Italian pasta dish calls for Chianti, *boeuf bourguignon* for a Burgundy such as Gevrey-Chambertin or Pommard, an *entrecôte bordelaise* for a Saint-Emilion or Médoc, and a grilled steak can be accompanied by a California Zinfandel or Cabernet Sauvignon. It's always more fun to experiment, guided by your own common sense, than to stick to a few safe but unimaginative rules.

So far we have been matching a dish with a wine, but for more elaborate dinners you may want to serve more than one wine. There is certainly nothing unusual or particularly fancy about serving two or three wines with a meal, and it can be more fun than serving two or three bottles of the same wine, especially when you have several enthusiastic wine drinkers at the dinner table. There are some traditional guidelines concerning the service of more than one wine: white before red, dry before sweet, young before old.

White before red simply conforms to the normal sequence of food, assuming you are having a light appetizer, or shellfish, or even a cooked fish dish, before a main dish of meat. Also, because red wines are usually richer and more complex than white wines, serving a dry white wine second would diminish its qualities by comparison. Dry before sweet is traditional because sweet foods dull our taste buds (and our appetite) for the more delicate foods to follow (which is why dessert is served last). This rule supersedes the previous one in that a sweet white wine such as Sauternes or a German Auslese is usually served at the end of the meal, and therefore after the red wine.

Young before old is a traditional rule in most wine regions, and indicates that similar wines are usually served in order of increasing age and interest, to avoid an anticlimax. For example, if you are serving two red Bordeaux or two California Cabernet Sauvignons, the older one, presumably more mature and distinguished, will be preceded and, so to speak, introduced by the younger wine. If you are not serving different vintages of the same or similar wines, however, you may find it more appropriate to serve the best wine of the evening with the main course. You can then continue with a completely different wine that need not be older and finer, but that should be interesting enough to follow the previous bottle.

Champagne is often suggested as the one wine (along with rosé, I suppose) that can be served throughout a meal. Although this is a generous gesture and will be greeted with enthusiasm, Champagne does not complement all foods, especially full-flavored meats, and its taste may pall at the end of an evening. One alternative is to serve Champagne as an aperitif before the meal. Another is to serve it with dessert, but in that case choose an Extra Dry rather than the drier Brut.

Cheese and wine are traditional partners, although a cheese course is not as common here as in Europe. Even restaurants of the highest caliber, for example, will rarely present a cheese tray that is adequate. At a dinner party, a cheese course, which precedes the dessert, gives the host or hostess the opportunity of serving a fine old wine. Although cheese is considered an ideal accompaniment to wine, many cheeses actually overwhelm mature and subtle wines. If you decide to bring out a good bottle at this point, select the cheeses carefully so that they enhance the flavor of a delicate wine. If you prefer rich, creamy cheeses, tangy goat cheeses, or strongly flavored blue cheeses, it may be best to choose a younger and more vigorous wine.

Sweet white wines such as Sauternes, Barsac, and German Auslese are not often served these days, but if they are, they usually accompany dessert. Actually, the sweetness of most desserts diminishes the richness and concentration of flavor that characterizes the best sweet white wines, thereby depriving you of the qualities that make these wines so distinctive. German winemakers, for example, prefer to serve Auslese and Beerenauslese wines by themselves, without food, and in Bordeaux most vineyard proprietors in Sauternes and Barsac prefer not to serve their wines with rich desserts. You might consider serving Sauternes, German Auslese wines, and such sweet California wines as Late Harvest Johannisberg Riesling as an alternative to dessert, or perhaps with nothing richer than plain cake or ripe fruit. Because sweet wines are not consumed in large quantities, it's not inappropriate to open just a half-bottle for three or four people at the end of a meal.

Cooking with Wine

There is really no such thing as cooking wine, and it's a mistake to imagine that you can cook with a wine that you wouldn't want to drink. Most of the alcohol in wine will evaporate during cooking, and what's left is its flavor. It's not necessary to use an expensive bottle of Chambertin to make a *boeuf bourguignon* or a *coq au vin,* but if you try to economize by using a poor wine, all of its defects will be concentrated in the sauce.

Furthermore, it may actually be uneconomical to buy cheap wine for cooking. Say that an elaborate seafood dish calls for a spoonful or two of white wine to heighten its flavor. A cook who runs out to buy a bottle of cheap wine may spoil several dollars' worth of food and perhaps an hour or more of preparation with a dime's worth of wine. What's more, because the wine is not good enough to drink, the spoonful of wine has, in fact, cost the full price of the bottle.

WINE IN RESTAURANTS

One of the pleasures of dining out in Europe is the opportunity to drink wines inexpensively and without fuss. Winemaking is so widespread in Europe, and particularly in France and Italy, that a bistro or inn almost anywhere will feature local wines, often served in carafes, and no more expensive than a bowl of soup or a dessert. Unfortunately, wine drinking in American restaurants is neither so easy nor so cheap. All too often restaurant lists are both unimaginative and expensive, and the service of wine ranges from the indifferent to the pretentious. Ideally, the service of wine should be both correct and unobtrusive, but the sad fact is that most waiters know less about wine than all but the least knowledgeable of their customers.

Most of the elements of service that apply in the home are equally valid in restaurants. There are some aspects of wine service, however, that are more relevant to restaurants, and these are reviewed here briefly. If you plan to have wine, ask for the wine list while you are looking at the menu, otherwise you may be subject to a long wait between the time you order your meal and the moment when a wine list is finally put into your hands. Once you've ordered a wine, make sure that it is brought to the table and uncorked as soon as possible, to avoid the possibility of a forgetful waiter opening the bottle long after he has served the dish that the wine was meant to accompany. Getting wine brought to the table in time is particularly important if you plan to have a bottle of wine with the first course, which is often prepared ahead of time and brought to your table minutes after you've ordered it.

White wine should be chilled, of course, but not too cold. If a wine is placed in an ice bucket at the beginning of a meal, and then served with the main course, it may well be overchilled and have lost almost all its taste. Don't hesitate to take the bottle out of the cooler and stand it on the table. Also, note that many restaurants use ice buckets that are not deep enough for a bottle of wine, especially German or Alsatian wines. The easiest solution is to turn the bottle upside down for a moment before the first glass is poured: this may look odd, but the alternative is to drink the first two or three glasses of white wine at room temperature.

Red wines are sometimes served in wine baskets, but they are actually pointless as used in most restaurants. An older red wine lying on its side in the cellar will have thrown a deposit. Because it is not possible in a restaurant to stand the wine up for a couple of hours to let the sediment fall to the bottom of the bottle, the alternative is to move the bottle carefully, always on its side, from its bin to a wine basket, and then bring it to the table without disturbing the sediment. Ideally, the wine should be decanted at this point, or at any rate poured very carefully into large wineglasses. What actually happens four times out of five is that the waiter grabs the bottle any which way and carries it carelessly to the service station. There he puts the bottle into a waiting basket and brings it to the table. To make the farce complete, some waiters insert a corkscrew by rotating the bottle in its basket. If you order a young red wine without sediment, as most people do in a restaurant, there's no reason at all to use a basket.

When you've ordered a wine, the waiter or captain should always show you the bottle before he opens it to make sure the wine is exaclty the one you ordered, and of the vintage specified on the wine list (or at any rate, one acceptable to you). If it's a better-than-average wine that you've ordered, especially an older one, be sure that there is no more than the usual space between cork and wine: older wines sometimes develop too great an air space, and this may in turn affect the wine adversely. If you note too much ullage, as this is called, draw it to the waiter's attention to let him know that you'll be on your guard against an oxidized wine.

After opening the bottle, the waiter may show you the cork, or even hand it to you: the cork should be sound and the wet end should smell of wine, not of cork. You can give the cork a squeeze and a sniff if you want, but the wine in the glass is what's really important. The waiter will then pour some wine into the glass of whoever chose it, so that he or she can determine whether or not it is defective in any way. If you happen to be eating your first course when the red wine is poured, don't try to judge the wine against smoked salmon, tomato salad, creamed herring, vichyssoise, or whatever may be in your mouth. Take a piece of bread first, or else tell the waiter that you'll taste the wine a little later, at your convenience. If a wine is corky or spoiled, it should naturally be sent back. Some restaurants will do this more gracefully than others. Even the most accommodating restaurateurs will privately complain, however, that most of the wine that is sent back is perfectly sound—either the customer was trying to show off, or he had made an uninformed choice and mistakenly expected the wine to have a different taste. Actually, corky wine is rare and easily detected—it's a wine contaminated by a faulty cork, and tasting strongly of cork rather than wine.

Wineglasses in restaurants are often too small, and those ubiquitous three- and four-ounce glasses are inappropriate not only because they don't permit a good wine to be swirled and sniffed, but also because using a small glass seems such a mean and unpleasant way of drinking wine. The simplest solution is to ask for empty water goblets and fill them only a third. You can expect six to eight glasses of wine from a bottle, depending on how generously the waiter pours. It's a pity to run out of wine halfway through a meal, and if a second bottle seems too much, an extra half-bottle might be the answer.

Choosing a wine can be complicated by an assortment of dinner choices in a party of four or more. Rosé is one solution, but certainly not the best one, especially if fine food is being served. It's easy enough to order a half-bottle each of red and white. Another possibility is to order a bottle of white and a half-bottle of red. Everyone gets a glass of white wine with his or her first course, then those having fish as a main dish continue with white wine, those having meat go on to the red.

These general observations aside, the most important question is, Which wine to order? This will naturally depend on the kind of restaurant you're in, the food you plan to eat, and the variety and prices of the wines offered. Today, many people simply order a glass of the red or white bar wine. This is likely to be an acceptable, but inexpensive, California jug wine. Since many restaurants now charge as much for a four- or five-ounce glass of wine as for a cocktail, you may end up paying a rather high price for twenty cents' worth of wine. If wine is available by the carafe, it's usually a better value, especially if the restaurant uses liter carafes, which hold thirty-three ounces. An increasing number of restaurants now offer carafe wines, including relatively expensive establishments. Many restaurateurs have discovered that even knowledgeable customers don't always want to take the time to pore over a wine list.

There are now a great many restaurateurs around the country who take particular pride in their wine lists, and a selection of fifty or more wines is no longer as unusual as it was only a few years ago. Unfortunately, the majority of wine lists are still inadequate. Far too many neglect to indicate the producer or shipper of a wine, or the vintage. This gives the restaurateur some flexibility in replacing a wine if his supplier runs out, but it also makes it difficult for his patrons to make an intelligent choice. If you walked into a retail store you'd be surprised to see shelves marked Beaujolais, Nuits-Saint-Georges, or Chianti on which were standing bottles wrapped in paper bags. Yet a restaurateur who doesn't list the producer is asking you to make the same blind choice and at much higher prices. One solution is to pick out two or three potentially interesting wines and ask the waiter to bring the bottles to your table. After you examine the labels, you can select one and send the others back

As for vintages, they always matter, if only to indicate the age and relatively freshness of the many popular wines meant to be consumed young. And when you turn to the pages listing wines at $15, $20, or more, vintages naturally matter a great deal with respect to both quality and value.

Fortunately, many restaurateurs do list producer and vintage and are also committed to reprinting or rewriting their wine lists at frequent intervals. Others, with smaller budgets, have adopted the sensible policy of using well-designed typewritten lists that are easy to read, contain the relevant information about each wine, and are easily updated. These lists are a welcome change from the cumbersome leatherbound books that, as often as not, offer a limited choice.

When looking over a list, remember that the least-expensive wine is often a poor value, since its price is based, not on its cost, but on what the restaurateur feels is the minimum he or she should charge for a bottle of wine. For example, in most Italian restaurants, the least-expensive wines are Soave and Valpolicella. If you visited a dozen restaurants, you'd find that although most of them are offering the same two or three popular and similarly priced brands, the wines might be listed at anywhere from $6 to $12. Obviously, the price of the wine has more to do with the decor of the restaurant and the price of the food than with the actual cost of the wine. Usually, if you spend another dollar or two, you are likely to get a wine whose price more accurately reflects its value.

Just as it is usually a bad idea to order the least-expensive wines, so should you avoid the most-expensive wines, whatever your budget. Even if, for example, fine red Bordeaux châteaux are listed, they are likely to be of recent vintages and therefore too young to drink. It's a waste to pay what is inevitably a great deal of money for glamorous wines that are not yet showing the qualities for which they are famous. As for ordering mature red wines, if they are listed, remember that they are likely to contain sediment, so you must make sure that the waiter or captain is knowledgeable about old wines and is prepared to decant the wine carefully for you.

Looking through a wine list can often be a frustrating experience, and there are times when you find yourself not so much making a choice as resigning yourself to ordering the least-objectionable wine. Nevertheless, varied and fairly priced wine lists are not as uncommon as they were, and there seem to be a growing number of restaurants throughout the country that are even better known for their wine cellars than for their kitchens.

VINTAGES

For some reason, many people who are relatively unfamiliar with wines are nevertheless unduly concerned about vintages. Some pontificate about what they imagine to be the best vintage years, others simply become uneasy about whether or not a particular wine represents a good year. It seems to me that a wine's vintage is almost always the last fact to consider when deciding what to drink with dinner: the primary consideration should be the kind of wine that you would like. Often enough, its vintage will turn out to be of little importance. After all, more than three-quarters of all the wine produced in the world is meant to be consumed within a year of the harvest, and a great deal of what we drink is at its best within two years. Since the chief attribute of many wines is their freshness, the vintage date is often more useful as an indication of the wine's age than of its quality.

The importance given to vintages is of relatively recent origin. For centuries new wines were poured into goblets directly from the barrel. If bottles were used as an intermediate step, they were loosely stoppered up with oil-soaked rags or a wooden peg. In the eighteenth century, when an effective cork made of bark first became generally available, it was discovered that Port improved with a certain amount of bottle age. In consequence, the Port bottle evolved during the eighteenth century from a squat shape to the kind of bottle that we see today. What emerged was the binnable bottle—a bottle that could be stored on its side, thus keeping the cork wet and expanded, and preventing air from entering the bottle and spoiling the wine. It is possible that the first Bordeaux to be bottled and stored away was Lafite 1797, and a few bottles are still displayed today at the château. The effects of bottle age became so greatly admired that in the second half of the nineteenth century red Bordeaux was vinified in such a way as to retain its qualities for forty or fifty years, and these wines were rarely drunk before they were fifteen or twenty years old.

The concept of a vintage year or a vintage wine is often misunderstood. A vintage, or harvest, occurs every fall in all of the world's vineyards. Consequently, every year is a vintage year, although some are better than others. Now, in the case of Port and Champagne, it is traditional to blend together the wines of several years. When an exceptionally good growing season results in better-than-average wines, the producers may decide to bottle part of that crop without blending in wine from other years, and the resulting wine bears on its label the year in which the grapes were harvested. In all other wine-producing regions, however, the words vintage year or vintage wine have no special meaning.

There are a number of factors that make one vintage better than another in a particular region, but the most important is the amount of sunshine and heat between the flowering of the vines in June and the harvest in late September or early October. As grapes ripen in the sun, their natural acidity decreases and their sugar content increases. Ideally, the vintage takes place when the sugar/acid balance is in correct proportion. The wine will consequently have enough alcohol (from the sugar in the grapes) to be stable, and enough acidity to be healthy and lively. Cold and rainy summers result in immature grapes that produce less alcohol, more acidity, and less coloring matter in the skins for red wines. The wines are therefore weak, tart, and pale. In general, there are more good vintages for white wines than for reds—within a given district—because white wine grapes normally ripen earlier and do not require as long a growing season as do red grapes, and they make fine wine at lower levels of sugar. In addition, color is not as important to the appearance of white wines, extra acidity does less harm to their taste, and they do not need the depth of flavor that is expected of red wines.

The quantity produced in a vintage may be affected by poor weather during the flowering, which will diminish the crop, or by brief summer hailstorms, which can destroy part of a vineyard's production in minutes. A sudden frost in the spring may kill the new growth on the vines and can drastically reduce the crop in a wine region overnight. Many growers in northerly vineyards are now using modern frost-control devices to protect their vines during cold spells, but frost is still a danger.

Although it is axiomatic that a wine cannot be judged before it is made, it is not uncommon for a vintage to be publicized as excellent—by the wine trade and by the press—before the grapes have even been picked. Unfortunately, even an excellent growing season that gives every promise of producing fine wines can be marred by bad luck. Rain just before a harvest can swell the grapes and dilute the intensity of the wine, and continued rain can transform ripe grapes into rotten ones. Rain during the vintage means that the pickers are harvesting water along with grapes, which may result in weak wines lacking in flavor. Although the personality of a vintage can be determined once the wines have finished fermenting, many winemakers and professional tasters prefer to reserve judgment until the following spring, when the wines have become more clearly defined. This suggests that the first impression of a vintage, even a good one, may not be completely accurate, but by the time knowledgeable wine people have determined the character of an overpublicized vintage, consumers may have already heard and read too much about it for their impression to be corrected, much less reversed.

Any discussion of vintage years must take into account two basic factors: How accurate is the vintage date on the label? How useful is it?

The first question is basic, because if vintage dates are inaccurate, then it's obviously a mistake to attach too much significance to them. California wines must be made 95 percent from grapes harvested in the year shown on the label. German wines can be blended with up to 15 percent of wines from a vintage other than the one shown. (Before 1971, a third of the wine could come from another vintage.) French wines must come entirely from the vintage indicated, but since vintage years are not part of the *Appellation Contrôlée* laws, but another set of laws, it is possible that the labels of some blended wines are not as accurate as those of single-vineyard wines. In many other countries, vintage years are not taken seriously except for the finest wines, and even then it is not unusual for wines that undergo long barrel aging to be refreshed with younger wines.

Even when vintage dates are accurate, how useful is the information? Although many consumers have at least some acquaintance with the best recent vintages in Bordeaux, Burgundy, and perhaps along the Rhine and Moselle, what do most of us know about good and bad vintages for Barolo, Valpolicella, or Chianti; for Rioja; for Hungarian Tokay, Austrian Gumpoldskirchner, or Yugoslavian Cabernet; or for the wines of Chile or Argentina (where their harvest takes place in our spring)? For that matter, what are the best recent years for Napa Cabernet Sauvignon, Sonoma Zinfandel, and Monterey Chardonnay?

There are, however, many wines whose vintages are both accurate and important. These include most of the world's fine wines, and as a general rule, the more you pay for a bottle, the more important its vintage becomes. Most fine wines are made in regions where hot and sunny summers cannot be taken for granted, and where wide variations exist from one year to the next. Furthermore, in such regions as Bordeaux and Burgundy and along the Rhine and Moselle, the finest and most-expensive wines come from individual vineyard sites whose proprietors are not even permitted to blend together wines from neighboring vineyards or villages to offset some of the deficiencies of a lesser year. Even the best varietal wines of California display greater variations from one year to another than many people imagine. Although the weather in northern California is more consistent than in Burgundy or along the Rhine, there are nevertheless differences between, say, Napa and Monterey, which are nearly two hundred miles apart. Furthermore, if a number of different grape varieties are planted side by side, the same growing season is unlikely to be equally successful for each of them.

The problem with evaluating vintages of fine wines is

that knowing just a little is usually not enough, and as these wines are often expensive, mistakes can be more costly than for most other wines. Consumers generally seem to be most familiar with the best years for red Bordeaux, and the reputation of those vintages inevitably has an effect on many people's perception of vintages years in other regions. Actually, the best vintages in Bordeaux are not even the same for fine red wines and for the sweet white wines of Sauternes. Vintages for red Bordeaux and red Burgundy do not match, nor do those for red and white Burgundy. Bordeaux and Burgundy vintages do not necessarily have any relevance to the best years in the Rhône Valley or along the Loire, and of course, French vintages do not correspond with those of Germany or Italy. The best years for Vintage Port bear no relation to those for most other European wines, and European vintages are quite different from those for the best California varietals, produced six thousand miles away.

Vintage charts, with their numerical rating system, can be useful as a rough guide to recent years for the best-known wines. The system is too summary, however, to indicate much more than the comparative overall reputation of those vintages. The basic flaw in vintage charts, most of which are prepared by shippers and importers, is that they are so often inaccurate and self-serving, especially for recent vintages that are still currently available. Good years are rated as excellent, poor years are rarely rated as less than acceptable. It is often pointed out that not all the wines of a top-rated year are equally good, and conversely, that certain vineyards may have produced decent (and less-expensive) wines in a year rated only fair. While variations naturally exist between the wines of one producer and another within a vintage, the main characteristic of poor years—those in which wines are made from unripe or even partially rotted grapes—is that they are unsound and cannot last. Even if there are a few bargains to be found, they are unlikely to maintain what little quality they possess for very long. Although vintage charts may be faulted for perpetuating the public's tendency to focus only on the best vintages, it is nevertheless true that, among fine wines, it is the best wines of the best vintages that are the most dependable, the longest-lived, and that will eventually provide the greatest pleasure.

On the other hand, an unfortunate result of the attention given even to indisputably fine vintages is that the public, anxious to buy these wines as soon as they appear, consumes the best wines of each vintage long before their prime. The wave of anticipation that accompanies a publicized vintage carries in its wake the disappointment that must inevitably occur when a good red wine is drunk too young. A fine Bordeaux or California Cabernet Sauvignon will demonstrate its quality only with the passage of years, when it has fully matured. If you drink such a wine soon after it has been bottled, you can perceive only in rough outline the particular qualities that have made it sought-after and expensive. Of all the comparative tastings that can be arranged, few are more instructive or surprising than to compare fine red wine from the same vineyard or the same winery in two good vintages that span at least three or four years. You will understand, as you taste the more mature wine, why certain wines are so highly acclaimed, and you will also realize, as you taste the younger wine, that to drink expensive red wines too young is pretty much a waste of money.

The success of a vintage is one element in a wine's quality and appeal, its ability to age is another. While it's true that all wines change during their life in the bottle, not all wines change for the better. The consideration of a vintage takes on a different dimension for wines whose virtues are charm, lightness, and fruit, than for wines characterized by tannin, depth of flavor, and a slowly developing bouquet. On most vintage charts a great year is great forever, but every wine has a life cycle of its own, based on the combination of soil, grape, and climate that produced it, as well as on grape-growing and winemaking techniques that may differ from one producer to another. Some wines are at their best when they are bottled, remain good for a year or two, and then decline rapidly. Others reach maturity only after a few years in bottle, maintain their excellence for several years, and then very gradually decline. Age alone is no guarantee of quality, nor is a good vintage, in itself, a guarantee that the wine will be enjoyable today.

Finally, an observation about nonvintage wines, those on whose labels the year of the harvest does not appear. The trouble with such wines is not that they are blended from wines of more than one year, but that it is difficult for the consumer to determine just how old a particular bottle is. As most nonvintage wines are inexpensive (except for Port and Champagne) and meant to be drunk without any bottle age, not knowing how long such wines have been around means that you will sometimes come across faded and disappointing examples.

PRONUNCIATION GUIDE

Abboccato	ah-bo-*kah*-toe
Alella	ah-*lay*-l'yah
Aligoté	ah-lee-go-tay
Aloxe-Corton	ah-lox cor-tawn
Alto Adige	*ahl*-toe *ah*-dee-d'jay
Amabile	ah-*mah*-bee-lay
Amarone	ah-ma-*roe*-neh
Amontillado	ah-mon-tee-*yah*-doe
Anjou	ahn-joo
Auslese	*ow*-slay-zuh
Auxey-Duresses	oak-say duh-ress
Baco	bah-coe
Barbaresco	bar-bah-*ress*-coe
Barbera	bar-*bear*-ah
Bardolino	bar-doe-*lee*-no
Barolo	bar-*oh*-loe
Barsac	bar-sack
Batârd-Montrachet	bah-tar mon-rah-shay
Beaujolais	bo-jo-lay
Beaune	bone
Beerenauslese	*beer*-en-*ow*-slay-zuh
Bereich	buh-*rye'k*
Bernkastel	bearn-castle
Blanc de Blancs	blahn duh blahn
Blanc Fumé	blahn foo-may
Bocksbeutel	*box*-boyt'l

Bodega	bo-*day*-gah
Bonnes Mares	bon mar
Bordeaux	bore-doe
Bourgogne	boor-*gon*-yuh
Brouilly	brew-yee
Brunello di Montalcino	brew-*nell*-oh dee mon-tahl-*chee*-noe
Brut	brute
Bual	boo-ahl
Cabernet	ca-bear-nay
Calvados	cahl-vah-dohss
Carruades	cah-roo-ahd
Cassis	cah-seece
Cave	cahv
Chablis	shah-blee
Chai	shay
Chambertin	sham-bear-tan
Chambolle-Musigny	shahm-bol moo-seen-yee
Chardonnay	shahr-doe-nay
Chassagne-Montrachet	shah-sahnyuh mon-rah-shay
Chasselas	shass-lah
Château	shah-toe
Châteauneuf-du-Pape	shah-toe-nuff-doo-pahp
Chénas	shay-nahss
Chenin Blanc	shay-nan blahn
Chiroubles	shee-roobl
Climat	clee-mah
Clos de Bèze	cloh duh behz
Clos Vougeot	cloh voo-joh
Colheita	cul-*yay*-tah
Consorzio	con-*sorts*-ee-oh
Corbières	cor-b'yair
Corton	cor-tawn
Cosecha	co-*say*-chah
Côte de Beaune	coat duh bone
Côte Chalonnaise	coat shah-lo-nayz
Côte de Nuits	coat duh nwee
Côte d'Or	coat dor
Coteaux Champenois	coat-toe shahm-pen-wah
Côtes du Rhône	coat doo rone
Côte Rotie	coat ro-tee
Crémant	creh-mahn

Cru	crew
Cru Classé	crew clah-say
Cuvaison	coo-vay-zohn
Cuvée	coo-vay
Dão	down
Dolcetto	dole-*chet*-toe
Douro	doo-roe
Echézeaux	eh-shay-zoh
Edelfäule	ay-del-foil
Einzellage	*ein*-tsuh-lah-guh
Egri Bikavér	egg-ree bee-ka-vair
Entre-Deux-Mers	ahn'tr-duh-mair
Erzeugerabfüllung	*air*-tsoy-guh-*ahb*-foo-lung
Estufa	esh-*too*-fah
Fendant	fahn-dahn
Fiaschi	fee-ahss-kee
Fino	*fee*-no
Fixin	fix-ahn
Fleurie	fluh-ree
Framboise	frahm-bwahz
Frascati	frahss-*ca*-tee
Freisa	fray-zah
Frizzante	free-*zahn*-tay
Friuli	free-*ooh*-lee
Gamay	gam-may
Gattinara	gah-tee-*nah*-rah
Gevrey-Chambertin	jev-ray shahm-bear-tan
Gewürztraminer	guh-*vurts*-trah-*mee*-ner
Gigondas	jee-gon-dahss
Grands-Echézeaux	grahnz eh-shay-zoh
Graves	grahv
Grenache	greh-nahsh
Grignolino	gree-n'yohl-*ee*-no
Grosslage	*gross*-lah-guh
Gumpoldskirchen	goom-poles-*kir*-ken
Haut	oh
Hermitage	air-mee-tahj
Heurige	*hoi*-ree-guh
Hospices de Beaune	oh-speece duh bone

Jerez	hair-reth
Johannisberg	yoh-*hah*-niss-bairg
Juliénas	jool-yeh-nahss
Kirsch	keersh
Labrusca	la-*broos*-ca
Lacryma Christi	*la*-cree-mah *kriss*-tee
Mâcon	mah-kohn
Maderisé	mah-dair-ree-zay
Malmsey	*mahlm*-zee
Manzanilla	man-zah-*nee*-ya
Marc	mar
Margaux	mahr-goe
Médoc	meh-dock
Merlot	mehr-loe
Meursault	muhr-soe
Mise en bouteilles	meez ahn boo-tay
Montilla	mon-*tee*-yah
Montrachet	mon-rah-shay
Morey-Saint-Denis	moh-ray san-deh-nee
Moulin-à-Vent	moo-lahn-ah-vahn
Mousseux	moo-suh
Müller-Thurgau	*moo*-lair-*toor*-gahw
Muscadet	muhss-ka-day
Musigny	moo-see-nyee
Nahe	nah
Nebbiolo	neh-b'*yoh*-low
Neuchâtel	nuh-shah-tell
Nierstein	neer-shtine
Nuits-Saint-Georges	nwee-san-jawrj
Oechsle	*uhk*-sluh
Oloroso	oh-lo-*ro*-so
Oltrepó Pavese	ohl-treh-*poe* pah-*veh*-seh
Originalabfüllung	oh-*rig*-ee-nah-*ahb*-fuh-lung
Orvieto	ohr-vee-*ay*-toe
Pauillac	paw-yack
Pays	pay-yee
Pétillant	pet-tee-yahn
Petit	puh-tee
Phylloxera	fil-*lox*-uh-rah
Piesport	*peez*-port

Pinot Grigio	pee-noe *gree*-d'joh
Pinot Noir	pee-noe nwahr
Poire	pwahr
Pomerol	pom-uh-rohl
Pommard	poh-mar
Pouilly-Fuissé	poo-yee fwee-say
Pouilly-Fumé	poo-yee foo-may
Pourriture noble	poo-ree-toor nohbl
Premier Cru	preh-m'yay crew
Puligny-Montrachet	poo-lee-n'yee mon-rah-shay
Puttonyos	puh-tohn-yosh
Qualitätswein mit	kvah-lee-*tayts*-vine mitt
Prädikat	*pray*-dee-kaht
Quincy	kan-see
Quinta	*keen*-tah
Recioto	ray-*t'shot*-oh
Retsina	ret-*see*-nah
Rheingau	rine-gow
Rheinhessen	rine-hessen
Rheinpfalz	rine-faltz
Richebourg	reesh-boor
Riesling	*reece*-ling
Rioja	ree-*oh*-ha
Rosé	roh-zay
Ruwer	*roo*-vuh
Saar	sahr
Sancerre	sahn-sair
Sangiovese	san-joh-*vay*-zeh
Sauternes	saw-tairn
Sauvignon Blanc	saw-vee-n'yohn blahn
Scheurebe	*shoy*-reh-buh
Secco	say-co
Sekt	sekt
Sémillon	seh-mee-yohn
Soave	so-*ah*-vay
Solera	so-*lair*-ah
Sommelier	so-mel-yay
Spätlese	shpaht-lay-zuh
Spumante	spoo-mahn-tay
Sylvaner	sil-*vah*-ner

Tafelwein	*tah*-fell-vine
Tastevin	taht-van
Tavel	tah-vell
Terroir	tehr-wahr
Tête de cuvée	teht duh koo-vay
Tonneau	tun-oh
Traminer	trah-*mee*-ner
Trentino	tren-*tee*-no
Trockenbeerenauslese	*trok*-en-*beer*-en-*ow*-slay-zuh
Valdepeñas	val-day-*pain*-yass
Valpolicella	val-poh-lee-*t'chell*-ah
Valtellina	vahl-teh-*lee*-nah
Vaud	voh
Veltliner	velt-*lee*-nuh
Verdelho	vehr-*dell*-yoh
Verdicchio	vehr-*dee*-kee-oh
Vinho Verde	*veen*-yoh *vair*-day
Vinifera	vin-*if*-uh-rah
Vosne-Romanée	vohn ro-mah-nay
Wachau	*vah*-kow
Wehlen	*vay*-len
Yquem	ee-kem

INDEX

ABOUT THE AUTHOR

ALEXIS BESPALOFF is the author of *Alexis Bespaloff's Guide to Inexpensive Wines* and editor of *The Fireside Book of Wine*, a literary anthology. He writes about wine for *New York, Travel & Leisure,* and other publications.